THE UNFORGIVING MINUTE

Books by Beverley Nichols

PRELUDE

PATCHWORK

SELF

TWENTY-FIVE

CRAZY PAVEMENT

EVENSONG

DOWN THE GARDEN PATH

ARE THEY THE SAME AT HOME?

THE STAR SPANGLED MANNER

WOMEN AND CHILDREN LAST

FOR ADULTS ONLY

FAILURES

CRY HAVOC!

THE FOOL HATH SAID

NO PLACE LIKE HOME

NEWS OF ENGLAND

MESMER

GREEN GROWS THE CITY

REVUE

THE GIFT OF A GARDEN

THE GIFT OF A HOME

NO MAN'S STREET

THE MOONFLOWER

MEN DO NOT WEEP

VERDICT ON INDIA

THE TREE THAT SAT DOWN

ALL I COULD NEVER BE

THE STREAM THAT STOOD
 STILL

SHADOW OF THE VINE

THE MOUNTAIN OF MAGIC

A PILGRIM'S PROGRESS

THE SWEET AND TWENTIES

CATS' A.B.C.

CATS' X.Y.Z.

GARDEN OPEN TODAY

POWERS THAT BE

A CASE OF HUMAN BONDAGE

GARDEN OPEN TOMORROW

THE ART OF FLOWER
 ARRANGEMENT

THE SUN IN MY EYES

FATHER FIGURE

DEATH TO SLOW MUSIC

THE RICH DIE HARD

MURDER BY REQUEST

DOWN THE KITCHEN SINK

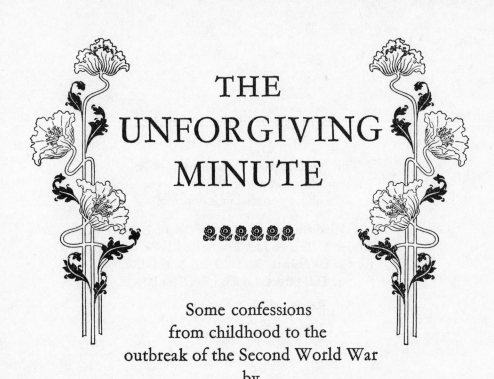

THE
UNFORGIVING
MINUTE

Some confessions
from childhood to the
outbreak of the Second World War
by

Beverley Nichols

W. H. ALLEN · LONDON
A Howard & Wyndham Company
1978

Printed and bound in Great Britain by
Butler & Tanner Ltd, Frome and London,
for the Publishers, W. H. Allen & Co. Ltd,
44 Hill Street, London W1X 8LB

Reprinted November 1978

ISBN 0 491 02444 4

For

Blanche and Eric Glass

*The Guides, Philosophers
and Friends of my literary
life, with love and gratitude*

If you can fill the unforgiving minute
With sixty seconds' worth of distance run
Yours is the Earth and everything that's in it
And—which is more—you'll be a Man, my son!
Rudyard Kipling

In preparation—*Distance Run*—covering
the remaining years of the author's life.

CONTENTS

CHAPTER I

THE SACRED
AND THE PROFANE

I am entirely self-taught.

With a background of Marlborough and Balliol, this may sound unlikely, but it probably applies to the majority of my countrymen who have gone through the mill of British middle-class education.

When I was President of the Union at Oxford one of my two guests of honour was an endearing scoundrel called Horatio Bottomley. (The other was Winston Churchill, and if they had been born in different bedrooms they might well have played each other's roles in history.) Bottomley had no pretensions to gentility; he was brash and uncouth, and when he rose to speak there were titters. He silenced them with a single phrase. 'Gentlemen,'—and he subtly accented the word—'I have not had your advantages. Such poor education as I have received has been acquired in the University of Life.' The titters were hushed and at the end of his speech there was a standing ovation. Yes—if he had been born in Blenheim he might well have trod the Churchill road. Perhaps the most important thing in life is the bedroom in which one is born. I was born in the wrong one, very much the wrong one.

Nobody has ever taught me anything whatsoever. I speak reasonably good French but I learned it from friends and from the bistros in the Place Pigalle. Such German as I can manage was picked up in the streets of Berlin and, of course, in bed, where at least one gets down to fundamentals. I was obliged to study Greek at Marlborough, but it was taught as though it were not merely dead but as though it had never lived at all. Greek only fluttered to

I

life on my first visit to Athens and I did not learn it while poring over guide-books in the Parthenon but during trips to a shady casino in the Piraeus. (I seem to be painting a rather lurid past.)

It was the same with history. At Marlborough we spent a whole term studying the dusty details of the Elizabethan Ecclesiastical Settlement. We memorised the strategic techniques of long-forgotten battles. I learned my history from cathedrals and museums and picture galleries. Geography was a question of capes and bays and peninsulas and archipelagoes, which bored me to tears. At a very early age I decided that the only civilised way of learning geography was to go round the world, and in order to do this one needed money. So I earned the money, and went round the world. In both directions.

Poetry—and indeed the whole field of English literature—I had to discover for myself. There were no books of poetry in our home, and our scanty library was a load of trash. True, my father taught me one quatrain of Tennyson which he had learned by heart when, for a brief space, he was one of the rising hopes of his local Tory party. You probably know it.

> I held it truth, with him who sings
> To one clear harp in divers tones,
> That men may rise on stepping-stones
> Of their dead selves to higher things.

My father never rose to higher things. He fell off the stepping-stones and sank deeper and deeper into the mire of hopeless alcoholism. But that is another story, which I have told elsewhere.*

So it was, across the whole spectrum of art and letters; I was a lone figure, desperately seeking guidance and never getting it. Self-pity? Why not? If one has pity for others, why should one not spare some for oneself? Perhaps it was all my own fault, perhaps it was due to some inherent defect of character. All the same I still bitterly regret that the background of my 'home', which came

---

* *Father Figure:* William Heinemann Ltd, 1972.

increasingly to resemble an institution for the criminally insane, compelled me to approach everything from the wrong way round.

Repeat . . . I am entirely self-taught.

As if anybody cared. And yet, the matter may have interest, if only as an example of one man's capacity, not only for survival, but for spiritual development, against considerable odds.

Let us consider the visual arts. When I was sent to Marlborough, where I learned absolutely nothing whatsoever during three cold and wasted years, it was not long before I began to collect my share of prizes. The first of these was the annual award for the best essay on 'an artistic subject', which was certainly a wide enough definition. I won it with a piece on the French Impressionists.

How did I come to write this piece? How indeed did I come to hear about the French Impressionists at all? The year was 1913; my home was in Torquay, a citadel of Philistinism; I had never been abroad; and on my one and only trip to London my cultural excursions had been confined to Madame Tussaud's, the Zoo, and the Tower, all of which I detested because I dimly realised that they were all monuments to human cruelty. But let us return to the aforesaid 'capacity for spiritual development'. In Torquay there was a little arty-crafty shop on the Queen's Parade which dealt in the sort of fragile rubbish which one finds in all such sea-side establishments—china mugs with the inscription 'A Present from Torquay', brooches from the wings of blue butterflies, 'ivorine' models of the Taj Mahal, shelves of calendars and Christmas cards. I was in search of Christmas cards, and went inside. Life suddenly acquired a new dimension. Facing me was a tray of cards marked 'Reduced to One Penny . . . One Dozen for Tenpence'. They were crude early reproductions, printed in Paris, of the French Impressionists. I stared at the brilliant colours as though I were gazing at a stained glass window. 'French they are,' said a voice behind me. And then . . . 'You can 'ave the lot for two bob.' Two shillings was a lot of money; I should be skint till Christmas, but I bought the whole tray. When I got home I had my own private art gallery—Renoir, Monet, Cézanne, Manet, Degas, Matisse, Utrillo, Pissarro—the lot.

3

Fifty years later I was to use two of those pictures, a Renoir and a Manet, to illustrate a book of my own, which was more a labour of love than any that I have written.*

I cannot remember how I learned enough about the Impressionists to write the Marlborough essay. It must have been jejune, but maybe the boyish enthusiasm compensated for the lack of erudition.

A side-light on British public-school morality in the days before the war. When I went to the headmaster's study to read him the essay, as was the custom on these occasions, he placed me by the fire-place and came to stand by my side. He then proceeded casually to slide his hand down the back of my trousers and pinch me gently on the behind throughout the entire reading. This struck me as rather peculiar behaviour from the headmaster; it was more what one had come to expect from the senior prefects. Besides, it was a very cold day and his fingers were icy. However, it was nothing to write home about, and I cherished the hope that he was really more interested in my prose than my posterior.

The reaction of my form-master was even more curious. I loved my postcards so much that I stuck two of them inside my desk. One of them was Manet's picture of spring flowers which now hangs in the Louvre; the second was Cézanne's 'Les Baigneurs'. He ignored the Manet and glared at the Cézanne.

'Do you like this stuff? Do you like looking at the bodies of naked young men?'

I will not employ the device of inventing dialogue, so I will not 'remember' my reply. In any case the question was so idiotic that it was unanswerable. I did not like 'looking at the bodies of naked young men'. One had more than enough of that sort of thing in dormitory and in the swimming pools. What I did 'like' was the magical play of light and shade, the miraculous handling of the flesh tints, and the musical perfection of the design, which had the mathematical authority of a Bach fugue. But a curly-headed sixteen-year-old school-boy, shivering at his desk, could hardly be expected to defend his aesthetic credo with conviction, and I made

* The *Art of Flower Arrangement*: William Collins & Co. Ltd, 1967.

no protest when he seized my little Cézanne, tore it up and threw it into the fire, to the evident delight of my class-mates.

In retrospect I have sometimes wondered whether he was indeed so outraged by the Cézanne. His subsequent conduct suggested that he was activated by the same motives as the headmaster (who was later elevated to the bishopric of Bath and Wells, after marrying a tobacco millionairess). What really worried him was an urge to pinch my behind.

It is time that we began at the beginning.

The first sentence of this book, if you are still with me, is . . . 'I am entirely self-taught.'

This is not quite true. From the outset I was instructed, in the most passionate, positive and primitive manner in the reality and omnipresence of God. The lessons were given by my first governess, Miss Herridge, who was later to play a major role, under the pseudonym of 'Miss Hazlitt', in a book called *A Village in a Valley*.* After forty years I still receive letters addressed to her personally, which is gratifying, because she was a saint—the only authentic saint whom I have ever known—and it makes me happy to think that her spirit still marches on. Miss Herridge was a member of the Plymouth Brethren, who were also saints, but not of quite so attractive a nature. For *her* the presence of God was like birdsong in the morning skies. He was a symbol of Joy and her heart longed to sing back to Him. For most of the Brethren God was a Thunderer, forever growling and threatening from behind a dark curtain lit by the fires of Hell. I was lecturing in America when she died and on my return I got in touch with one of the Senior Brethren to find out where she was buried. It was somewhere in Wiltshire and I wanted to go on a pilgrimage to lay some flowers on her grave. For reply I received a harsh reproof. Miss Herridge, wrote the Brother, was now in Heaven where she would have all the flowers she wanted. She had no need of any mundane blossoms from the likes of me. He declined to forward the address.

* Jonathan Cape Ltd, 1934.

5

Perhaps it was foolish to be distressed by so uncouth an epistle, but it hurt me. Flowers and Miss Herridge—they went hand in hand. To say that she 'taught' me to love flowers would be absurd; the love was already there, and always had been, since I made my first daisy-chain. But she gave direction to that love and a sound foundation of scholarship. On our walks through the Devonshire lanes we would pick bunches of wild flowers, which she showed me how to press in sixpenny albums, and when they were fixed she taught me their names—the Latin name and the popular country name. To my dying day I shall always remember that *Lychnis flos-cuculi* is the botanical name for the Ragged Robin. It seemed a pompous appellation for so charming a little ragamuffin of the hedgerow.

But her main preoccupation was to lead me to God—*her* God, who was everywhere, but everywhere, day and night, upstairs, downstairs, measuring every breath, guiding every step. In our home her task was difficult, to say the least of it. My father did not believe in God, he did not even believe in hell-fire, which was a matter of regret to me, for such a belief might have acted as a check on some of his grosser excesses. My mother tried to 'believe', and went to church, but she had no conviction and gained small comfort. She once said to me, 'I cannot visualise Jesus; I cannot see him as a Person.' In which she showed her very good sense; most of the legions of painters who have seen Jesus as a 'Person' have certainly got him wrong. Instead of seeing Jesus as a tortured, emaciated, fanatical Jew they have seen him as a handsome, highly photogenic Aryan. The last 'authentic' portrait of Jesus which was presented to me—(it was revealed to a spiritualist lady in a vision and got a lot of publicity)—might well have served as a model for the Hitler Jugend. Of my two brothers, the elder, Paul, took holy orders, though I do not think that he was truly destined for the Church. My other brother, Alan, never thought of anything but football. I was therefore left to bear the full brunt of Miss Herridge's missionary fervours, and obviously they must have had their effect. No child can be brought into prolonged contact with such burning convictions without being scorched, and the scars—if they are to be regarded as such—remain for life.

6

If anybody, in years to come, were to appraise the Collected Works of Beverley Nichols—and there might be some Californian professor, as yet unborn, who would be eccentric enough to attempt the task—he would be obliged to observe that Mr Nichols, throughout his long life, had been greatly concerned with God, and had recorded his concern in tens of thousands of words. An early example may be discovered in a book called *Are They The Same at Home?** which was published in the late twenties. This was a collection of 'profiles' written for the *Sketch* and it had considerable success. My immediate reaction on turning over its dusty pages is one of astonishment, almost of incredulity. Did one really meet all those important people, explore their souls, crystallise their personalities, and pin them, so adroitly, on the printed page? Where did one find the energy? Here is the not very exceptional record of a single day:

> Breakfast with Lloyd George
> Lunch with Diaghilev
> Tea with Sean O'Casey
> Cocktails with George Gershwin
> Dinner at the Garrick Club with H. G. Wells

Since everything and everybody in those days was grist to my mill these encounters usually found their way into print, with the permission though not always with the approval of those concerned. When the series was in full swing the *Sketch* suggested that I should write a profile of myself and it was here, in this very mundane *galère*, that I thought it incumbent upon me to declare my faith, or rather my lack of it, which comes to much the same thing. I quote . . .

Faith is a musty lisping word to me. It is no more a virtue than measles or an ear for music. I believe that when I die I am snuffed out like a candle and that no God will ever again set me alight. I see no use in trying to cheat myself. I long to believe in an after-life; I long to think that the

* Jonathan Cape Ltd, 1927.

shadows which even now are slowly lengthening over the lawns of life will, when the night comes, be chased away by some as yet unrisen moon. But I cannot. All my searching, my questioning, my endeavour, lead me nowhere.

This was not the sort of stuff that the *Sketch* was in the habit of publishing. I should be the last to suggest that it is either profound or original, and the metaphor about 'the lawns of life' is decidedly embarrassing. But that is not the point. The point is the declaration of a spiritual interest at so early an age and, even more, the fact that this declaration, in the years to come, was to be so constantly modified and so drastically reversed that my imaginary American professor, writing his thesis in the year 2000, would find himself incapable of describing what Mr Nichols really did believe at any given period in his life.

Actually my spiritual awareness was very much alive at the age of nine, when I not only recorded it but got it into print, in the year 1907. Our local newspaper was a weekly sheet called the *Torquay Directory*, which, if studied today, would vividly recall the Domesday Book. The main function of the *Directory* was to record the activities of the local gentry and its most popular feature was a column headed 'Arrivals and Departures'. My father was a keen follower of the *Torquay Directory*; indeed, he frequently saw to it that our family was represented in the social section. My brother Paul had an amiable but rather dreary Oxford friend called Lord St Audries, who often came to stay with us at our home, which bore the ludicrously pretentious name of Cleave Court. Each of his arrivals was chronicled in the *Torquay Directory*, which had been duly informed of this momentous event by my father, in a drunken sprawl, on crested writing-paper. 'Lord St Audries has arrived at Cleave Court.' A very impressive item to show to his favourite barmaid at the Queen's Arms. And a few days later . . . 'Lord St Audries has departed from Cleave Court.'

I had other interests in the *Torquay Directory*; I saw it as a platform for my burgeoning talents. So one day I sat down and wrote a sonnet to buttercups, inspired by a secret field which I used to visit

8

when life at Cleave Court was more than usually stormy and frightening. As a poem it was probably neither better nor worse than the average sonnet written by a boy of nine, but it had one image that lingers in my memory. Staring out over the yellow fields I saw the flowers as a sort of celestial coinage and I wrote down the words 'God's money', which became the title of the poem. No two words could have been more significant of the life that I was destined to lead—the first stirring of the spirit and the precocious awareness of the material struggles that lay ahead, the eternal conflict of the sacred and the profane.

Is this authentic 'autobiography'? I think so, because any work that can be classified as autobiographical must be to some extent a record of spiritual experience.

In referring to the 'eternal conflict between the sacred and the profane' I was not suggesting that my life has been one long struggle between these two forces; I was merely noting that the battle has been incessant and has sometimes been waged in the most bizarre circumstances.

Here is an example. The only blazing row concerned with religious matters which I have ever had occurred in—of all places—the Café de Paris, and it was with—of all people—Noël Coward. He had sent me seats for the première of one of his cabaret seasons, accompanied by a note asking me to come round for a drink afterwards. I have it still. 'Beverley darling, I know that you are the supreme protagonist of the early-to-bed-and-early-to-risers but in this case you must make an exception fondest love Noël.'

So there I was at a ringside table at midnight lapping it up, the timing, the exquisite understatement, the crisp, crackling expertise, sparkling as brightly as the champagne which he had kindly ordered for my table. Until, just before the finale, he sang 'Don't put your daughter on the stage, Mrs Worthington'. Since the words of this song are probably more familiar to the younger generation than the words of the National Anthem, we need not quote the lyric in its entirety. It was only a matter of the last three lines. They should have been . . .

9

> Please Mrs Worthington
> *On my knees*, Mrs Worthington
> Don't put your daughter on the stage!

But when the song rippled to its familiar conclusion Noël suddenly changed it. He sang . . .

> Please Mrs Worthington
> *Christ* Mrs Worthington
> Don't put your daughter on the stage!

There was great applause at the end of the song. The audience, as always, was enchanted. And Noël swept off.

Should I go round to the party? I went upstairs, out into the cold winds of Leicester Square. I was suddenly very angry; the use of the word 'Christ' in such a context was excruciatingly vulgar; in some respects it could be regarded as obscene.

We need not write a saga about the next five minutes. I remember entering a crowded room, blue with cigarette smoke. A cacophony of adulation. Marlene Dietrich, a miracle of artifice, propped against the wall. Me, telling Noël that he should be ashamed of himself.

And Noël, looking more Chinese than the thoughts of Mao Tse-Tung, spitting out the only sentence that I care to recall in a dialogue that brought the party to a swift and embarrassing conclusion. 'My dear Beverley, if you have come here in your role of a professional evangelist you have misjudged your audience.'

So that was that. Noël is dead and I am extending an arthritic ankle towards the grave. Our little fracas had no permanent effect on our friendship; Noël was an honest man and he respected honesty in others. Only once, many years later, did he betray that he remembered our disagreement. It was at his villa in Switzerland, a few weeks before his death. For a moment we were alone together. Suddenly he looked up from the bed in which he was lying. Abruptly he said . . . 'Beverley. About Christ. I haven't come round to your way of thinking. But . . .' Long pause. Perfect timing '. . . But I do agree with you that He had star quality.'

*   *   *

This, I claim, *is* legitimate 'autobiography'. But where is the pattern? How does one disentangle it all? I will recall a few dates.

In 1927, I was waving the banner of agnosticism against the unlikely backcloth of a fashionable magazine.

Nine years later, in 1936, after long periods of painful introspection, I exploded into a book called *The Fool Hath Said*.* This was as passionate a defence and interpretation of the Christian faith as G. K. Chesterton's *Orthodoxy*. Though neither of these titles, in these days, can arouse much interest, they both caused something of a stir at the time. Mine would have caused even more of a sensation if it had carried a preface informing the reader that it had been composed in the Martinez at Cannes, between visits to the Casino at Monte Carlo. Well—why not? Faith is faith whether it comes to you in a monastery or on the top of a bus.

The mention of buses gives me a chance to give some shape to this tangled story.

1952. Sixteen years have passed since *The Fool Hath Said*. Suddenly the buses of Britain charge through the cities, plastered with further evidence of my crusading zeal. Bright red buses blazing with the slogan '. . . Read Beverley Nichols in *A Pilgrim's Progress*'. I was nearly run over by one of them outside White's Club and when I staggered into the club for a recuperative brandy and soda I met Evelyn Waugh in the hall. 'It would have served you right, Beverley, if it *had* run you over. All those buses!' Evelyn never got onto a bus unless he was quite sure that nobody was looking. I got onto hundreds of buses and I welcomed them as a weapon of propaganda. Also, to be scrupulously honest, and admitting the frequent prevalence of the profane over the sacred, the buses flattered me. It is an exhilarating sensation, when you are on the top of a Number 6, speeding from Marble Arch, to find yourself suddenly confronted by a Number 9, hurtling towards the Thames Embankment, bearing your own image. You find yourself thinking what a good news story it would make, if there were a collision.

What has this got to do with spirituality? Any 'sensitive' person

* Jonathan Cape Ltd., 1936.

would say nothing at all, and would retreat with Evelyn Waugh to a corner of White's with a fusillade of superior sniffs. I say that it has everything to do with it—though 'spirituality' is not my favourite word. Anyway, it is autobiographically and historically apposite. *A Pilgrim's Progress* came out in 1952 and was a record, a very vivid one, of all the warring faiths which in those distracted days were clamouring for the attention of the British people. The death cries of the Church of England, the complacent chants of the Roman Catholics, the even more complacent murmuring of the Christian Scientists, the shrill shouts of the Jehovah's Witnesses, the soothing syrups of the Spiritualists, the eternal, mystical music of the Jews.

I was intensely absorbed by all these claims and counter-claims. I was no longer the bright-eyed believer of 1937. Fifteen years had passed. There had been a very big and a very beastly war, in the course of which I had come to the cliff-edge of death. Not in any glorious circumstances, but in a flat in Bombay, during one of the all too numerous physical crises of my erratic life. Being sent out as a war correspondent, ending up in hospital, being slashed and counter-slashed. With Reuter's news agency ringing up and asking if I was dead yet. With a rather nasty Anglo-Indian nurse saying brightly, 'No. But if you ring up tomorrow we *may* have some news for you.'

The war—India—the confrontation with death—the struggle back to life—the return to England—back to an empty house ... to an utter loneliness, all the squalid routine of coping with the daily chores of existence in a beleaguered city. What cause had I to complain? None. I was all in one piece. I was out of pain. Millions of my fellow-men were enduring greater tribulations.

But what had it all been *about*? And why had God ordained the crucifixion of so many millions of His creatures? These were the primitive questions which were being asked by every man who was not comfortably encapsulated in any of the orthodox religions. But I had already explored all the orthodox religions and found them wanting. In India I had even been allured by the mystique of Hinduism, and tried to make sense of it; but I had not the temperament of a Christopher Isherwood; I had not his enviable capacity for swallowing spiritual nostrums. A week in Benares put paid to *that*. The most penetrating observation about the Hindu religion—(which is in fact a bewildering complex of a thousand warring creeds)—was made by Mark Twain. When he was in Benares he discovered that if an orthodox Hindu were to have the misfortune to die on the wrong side of the river he would be reincarnated as a donkey. 'If I were a Hindu,' said Mark Twain, 'and I found myself dying in Benares, I should take the earliest possible opportunity of crossing to the wrong side of the river.'

A brief recap.

If you have followed me so far you will have the picture of a middle-aged gentleman, in a state of bewilderment, turning this way and that, in an effort to discover what life was all about. You will have noted his acceptance of orthodox Christianity, his sub-sequent doubts, his divergence to other faiths, his exile to the desert of 'agnosticism'—perhaps the most arid word in the English language. You will also have noted how these explorations into the territories of the spirit were constantly interrupted by the conflicting claims of the world of the profane.

This is an all too familiar struggle, which has been told in countless autobiographies by men and women of varying convictions, but in my case it had a new twist. For my final spiritual convictions—though I did not realise it at the time—came not through prayer or study or meditation but through the bright lights of the theatre.

It is a very curious story.

We must flash back to 1934. In that year I was scribbling away with the customary frenzy, producing at least two books a year, when I happened to read a review by Rebecca West in *The Sunday Times* of a book by Stefan Zweig called *Mental Healers*. The healers were Mesmer, Freud and Mary Baker Eddy. I was already reasonably *au fait* with Freud and Mrs Eddy, but Mesmer was only a name to me, and I decided to get to know more about him, and began to haunt the British Museum, seeking every scrap of information about this extraordinary man who, more than any other, was the father of modern psycho-therapy. I also decided that he would make an admirable subject for a play, which I proceeded to write with unbridled enthusiasm, far too quickly, as though I were catching an aeroplane to a distant country in search of hidden treasure. Which, in a sense, was precisely what I was doing.

In ten days the play was finished.* I sent it to Cochran who decided to put it into immediate production. A famous actor called Oscar Homolka flew from Vienna to play the lead, a brilliant actress called Peggy Ashcroft was cast as the heroine, and a celebrated producer called Komisaryevsky was engaged to direct. Never was a play presented under such brilliant auspices and never was there such a resounding flop. No—that is the wrong word. There was no 'resounding'. There was neither acclamation nor approbation; there was a silence that could be heard from Land's End to John o'Groat's.

I have nothing but contempt for dramatists who moan about their failures. If one writes a play which nobody wants to pay to see one should shut one's trap, and shrug it off, and go to lunch at the Garrick Club and accept the commiserations of one's fellow-dramatists with a gentlemanly smile.

The mention of the Garrick suggests that I might be permitted a momentary 'aside', if only to draw attention to the rather exceptional time-span of these recollections. For suddenly, we are back in the days of The Second Mrs Tanqueray. It happened like this. The only outstanding commercial success I ever had in the theatre was with a play called *Evensong*, in which Edith Evans gave one of the finest performances of her career. After a brilliant première I sat up all night to read the notices. They were without exception appalling. Never had the critics been obliged to listen to such a load of rubbish. *But* . . . on this they were unanimous—Miss Evans had been magnificent. Electrifying. She had saved the evening from disaster.

---

* *Mesmer:* a play in three acts by Beverley Nichols. Jonathan Cape Ltd, 1935.

After fortifying myself with a large Bloody Mary, which seemed an appropriate potion, I went down to the Garrick to read the rest of the papers which were, if possible, worse. Ghastly play. Superb Edith Evans. I began to hate Miss Evans. Then into the room walked Sir Arthur Pinero. He came up to me and put his hand on my shoulder.

'You remind me of myself forty years ago,' he said, 'after the first-night of *Mrs Tanqueray*. I went through much the same ordeal. But never forget this. No actress can give a great performance if the dramatist has not given her a great part.'

That was a maxim from a master of the theatre which I think is worth recording, not only for the benefit of aspiring dramatists but of popular actresses and omniscient critics.

This 'aside' has gone on longer than I intended. We were talking of Mesmer, the date was 1934, and all that matters, autobiographically, is that from this year, Mesmer the man, Mesmer the mysterious genius, Mesmer the bewildering complex of charlatan and prophet, continued to haunt me for ten, twenty, thirty years. He was constantly looking over my shoulder, at the most unexpected moments. I would read a paragraph about faith-healing, and there he was, his voice echoing the same language. I would hear a conversation about water-divining, and make tentative experiments of my own accord with hazel-twigs, on deserted lawns, and find that I had the gift in my own hands, that I was receptive to the inexplicable forces, the surge of some unexplained radiation. That is the key word . . . 'radiation', and once you have got that word in your head, life is never quite the same. In the end, everything comes down to words. They are the only coinage of communication, and one of the reasons for the agonies of the world is that this coinage has been so debased.

> 'Radiation'
> 'Vibration'
> 'Resonance'

These were some of the words—and there were many others, which began to echo through my head, like the key notes in a tune which will not sing itself into shape, which fits into no conventional rhythm, which is always running off the stave. What did these words mean? Everything, or nothing?

More and more urgently the words clamoured for clarification. Could the 'vibrations' of spiritual healing, for example, be scientifically assessed? To what extent was the 'resonance' of water-divining actually measurable? How did one account for the extraordinary phenomenon of telepathy, for which there is so impressive a volume of evidence? How did one define the word which is perhaps the key to this whole bundle of mysteries . . . the word radiesthesia?

Radiesthesia? The great majority of readers have probably never even heard of it, and it has not attained the distinction of being included in the Oxford Dictionary. And yet it is one of the most important words in the English language, or should be.

I cannot hope to condense the painful researches of five years into a few pages. I can only hope to jog the reader's attention with a couple of stories.

Among my honoured friends is Mervyn Stockwood, the Bishop of Southwark, one of the few churchmen to whom these matters are the legitimate concern of the Christian who relates his religion to the realities of the contemporary scene. One day, not so long ago we went up to the de la Warr Institute at Oxford to examine the mysteries of the Black Box. It would need a whole book to explain the Black Box, the claims and counter-claims that have been made for it, what is in it, what is not in it. All one can say with assurance is that thousands of highly intelligent people have used it and are using it with results which they claim, with reason, to be miraculous. The trip to Oxford was among the most exhausting experiences that I have ever known; one felt as if one were climbing mountain ranges in which the air was too rarefied for common mortals. At the end of the day we sank into the car that was to take us back to London.

I said to Mervyn, 'I only understood about ten per cent of all that. How much did you understand?'

'At the most, one per cent. But I feel totally convinced of the

integrity of the work that Institute is doing, and of its importance.'
Pause. 'I also feel that we have both earned a large gin and tonic.'
Mervyn, as you may gather, is a complete human being, for whom the
co-existence of the sacred and the profane is a source of strength.

My last story is one which ought to make headlines all over the
world if the press had any inkling of what is news and what is not.
I have already told it in *Powers That Be*,* the book that was the final
outcome of these years of very difficult research. Nobody took any
notice of it at the time so I shall tell it again, very briefly. Nag, nag,
nag. Quite. But it is the nagnagnaggers of the world—a word that
might have appealed to Swift—who sometimes get things done.

Try to visualise a middle-aged woman, with grey hair and keen,
kindly eyes, stretching out her hand over a large-scale relief map.
It is an odd sort of map, because there are no names on it, only
contour lines, signs of afforestation, and tracings of meandering
streams. From her fingers hangs a piece of raw copper attached to
a pendulum, which swings in a regular rhythm. As it swings, she
makes notes on a sheet of paper, and after a few minutes she sighs,
and leans back, and says to the little group of men who are watching
... 'I am afraid that's all I can do for the moment. Has it been any
use?'

The men smile at the woman, whose name is Evelyn Penrose.
They are very tough, hard-headed business-men, with considerable
interests in an East African mining complex. They had presented
Miss Penrose with this map, without giving her the smallest idea of
where it was. She did not even know which continent she was
examining. All she knew was that they had wanted her to look for
copper. She had found it.

Yes, they told her. She had discovered what they wanted. She
had confirmed the speculations of their chief geologists, and added
details of the greatest value, such as the depth and quality of the
deposits. All from a printed map. And she had never been within
a thousand miles of the mines in question.

If this is not a miracle I do not know what is. Moreover, it is a
miracle that would stand up to the most ruthless scrutiny in a court

* *Powers That Be:* Jonathan Cape Ltd, 1966.

of law. Among the areas of the world where Miss Penrose has exercised her astonishing gifts, researching for oil, water and minerals, is British Columbia. And among the men who have unanimously testified to her 'miraculous' gifts are the Minister of Finance, the Attorney General, the Minister of Mines and the deputy Minister of Agriculture. I have their statements and have published them, without contradiction.

One miracle implies another. Miss Penrose is dead, but her work goes on, her pendulum swings in other hands; knowing that these extraordinary forces are still at work, the airs of the world are alive with these strange echoes and radiations.

Hardly anybody seems to care. I care very much indeed, though I do not pretend to understand, and I shall go on caring until I die.

When one is in a muddle, spiritual, literary, physical, domestic or financial, there are really only three things to be done. Go to the piano and play some Chopin. Go into the garden and pull up some weeds. Go to the bookshelf and take down a book of poetry. I cannot conduct you to the piano nor lead you down the garden path, but I can guide you to the bookshelf and read you a poem.

> All things, by immortal power
> Near or far
> Hiddenly
> To each other linked are,
> That thou canst not stir a flower
> Without troubling of a star.

The man who wrote those twenty-six words of magic was called Francis Thompson. He danced in and out of the gates of Heaven and he knocked on the doors of Hell. He was one of the guiding stars of my boyhood. The three collected volumes of his works were the books which I chose for my first prize at Marlborough College. They were presented to me by the same headmaster who displayed so tender an interest in my posterior when I read him the essay on the French Impressionists.

Which might be a reminder that it is time to go back to the beginning of it all.

CHAPTER II

⚜⚜⚜⚜⚜⚜

VIRTUTE STUDIO LUDO

I am a great believer in putting carts before horses, particularly when travelling in Arabian countries where horses are regarded as legitimate objects of torture. No prospect would give me greater satisfaction than the sight of an emaciated horse, reclining in a heavy cart while its Arabian owner sweated in the traces, occasionally receiving sharp bites on his behind.

I have been putting the cart before the horse in this volume, but autobiographically this may not be such a bad idea. If the reader has some concept of the end product of the human being whom he is studying, he may take more interest in the process which moulded him. To quote Browning . . .

> All I could never be
> All men ignored in me
> This was I worth to God
> Whose wheel the pitcher shaped.

> In virtue I study and I play.

This was the motto of Marlborough College in the County of Wiltshire, whither I was sent in the Autumn of 1912. As far as the 'virtue' was concerned we were left to formulate our own ethics and to construct our own codes of conduct, under the guidance of gangs of gauleiters disguised as senior prefects. Our 'study' was haphazard and unimaginative; the operative word was 'ludo'. Not only did we play, but we were compelled to play, day in and day

19

out, at all seasons and in all weathers. If a boy was good at games he could get away with murder; nothing else mattered. I learned this within a few hours of my arrival, and the discovery filled me with apprehension, because I was never good at games. The only athletic distinction I ever achieved was in the sphere of sports. I found that I could run rather faster than most people, and I broke the school record for the quarter mile.

This might have a fleeting interest for the student of juvenile psychology. For I was not trying to win a race. What I was really doing was running *away*, with the devil at my heels, away from the horrors of it all.

I do not know what decided my father to pack me off to Marlborough, which was and is among the most expensive schools in England. He certainly could not afford it; he was probably attracted by its Spartan reputation. There was no nonsense about Marlborough; it was a school where they made full use of the cane and where, throughout winter's rages, the windows of the dormitories were always kept wide open so that one sometimes woke up to find that one was sleeping under a coverlet of snow.

That is my sharpest and most immediate reaction in recalling those desolate years. Cold. We were always cold. There was an institution called Early School, which was enforced throughout the year. Every morning we shivered out of bed and raced across a wind-swept courtyard, in the teeth of the wild Wiltshire gales, in order to sit in an icy classroom which, of course, had no central heating. If we were lucky we managed to gulp a mug of luke-warm cocoa on the way in. After which we sat chafing our fingers, making notes about matters of complete unimportance. News from Nowhere. Fiddling little battles and long-lost causes which would better have been forgotten.

After the cold, the accent was on cruelty. Here are some examples . . .

'DORMITORY PULL-UPS'
The details of this convention were revealed on the first day of term. The new boy arrived in a cab, entered a bleak building, met a

master, clattered up a stone staircase to his dormitory, in the wake of a prefect.

The prefect showed him his bed and pointed to the ceiling.

'See those?'

'Yes, sir.'

'You've got six weeks to get your muscles up. So you'd better get busy unless you want your bottom tanned to ribbons.'

Exit prefect.

What had the prefect been pointing at? A pair of steel gymnastic rings, hanging from the ceiling. And why the menacing reference to the boy's bottom? Because those rings were the symbol of Marlborough's insistence on muscular Christianity. At half-term we were expected to have developed our small biceps to a degree that would enable us to leap up, grip the rings, and twist about in a series of complicated gymnastic exercises. If we failed we were bent over the bed and given ten strokes in pyjamas, in the presence of the rest of the dormitory. If we cried out in pain, the strokes came harder.

I managed to perform the exercises, but a great many boys failed, and suffered accordingly, for the sole reason that their muscles were too weak. To be beaten for misconduct—well and good; to be beaten for a physical deficiency—this enraged me and still does. It also throws a sharply contrasting light on the contemporary educational scene. Nowadays, if the form-master in a comprehensive school is maddened by the outrageous behaviour of a gang of louts, and if he is rash enough to give one of them a clout, there is an immediate public outcry. Parents arrive demanding vengeance. Left-wing members of Parliament spring up in the House of Commons, foaming at the mouth. The Amalgamated Union of Boiler-makers threaten immediate strike action. This perhaps is exaggerated, but when I read the memoirs of some of the more successful men who have risen from the ranks of the workers, and am asked to sympathise with the hardships of their youth, I cannot help wishing that they might have had a taste of what was suffered by the ones of the comparatively upper classes. We were turned into 'Gentlemen', but my God we suffered in the process.

We were still living in the shadows of *Tom Brown's Schooldays*. And that shadow stretched into the grim distances of Dotheboys Hall. Another example . . .

'TURFING DOWN BASEMENT'

This was a form of punishment which could only have originated in the mind of a sadist, and every prefect had the power to enforce it. To 'turf' in this context meant to run, not only down the stone stairs to the basement but up again, and down again and up again, as though one were on a treadmill, as many times as the prefect might ordain. A hundred 'turfings' were not unusual, and the prefects used to stand at the top of the staircase, with grins on their faces, to make sure that their victims were not cheating.

Not all these tribal customs came under the heading of cruelty. Many of them were merely senseless; nevertheless they were rigidly enforced, not only by the boys but by the masters. Such as . . .

'CARRYING THE KISH'

The Oxford Dictionary definition of the word Kish is 'a large wicker basket which is used in Ireland for carrying turf'. At Marlborough it was applied to a flat cushion, like a large pad, which we tucked under our arms and used as a container for our books. This, heaven knows, was silly enough; the books fell into the mud and the cushions were soaked in the rain; but sillier is to come. During one's first year the kishes had to be carried so that there were exactly six inches more kish in front than at the back, and if these proportions were disregarded one was severely reprimanded and sometimes beaten. Have any of the tribes of Darkest Africa ever conceived taboos so totally inane? And yet the Kish complex was fervently upheld by the headmaster and his subordinates, and had the support of the Board of Governors. There was one Speech Day when a bishop of quite exceptional mediocrity (Marlborough produced so many bishops that one felt they were coming off an assembly line) made an oration in which he praised the Kish complex as 'one of those happy traditions of our younger days which have helped to mould the character of our people'.

SEXUAL CURIOSA

Did these strange conventions leave a permanent mark? Did they help to mould the characters of boys who were expected to provide the material for the ruling classes of a great Empire? The answer is probably yes. They certainly taught us to accept discipline as one of the essentials of our later conduct, and even though the methods of teaching were ludicrous and barbaric, once a boy has acquired the habit of discipline he never loses it, no matter where life may lead him. Even if he is destined to become a concert pianist.

In the sphere of sex things were very very different. There was no discipline, nor even any guide-lines. If my own sexual history was in any way typical of the average Edwardian schoolboy, it is surprising that the members of my generation—what remains of it —are not all incarcerated in lunatic asylums. To suggest that we were taught nothing about sex would not be quite true, for though there was no instruction there were a great many hints and mutterings, and they were all dark and dreadful and fraught with fear.

We did not learn from our parents. To Edwardian parents the word 'sex' was a sort of hiss, an evil echo against which they must shut the door, lest their children should be contaminated. It was not for them to raise the subject; the proper place to learn about sex was in the gutter. They would have been horrified if you had suggested that this was the implication of their attitude, but how else was it to be interpreted? Actually, the basic mechanics of sexual intercourse were taught to me by my brother Paul, during the holidays, after his first term at school. We were staying in Cornwall and he took me out and sat me down in a field and picked a lot of leaves and twigs and dandelion heads. These he formed into various mystic patterns which he jiggled up and down as though he were manipulating a puppet show. The climax came when he took a deep breath, puffed out his pink cheeks, and sent the seed pods flying up to the summer skies. He was trying to illustrate the nature of a sexual orgasm, and very kind and gentle of him it was, to think of this way of enlightening me. But it was not really so sensible. For I was not in the least enlightened and had no idea what he was going on about. I wondered if perhaps he had caught sunstroke.

When I eventually came to learn the meaning of this fumbling symbolism the shock was all the sharper. Sex—so my early boyish intuitions informed me—was a strange, disgusting, and probably painful exercise in which grown-ups indulged, for reasons best known to themselves. That my father should indulge in it was of course to be expected, but that my mother should have joined him—that was very hard to bear.

All these bewilderments and frustrations were probably common to the children of the Edwardian gentry. It was a difficult age for a child to be brought up in. The religious dogmas of the Victorians were losing their authority, parents were beginning to stay away from church, and even in Torquay there were quite respectable families who permitted croquet to be played on Sunday. But though this comparative laxity was to be welcomed it was not accompanied by any corresponding enlightenment. We were left in a vacuum. Sex was still a dirty word.

The sources of information came from cheap magazines—the equivalent of modern 'porn'—which we picked up at railway stations and sea-side book-stalls. In these we studied articles by 'medical correspondents' informing us that if we masturbated we should go mad. We read these articles with a mixture of horror and exhilaration. Were they true? Was it really the case that if friction was applied to our private parts, with the normal consequences ordained by nature, we should end up in a lunatic asylum? We asked ourselves these questions in bed, in the gymnasium, in the garden, lying under lilac trees on hot Sunday afternoons.

I was still asking them when I went up to Marlborough. It was not long before they were answered.

It began with a note from a senior prefect whom we will call Redwood, telling me to report to his study after evening prep.*
The note was handed to me by a rather nasty boy whom we will call Drake. I read it with dismay. What had I done wrong? Should

---

* 'Prep' was the hour of preparation spent in studying the lessons for the following day.

I be beaten for it? And in any case why did he have to write a *note* about it?

'It's an old Marlburian custom,' smirked Drake, who was not without an occasional flash of wit.

At the appointed hour I presented myself, and was duly initiated. Presumably the reader will not need to be told the details of what transpired, and in any case I have never been attracted by pornography, either in reading it or in writing it. What is apposite to the story—here I am thinking aloud—is my own reaction.

Firstly, I was not at all 'shocked'. After all, from the age of seven, my father had provided me with enough shocks to last a life-time. I knew all the four-letter words as a small boy, though I did not fully understand what they meant.

Secondly, young Master Redwood was extremely good-looking; and his requirements were very simple.

Thirdly, although he was obviously no stranger to the arts of masturbation, it had obviously done him no harm, either physically or mentally. He was a brilliant athlete, he later won a history scholarship at Cambridge and a military cross in the war. I don't know what happened to him nor even if he is still alive. If he is, I hope he remembers me with affection.

Four years go by, and in these pages I will make them pass swiftly, for though they marked the opening stages of the First World War, I am not writing a history of our times. Besides, during the first stages of the conflict, the war made little impact either on myself or any of my fellows. It was only a distant thunder of battle in the distant background.

Little by little this situation was to change; the thunder came nearer, the grey skies of Wiltshire were to be streaked with ominous flashes from the inferno of France. And I was to be swept into it.

Meanwhile, life went on much as usual. There were more encounters with Redwood and others, but it would be misleading to suggest that Marlborough—or Eton or Harrow or any other such similar institutions into which we were herded—were hot-beds of homosexuality. Even if they were, the corruption, if it is to be so regarded, cannot have gone very deep. Marlborough's exceptional output of bishops, field-marshals and pillars of the establishment is proof to the contrary.

In retrospect, what enrages me about these years—these dangerous, delicate, difficult years in which one's character was being moulded—is that nobody ever attempted to put sex in any sort of perspective, or suggested that it was a force that might one day play a role of importance in one's life, that it might even be a source of inspiration. Indeed, the only time I ever heard the word mentioned by an adult was from the pulpit. One of Marlborough's innumerable bishops came down and preached a sermon based on one of the epistles of St Paul—who certainly had strong views about sex, most of which are highly suspect. The bishop used the word 'sex' at the beginning of his sermon, and seven hundred boys sat up sharply. But they soon leant back in their pews again, for no enlightenment was to come from this distinguished ecclesiastic. All he had to say to us was 'keep your bodies clean'. In view of the fact that we were all obliged to take a cold bath every morning of our lives the injunction was superfluous.

We are back at the beginning. 'I am entirely self-taught.' Admittedly, there were some spheres in which nobody could have taught me anything at all. Confronted by the complexities of geometry my mind shut up like a clam. I could not even remember the verbiage, and the word 'hypotenuse' suggested something large and fierce that ought to be shut up in the zoo. Mathematics was an insoluble mystery. As for chemistry—very popular with most of the boys, who called it 'stinks'—my only reaction was one of alarm. I was always afraid that things were going to explode. Indeed, all through life I have had the fear that things are going to explode, and on quite a number of occasions the fear seems to have been justified.

And yet, surely there was *some* knowledge that might have been imparted? After all, as a Marlburian I was a member of the educational élite. I was Empire-building material. I might have played a role in foreign affairs, even if it were only running a second-rate consulate in a South American banana republic. Such a role would have demanded at least a smattering of French.

But French came to us via a master called Cartwright, whose accent was so atrocious that if he had ever tried to order an omelette in a French restaurant he would probably have found himself confronted by a steak au poivre. This irritated me inordinately because at one of my numerous preparatory schools my best friend had been a small boy called Victor de Polignac, whose great-great-great-grandmother had accompanied Marie Antoinette on the Flight to Varennes. Presumably in such circles they spoke French correctly, and so did Victor, whose family seemed charmingly unaware that the French Revolution had ever occurred at all. But when Mr Cartwright called me to stand up in class, and read a passage of French aloud—it was of the more boring fables of La Fontaine—and when I proceeded to deliver it, *à haute voix*, in the authentic accents of Marie Antoinette, Mr Cartwright banged on his desk and told me to stop 'showing off'. One couldn't win.

German was even worse. It was taught to us by an arrogant martinet called Colonel Wall, whose hatred of the Germans was so intense that when he attempted to speak their language he almost throttled himself. He reminds me of Churchill during the last war, and his snarling references to 'Mosserleeny' when he was attacking the Duce.

And then there was 'art', administered by a dear old gentleman called Wallace, who had obviously been destined to be a vet. His lessons were a farce. Surrounded by mouldering plaster casts of Greek statues he endeavoured to make himself heard through a Babel of ribald comment, accompanied by a fusillade of paper darts.

As for 'music' ... but I have written about this before, and won't go on about it. There was a thrilling occasion when I won the Marlborough music prize, and played a prelude of my own composition at the annual Speech Day, and was acclaimed in a London newspaper as a 'Schoolboy Chopin'. My male parent soon put a stop to all that, and my music lessons were abruptly terminated.

*   *   *

Moaning can become monotonous, so we will change the mood. This will involve a flash forward from 1917 to 1920, the year when I came of age, and when I published my first novel . . . *Prelude*.*

The fact that nearly sixty years have passed since the publication of *Prelude* must be my excuse for suggesting that this was an exceptional work to come from the pen of a schoolboy. *The Times* referred to it as 'the most remarkable study of a boy since Compton Mackenzie's *Sinister Street*—indeed one of the most remarkable studies of a boy that can ever have been written'. And who am I to quarrel with *The Times*? After all, one is a totally different person, not only mentally but physically. One is writing about a stranger, in whom one has no vested interest. Sometimes I think that the physical side of it is the more important. One's mind dances on, the words continue to scurry across the page like Shelley's 'leaves before an enchanter flying', but the pen falters, and one catches a glimpse of one's face in the mirror and mutters 'Oh, my God'.

So I have no false modesty in quoting *The Times*. *Prelude* was a remarkable book and perhaps the most remarkable thing about it was that it came out as a love story. In spite of the cold, the cruelty, the barbarism and the sheer stupidity of the tutorial system, I must have been in love with the place when the time came to leave.

And obviously I must have learned a great deal more than this record would suggest; the pages crackle with schoolboy dialogue that is intelligent and curiously contemporary. We had not only read our Bagehot's *The English Constitution*, our Bryce's *The Holy Roman Empire*, our Guizot, Hobbes, Maine and all the rest of them, but we had also read our Shaw and Wells and Chesterton, and had no hesitation in putting them in their proper places, with Shaw well in the lead and Chesterton dismissed as a second-rater. Needless to say we all had our transient love-affairs with the decadents; one of the characters, drawn from life, plastered the walls of his study with Beardsley's drawings for Salome and another wandered about the playing fields with Pater's *Marius the Epicurean*, reciting it aloud. (Both of them, by the way, were to win the Military Cross on the

* Chatto and Windus Ltd, 1920.

battlefield and both of them were killed.) For one of my school prizes (prizes were always awarded in the form of books) I chose Baudelaire's *Les Fleurs du Mal*, which caused my French master to raise his eyebrows, but as he could scarcely have translated it, let alone understood what it was all about, I got away with it.

Where did we acquire this knowledge? Certainly not at Marlborough. How did we come to evolve our theories over so wide a spectrum of the arts? We could reasonably regard ourselves as an intelligentsia, though we were of course in a minority. But how does such a community come into existence at all, against such a background, at so early an age? There can be no firm answer to such questions. But I have a theory—that knowledge, and taste, and the aesthetic passions, are infectious; they are in the air, with a sort of microbic life of their own, and the intelligent boy catches the microbes as inevitably as the unintelligent boy is immune to them.

In spite of our teenage flirtations with aestheticism we were not living in an ivory tower. We had heated arguments about proportional representation and capital punishment and we were not fooled by the popular jargon of the war years. One of our bibles was E. D. Morel's *Ten Years of Secret Diplomacy*, a book which might still be read with profit. And though our politics were juvenile and ill-informed, we were political animals, in our various ways, and we were all firmly to the left of centre. *Plus ça change.*

And of course, we held fervent views on religion, or rather on a wide range of religions. At the age of sixteen, when we went to bed, we may not always have knelt in prayer; but when we looked out of the dormitory windows, up to the cold winter skies, the stars seemed to form themselves into mysterious symbols, glittering question marks, pointing here there and everywhere, and sometimes nowhere.

I am reminded, yet again, of the ceaseless conflict between the sacred and the profane. To turn back to one's own work, after a lapse of over fifty years, is a curious experience for an author. Until I fished out this old copy of *Prelude* from a battered cabin trunk I had completely forgotten that there was a time when I very nearly 'went over to Rome'. The way in which I describe this

phase is, I think, rather touching, in spite of its youthful sentimentality. I was drawn to Rome, like countless sensitive youths
throughout the ages, for aesthetic reasons, the perfume of the
incense, the magic of the ritual, the music of the mass. I bought a
crucifix and burned incense in my study, to the not unnatural
irritation of the heretics, who used to bang on my door shouting,
'Nichols you bastard, stop making that bloody stink.'

But it did not last for long, and the passage celebrating the end
of the affair would be a gift to any parodist. I made my hero walk
out of chapel, torn by conflicting emotions, carrying his crucifix in
his pocket. Then I walked him down to the swimming-pool, sat
him by the edge and—after a pause for melancholy introspection—
had him drop the crucifix into the pool. I quote . . .

He watched it fall with a flash of silver into the deep black weeds below.
He wondered if that was, in a way, symbolic of what Christ had done . . .
a flash of light, darkness again, and a crystal bubble breaking on the
surface of the waters. He stretched out his hand as though to drag it out,
for he felt dimly as though he had lost a friend.

Did I say that this old author of nearly eighty is so totally different
from the schoolboy of seventeen? I am beginning to wonder.

A final quotation from the last page. My hero was called Paul
and at the end of the book I sent him to the wars and killed him.
One does not need to have passed a very advanced course in psycho-
analysis to realise that I was in fact killing myself, subconsciously
rejecting all the struggles that lay ahead. The final passage comes
in the form of a letter which Paul writes from France to a friend
who is still at school. He is writing from a ruined billet behind the
front lines, a few minutes after an enemy air raid.

I try to picture you in the study, reading Bryce or Francis
Thompson, but it all seems so far away now. And in any case a
few months in the army gives you so much to say and takes
away whatever power you may have had of saying it. But I feel I
want to be a man and live more fully. I used to think that a poet
or a musician (as I believed myself to be) was so precious that

he shouldn't run the risk of mixing with other people, or he'd knock the bloom off. I don't believe this any more. Great art has its roots deep in the clay and the worms, and the deeper the roots the more lovely the flowers. I used to think that one could get everything in the world from a rose. But now I know that it's Life—wonderful, clean, dirty, ugly, beautiful, sordid, hideous, breathless Life—that's what matters. Art for Life's sake. And I am learning to fight. A singer is a fighter. He must be for everything in the world is eternally at war.

Some day, if I come out of this all right, I want to write a school-book about Martinsell. I dream of the time I can come on leave, and have tea in the study, and walk over the downs, when spring is making it fresh and green again, year after year, green for spring, red and gold for autumn, black for winter. Yet here it seems always grey.

Sorry, I'm getting morbid. I'm not really—only a bit sentimental. I feel so young and useless and rotten somehow. I shall have to get old George Herbert out of my kit-bag and read him again. Do you remember that poem of his which we learned by heart?

> I will complain, yet praise,
> I will bewail, approve;
> And all my sour-sweet days
> I will lament and love.

Thank God, I can still love.
Ever yours,
Paul.

The parodist may make what he likes out of all that. But if he has a generous nature, he will remember that it was written by a boy of seventeen. And he can console himself with the thought that there will be even richer material for his talent in the chapters that are to follow.

CHAPTER III

@@@@@@

FOR KING AND COUNTRY

If I were to claim that during the First World War I had a distin-guished career as an officer in the British army there might be some raising of eyebrows, though few people can be still alive who would regard the matter as of any importance. But it was important to myself, and the claim would be true, provided that we allow some latitude to the word 'distinguished'. My army career was distin-guished by its utter improbability, and by the totally unexpected sequence of causes and events.

I will tabulate.

The date is August 1917; the war has fifteen months to run, and I am in my last term at Marlborough, aged eighteen and a half. I have been seriously ill; for a year I have been unable to parade with the O.T.C., so that I am unfitted to go through even the elementary motions of soldiering. In spite of these disabilities ...

PHASE 1. August 1917: I am swept into the army and dis-patched to Cambridge to train for a commission.

PHASE 2. November 1917: I am duly commissioned, and hurtled to a 'Labour Camp' in Thetford, disguised as a Second Lieutenant. After three months of black comedy ...

PHASE 3. February 1918: I am shot back to London, where I enter the Secret Service. After which, having succeeded in arousing the suspicions of the Civil Police, I am promoted to the rank of First Lieutenant.

PHASE 4. May 1918: for no discernible reason I am rushed back to Cambridge in order that I may ... (here I really must write a warning *sic*) ... in order that I may 'instruct senior officers in the technical developments of modern European warfare'. But the best is yet to be, as Browning once observed, in a very off moment.

PHASE 5. October 1918: still in uniform—(having been no nearer to the battlefields than the Cafe Royal)—I am wafted to the United States in charge of an important propaganda mission.

PHASE 6. November 1918: I lunch with President Wilson at the White House.

Perhaps it may be agreed that such a career deserves a footnote in *The Guinness Book of Records*, particularly when one remembers that it was chalked up by a rather fragile curly-haired schoolboy whose sole desire was to be left alone in order that he could play Chopin nocturnes. Maybe my pen has betrayed me into a Freudian slip. Maybe the curly hair had something to do with it. Indeed, the curly hair probably had everything to do with it. But under the hair there must have been an intelligence, even if it was only a primitive instinct for self-preservation.

To appreciate the bizarre nature of this scenario we must return to the previous year, when I was stricken with an illness with which I will not bore the reader. My only reason for mentioning it is because it probably saved my life. 1916 was a year of carnage. Flanders was a gigantic slaughterhouse. The rolls of honour of Old Marlburians, painted in gold letters on the school notice boards, grew longer and longer; the puppet parades of the Officers' Training Corps began to assume a grim reality. Bayonet drill, which was now conducted by a group of exceptionally foul-mouthed sergeants invalided from the front-line, had the authentic touch; you could almost see the blood spurting from the straw sacks as the boys assaulted them. Most of them seemed to find it rather fun. From these unpleasantnesses I was saved at least for the moment. On returning from hospital I was summoned to the office of Colonel Wall, who commanded the O.T.C. He was reading a letter in which a high-ranking officer of the Medical Corps instructed him that I was to be excused all military duties.

'This is a bad business, Nichols.'

'Yes sir.'

'It looks as though you'll be out of it all.'

Colonel Wall assumed that I was straining at the leash to rush out to Flanders in order to stick knives into the stomachs of my contemporaries, whose only offence was that they happened to have been born on the wrong side of the Rhine. I was not anxious to do anything of the sort. From the outset of the war I had suspected that there was something phoney about it, if only because it was so fervently welcomed by my father, and anything that he supported must *ipso facto* be evil. I did not believe the propaganda; I was nauseated by the comic posters of Lord Kitchener with his gigantic moustache and I refused to believe that you could make the world a better place by blowing half of it up. These juvenile sentiments were later to be recorded in a book to which we might refer in a later chapter because it had some effect on the thinking of my generation.*

'A bad business,' repeated the Colonel.

It was not a bad business, nor was it a good business; anyway, it was a business in which I had played no part. I was merely obeying orders. Instead of drilling I went for walks, well wrapped up Winter came and dribbled into a miserable spring. I attended more medical boards, always with the same result. As far as I was concerned, I seemed to have been forgotten.

And then with a bang, things began to happen.

Once again I was summoned to the office of Colonel Wall.

'Good news, Nichols! Read this!'

He handed me a letter from the latest medical board which I had attended the week before. The board had changed its mind. Instead of being granted total exemption I was now to be graded 'C 3'. Admittedly, this was the lowest physical category in which one could be placed, but the fact that I had been graded at all meant that I was now liable to be called up.

'Very good news!' repeated the Colonel. 'You've made it after all, and you've got me to thank for it. I've been pulling a few strings!'

* *Cry Havoc:* Jonathan Cape Ltd, 1933.

I stood to attention while he informed me that in ten days' time I was due to report at Magdalene College, Cambridge, for a crash course of training which, if I passed it, would entitle me to a commission in the Labour Corps.

'And of course you *will* pass it, young man. No doubt about that!'

'What is the Labour Corps, sir?' I asked the question in all innocence. Most of one's friends had gone into historic regiments like the Guards or the Gordon Highlanders. They had been promptly annihilated for their pains, but at least they had died like gentlemen. The Labour Corps sounded as though it had something to do with plumbing.

The Colonel was vague about what the Labour Corps actually *was*, as indeed he might be, for—as I was later to learn—it was a sort of vast dumping-ground for the physical dregs of British manhood; those who were either so severely wounded or so congenitally incapacitated that they could not be assigned to normal duties. The official policy in those last tragic months seemed to be 'sweep 'em up and get 'em into uniform and see what happens.' What happened was that they were usually bundled off to France and huddled together in rearguard positions, doing 'field-work' for which there was not the slightest demand. While so engaged they were frequently blown up in even larger quantities than their fellows in the trenches.

Ten days later I was speeding to Cambridge in a state of advanced panic. I was wearing the uniform of an officer cadet with a white band round the hat, in which I felt like a rather dubious sort of page-boy at the Ritz. I had no idea what I was supposed to do, nor how, nor why. I had only a few shillings in my pocket. True, I had a cheque book with fifty pounds to my account but I did not know how to use it. I had never had a cheque book before.

Life now became totally surrealist. Standing in the porch of Magdalene College, peering this way and that, wondering where to report, I was accosted by a tall middle-aged man in a scholar's gown who suggested that I had the appearance of being lost. Yes, I agreed, I was very lost indeed. 'Then you had better come to tea.' said the middle-aged gentleman, and conducted me across a small quadrangle towards the Master's Lodge. There were a number of cadets running about and as soon as they saw us they sprang to attention.

In the space of two minutes my war—my very special war—seemed much less unpleasant, because my new friend was none other than the Master of Magdalene, A. C. Benson, whose father had been one of Queen Victoria's favourite Archbishops. There were three Benson brothers, all distinguished in their separate ways, though the only one who is nowadays remembered is E. F. Benson, who is currently enjoying a belated revival as a writer of Edwardian comedy.

A. C. Benson, whom I came to know very well indeed, was a true scholar and an admirable administrator, with a knack of coaxing large sums out of American philanthropists for the benefit of Magdalene, which was his chief love. A beautiful little college it was, with a library of exceptional distinction, founded on the original bequest from Samuel Pepys. Benson was a mixed-up man, who had a habit of developing sentimental attachments at a moment's notice, and no doubt this was what had occurred when he met me in the porch, though I did not at first realise the full implications of the encounter.

After tea I felt much sustained, particularly when A.C.B. conducted me to the billet to which I had been assigned. This was a large room with four beds and the occupants were suitably impressed when they saw my illustrious companion. Perhaps they had hopes of benefits to come, for at Magdalene Benson was monarch of all he surveyed. Whatever their motives, they made me welcome and took me under their wing. They were an odd trio, a typical cross-section of the human débris from which the Labour Corps was being recruited. There was a young portrait painter in a state of incipient consumption who kept us awake with his coughing. His name was John Wells, and a few years later he painted the picture of the year in the Royal Academy. He also designed the cover for my first novel *Prelude*, which was already shaping itself in my mind. There was a middle-aged clairvoyant, a large fat man with varicose veins and moonstone eyes who was always late for parade because he could not do up his puttees. He used to lie in bed making hair-raising prophecies about further slaughters in the Western Front, which were usually fulfilled. And there was Wally, an ex-corporal in the Welsh Guards, who had been heavyweight champion of his regiment. He was a gigantic young man, who looked indestructible, though he had been badly shell-shocked. He was unfitted to be an officer, and knew it. We became firm friends and he assured me that if anybody annoyed me I must inform him, and he would 'sort them out'. A great many people annoyed me but I did not report them. A 'sorting-out' from Wally would probably have been lethal.

So began Phase 1, and it was far less gruesome than I had expected. Indeed, it was not gruesome at all. There was a minimum of drilling and strutting about, for the simple reason that most of us were not physically up to it. The examination that one had to pass in order to qualify for a commission was so simple that any intelligent schoolboy could have done it on his head. The only thing that worried me was saluting—not saluting a superior officer but *taking* a salute in the role of an officer, on the assumption that one had already been commissioned. The C.O. was much concerned that this ritual should be properly conducted. 'You are going to be officers in His Majesty's army,' he warned us. 'This is an honour that entitles you to be saluted by lower ranks, and it is an honour which you must enforce.' So he used to lay traps for us to make sure that we insisted on our rights in case we were not properly saluted. Especially for myself, because I did not like being saluted at all; I felt that I had done nothing to deserve it and would much rather have said 'Good morning' or 'How do you do' or, best of all, looked the other way. And I was physically and psychologically incapable of acting with the sort of bull-throated ferocity which officers were supposed to display on any occasion when their rank was not respected.

Apart from the saluting problem, life at Cambridge was very agreeable. Thanks to the patronage of A. C. Benson I found myself moving in academic circles which would otherwise have been closed. One night he arranged that I should dine at the high table in King's College, which was indeed an 'occasion' . . . the historic setting, the mellow candlelight, the glitter of the Waterford crystal, the sparkle of the Queen Anne silver. One of the features of these dinner parties was the parade of snuffboxes which the stewards handed round with the port. There were seven blends of snuff, and they each had fragrant musical names, as evocative as the throb of an old guitar. One was supposed to take only a single variety, and only a small pinch of it. I took all seven, in generous portions, and had a violent fit of sneezing which brought a certain boyish stimulus to this rather antique celebration.

And always there was music. There were pianos all over Cambridge and I made the most of them . . . at sing-songs for the troops, at strange dimly-lit sherry parties for the shadowy remnants of a scholarly society which had been by-passed by the war, and sometimes with an authentic musician. Among these was the renowned Professor E. J. Dent, whose libretto for Mozart's *Marriage of Figaro* is still regarded as a standard work. He entrusted me with the key of his front door, and I used to go along to his small gatherings on Saturday evenings when he gave us cabbage soup and coarse red wine, and played us Scarlatti, not very well. Professor Dent was a rather wicked old man in a withered sort of way. He had a statuette of Paganini on the piano to which he invariably directed the attention of any new undergraduate who joined his circle, asking him what he thought of it. Most of the young men were embarrassed by the question because the artist had portrayed Paganini with an outstanding erection. However I had been forewarned and had my answer ready. I did not think very much of it, I said; I could do better than that myself. By this riposte the naughty old gentleman was much diverted.

So the weeks sped by, in a sort of trance. I was living two quite separate lives—the life of a scholar in a town that was peopled by phantoms, and the life of a soldier in a city whose streets echoed to the tramp of the cadet battalions, and neither of those lives bore any relation to the realities of the outside world. For all this, remember, was happening towards the end of 1917, when the young men of Europe were being torn to pieces, when they were at each other's throats, obeying the lunatic instructions of their betters that they must destroy themselves, that they must rend their bodies apart . . . bodies that might have been united in friendship.

Phase 2. November 1917. Suddenly it all came to an end.

On November 11th I received my commission. As far as I remember it looked like one of the standard contracts one signs with the B.B.C. Twenty-four hours later I was sitting in a first-class railway carriage speeding up to the Eastern Counties in order to 'report for duties' to the First Labour Corps, First Battalion. This was the section which was first in line for France.

Once again I was in a state of panic. Not because I was frightened at the thought of being sent overseas. This was not the heart of the matter. Of course I was frightened; we all were; no sensible young man walks willingly through the gates of Hell. But there were more immediate causes for apprehension, smaller, but no less disturbing.

'Report for duties.' *What* duties? I began this book by saying that I was entirely self-educated, that nobody had ever taught me anything, and this was poignantly true about the present situation. I was now an officer in the Labour Corps, with a brass pip on my shoulder, and as such I should presumably be put in charge of long rows of large heavy men, in order to shout at them and march them somewhere with the object of doing something or other . . . but *what*? Dig drains behind the lines? Run about with sandbags under shell-fire? I was being thrown into unknown territory, with no charts and no compasses of conduct.

The train sped on its way, the Eastern Counties rolled by the windows in a tapestry of gloom, we arrived at Thetford station as dusk was falling, and everybody began saluting as I stepped out of the railway carriage. This was agonising. I was the only officer around and was therefore the target for all the troops on the platform and they seemed to make a bee-line for me, saluting like mad. I was chilled to the bone. I longed to tell them all to go away and stop making these idiotic gestures so that I could escape somewhere to a quiet room and strip off this ghastly uniform and sit down at a cracked piano and practise arpeggios till the war was over.

But this was not to be. Chin up, Nichols. Act the man, even though your critics might describe you as a sickly epicene. Return the salutes. Push your shoulders back. Get into the lorry which is waiting outside. Sit bolt upright, and after an icy ride up a long and tortuous road, alight, and never forget that you are an officer in His Majesty's Labour Corps.

We reach the entrance to the camp. It seems to stretch to infinity —line upon line of tents strung across a desolate landscape. A sergeant emerges from a sentry-box, takes my name, checks it, and bawls to a private soldier to carry my sleeping-bag and show me to my quarters. We walk down several rows of tents and arrive at the one to which I have been assigned. The soldier shouts my name, somebody pulls open the flap, and I step inside. Five men are crouched on their truckle-beds; they glower at me, saying nothing. The soldier throws my bag onto an empty bed, salutes, and exits.

With a pitiful effort to appear at ease I hold out my hand and say, 'The name is Nichols.'

The gesture is ignored and the man to whom I have spoken stares at me as though I were a sort of freak.

'Nichols,' he repeats. 'You won't last long, not with that 'air.'

From the corner a little man with a face like a weasel raises himself on his bed. He too stares at me and then he grins.

The grin is welcome but I am not prepared for the remark that follows.

'Curly 'air,' he observes, 'always gives me the 'orn.'

This brief episode was not one of the major tragedies of the war; it would be more fittingly described as the black comedy. After a few abortive attempts on my virtue the little man on whom the curly hair had so stimulating an effect decided to leave me alone and a few weeks later he shot himself. Not on my account but because— as it transpired at the inquest—he was as nearly mad as makes no matter, and should never have been drafted at all.

Phase 2 lasted through the winter, from November 1917 to February 1918. With no records and no diaries a consecutive narrative is impossible, but a couple of isolated incidents may indicate the futility of it all.

The first incident occurred during an inspection by a senior general who had been dispatched from the War Office to find out how the Labour Corps was shaping. Imagine a wind-swept plain with groups of stunted pine trees keeping a witches' vigil on the horizon. In the foreground a long ragged line of 'officers' trying to stand up straight and present a passably military appearance. There is a lot of coughing and a fair amount of twitching. (The shell-shock cases.) Down the ranks struts a rosy-faced bigwig in a brilliantly beribboned tunic. He engages in brief bouts of conversation with random soldiers and then he pauses in front of the man standing next to me. His name was Hawkins and in civil life he was some sort of ironmonger. Hawkins was a nice little creature who kept a smile on his face in spite of the fact that he had almost every complaint which one can have without actually dropping dead. High blood pressure, incipient epilepsy, a double hernia that had gone wrong . . . the lot.

The beribboned bigwig addresses him. Hawkins—still smiling—begins to catalogue his complaints. (Not unnaturally he wants to be released from the army and go back to ironmongery.) When he gets to the double hernia the general has had enough.

'Never mind all that,' he observes, in ringing tones. 'Your heart's in the right place!'

To which Mr Hawkins replies . . . 'No sir. Displaced 'eart, sir.'

Half a century later I still find that remark amusing.

The second incident, in its consequences, was more serious, but it also had an element of comedy.

Among my duties was the morning inspection of the men's meals. I had to march out to the mess-tents, accompanied by a sergeant, push my head through the canvas flaps, and roar out the question 'Any complaints?' There was nearly always a high wind, and it was hard to make oneself heard above the uproar of the elements, but I steeled myself to go through the motions.

One morning something quite appalling happened. There *was* a complaint. A gigantic sergeant rose from his table and limped towards me. (He had been badly wounded in the thigh.) In his hand he bore a plate slopping over with some sort of stew. He pushed the plate under my nose. 'Yes, sir. We 'ave a complaint. Get a load of this.'

If I had been an officer—a real officer—I should have responded correctly. I should have ignored the plate so rudely proffered. I should have gone purple in the face, called the sergeant to attention, made the regulation bull-throated noises, and swept out.

But the devil must have entered into me. I sniffed the plate, grimaced, and said, loud and clear, 'It stinks.'

Sensation. The men were not accustomed to such reactions from their officers. Knives and forks were set down, plates were pushed aside, three hundred faces gaped at me.

In for a penny, in for a pound. 'Quite uneatable', I added in even more ringing tones. And then, since this was hardly an occasion for a discussion on the niceties of military cuisine, I fell back on the immortal phrase with which generations of incompetent young officers have extricated themselves from difficult situations. 'Carry on, sergeant!'

Outside the tent I expected the tumbrils to be waiting. I had committed the unforgivable sin; I had sided with the troops against the officers. Retribution was swift; half an hour later I was summoned to the commanding officer. He was outraged. In all his experience he had never known such conduct. He asked me, not once but several times, if Second Lieutenant J. B. Nichols was aware that there was a war on. Second Lieutenant J. B. Nichols was acutely conscious of this. But he did not regret his little gesture. On his next inspection, when he thrust his head through the flaps of the mess-tent ... Any complaints? ... he was greeted by three hundred friendly faces. There were no complaints. Somebody had spoken to the cook, and the food was quite eatable.

The army had actually taught me something. It had taught me that one should always speak to the cook, when the situation demands.

*   *   *

Phase 3. February 1918.

How did we ever win the First World War? If the military career of Second Lieutenant J. B. Nichols was in any way typical, how did we even survive the first few weeks?

For this was the moment when the powers that be decided to whisk me away from the glacial deserts of Thetford and established me in a Whitehall office in order to devote my talents to the machinations of His Majesty's Secret Service.

Which talents? My sketchy French? My even sketchier knowledge of the French Impressionists? My touch on the piano?

Or my curly hair? Your guess is as good as mine, but I have a feeling that it had something to do with the hair. (Now that I am almost bald I have no shame in recalling this vanished allurement.)

The hair brings us back to A. C. Benson, who had picked me up in the porch of Magdalene. Ever since my departure he had kept in touch through a constant stream of correspondence. No young man ever had a kindlier mentor; he wrote as an equal, drawing me out, seeking my opinions. He was not only kindly but practical. Realising that I had no means apart from my meagre Second Lieutenant's pay, he took some of my letters and sent them to an American magazine called *The Outlook* with the suggestion that they should be published anonymously. They were accepted, and the editors asked for more. Altogether I made five hundred dollars from *The Outlook*, which was a small fortune in those days. For the first time I knew the excitement of writing words on paper and selling them, of twisting my pen into symbols that could be exchanged for gold. Which is all that authorship has ever been about, or ever will be.

I do not know whether *The Outlook* still survives and Benson's letters to me have long since disappeared, with the exception of one, which I kept and cherished because I had a feeling that it was a landmark in my life.

My Dear Beverley,
We do not know each other as we might have done, but if you have come to know me at all you will have realised that one of

43

my 'complexes'—I believe that is the fashionable expression—
is a hatred of waste. Perhaps that is why I can claim some
success as the Master of Magdalene. I keep a very strict watch
on the outgoings of the Bursary! But it is not only a matter of
accountancy. It goes deeper than that. I am bewildered and
alarmed by the profligacy of Nature, and even more bewildered
and alarmed by the wastage of this hideous war.

I think that you are being wasted. You have many talents and
none of them is being used. With your precarious state of
health your sphere of activities must be limited, but that does
not mean that you can be of no use at all.

As soon as I see an opportunity I propose to do something
about this. Once you suggested to me—with that never-failing
impertinence which I find so engaging—that I was an 'intri-
guant'. (I had been telling you the story of the ingenious
manner in which I had persuaded a Chicago millionaire to give
us ten thousand dollars for our beloved Library.) You could
not have paid me a higher compliment. Intrigue, to me, is the
spice of life. I am an ancient spider, sitting in the centre of an
ancient web, weaving ancient spells. And some of them will
shortly be speeding in your direction.

My affectionate greetings,
A.C.B.

The ink of the letter has dimmed to a sickly sepia, and the address
on the envelope, with its faded penny stamp, is almost illegible.
But I still feel a glow of warmth as I read it, with half a century of
disillusionment behind me.

Once again I am 'summoned to the C.O.' (I shall have to set that
sentence up in type).

I remember a purple face against a background of dirty canvas.

'Nichols?' He makes my name sound like some sort of offence.

'Yes, sir.'

'You appear to have friends in high places.' He tossed me a buff-
coloured envelope which fell on the sanded floor. I picked it up
and began to open it but he checked me.

'You can read that at your convenience. No doubt you will
understand it. I do not. You will be granted a week's leave. If you

apply to the Adjutant's office you will be issued with a travel warrant. You may dismiss.'

I saluted and made my exit. I opened the envelope and blinked at the typed instructions inside. They were terse and to the point. Second Lieutenant J. B. Nichols would report on the following Monday, February 17th, at Number 2 Whitehall Court, and present himself to Major J. Darcy, D.S.O., Room 202, third floor, in order to be instructed in his duties.

Once again, panic. Who was Major Darcy, D.S.O.? What went on in Whitehall Court? And for what conceivable reason should my presence be required there? I was soon to learn that Whitehall Court was the holy of holies of the Secret Service, presided over by a very secret naval gentleman who—when he was mentioned at all —was referred to as 'M'. I knew nothing of these matters as I stood blinking outside the tent.

All I knew was that once again the winds of change were buffeting me, and hurling me into unknown territories. And that more than ever I wanted to escape to a quiet room and practise arpeggios, until the guns were hushed and the world came back to its senses.

CHAPTER IV

ଷ୍ଷ୍ଷ୍ଷ୍ଷ୍ଷ୍

A VERY SECRET SERVICE

London, February 1918. Grey, foggy, unwashed. A dull khaki city, swarming with troops of many nations, in which I am a drab speck of beige, wandering up a street near Marble Arch, in search of lodgings. The First War to End All Wars has still nine months to run.

After the passage of over fifty years I can scarcely paint an authentic picture of the contemporary scene which was not nearly as melodramatic as in the Second War to End All Wars, twenty years later. Apart from the occasional Zeppelin, the skies were clear. Presumably there was some sort of black-out but it cannot have compared with the deep darkness of the later conflict. I cannot recall the wail of sirens nor the skeletons of ruined buildings. The only ruins to be seen were human, and there were certainly plenty of *them*, bandaged and blasted and broken.

I arrive at the address which has been given to me, in Bryanston Street, near Marble Arch. The door is open by a Mrs Williams, a harassed lady in black. She has a couple of pleasant rooms on the first floor. There are papers to be signed and in the space for 'Occupation' I write 'Secret Service'. For a moment Mrs Williams hesitates, as though she were wondering whether her house is in danger of becoming a nest of international intrigue. Then she smiles, and motions me inside.

The farce began on the following Monday when I reported at Number 2 Whitehall Court. This was a luxurious building overlooking the Thames. After the war it became the London home of

46

Bernard Shaw, who had an apartment on the third floor, which was the scene of a rather startling interview he gave me twenty years later. At the time of which I am writing the whole building had been taken over by one of the branches of the Secret Service. Which branch, I never discovered, nor what it did, nor why. All I knew was that the presiding genius was a mysterious Being known as 'M'. Who was 'M'? Nobody knew, or perhaps it would be truer to say that nobody admitted that he knew. Sometimes I wondered if 'M' really existed at all, if it was not a letter chosen at random to endow the Secret Service with a bogus mystique of its own.*

I took the lift to the third floor, located the office of the head of the department, Major Darcy, D.S.O., and was admitted to the presence. We conceived an instant dislike for one another. He was a dapper little man with a ginger moustache. His belt was so tightly buckled that he gave the impression of wearing stays and he smelt of cheap lavender-water. His tunic blazed with ribbons, and I suspected that most of them were phoney.

Here, there will be no difficulty in refraining from the invention of dialogue because, with the exception of one sentence, there was no dialogue. After giving me instructions as to where to report, he leant forward, regarded me with obvious loathing, and hissed ... 'There is one other thing. In no circumstances will you refer to "M" by name. Is that clearly understood?'

'Yes, sir.'

'Perhaps you had better repeat it after me.'

I promised that in no circumstances would I betray the identity of 'M'. I was able to give this assurance with ringing sincerity because I had not the remotest idea what the letter implied, whether it stood for a he or a she or an it; for all I knew it might be a gloss for Fortnum and Mason's. It might even be a mask for the legendary 'Olga Petrova the beautiful spy'.

Having settled this little matter I gave Major Darcy a farewell salute and departed. It was not a very good salute because I never

* I now understand that there was in fact an actual 'M' in the person of a naval commander of outstanding ability.

learned how to do it properly; the right elbow was either too far up or too far down; the wrist was either too rigid or too limp. As for the correct expression on the face . . . that forever eluded me. Heroic? Subservient? Dogged and determined? I never learned. I really did try to be a good soldier, and I practised salutes in front of the looking-glass. The reflected image was not consoling; I still looked like a page-boy hailing taxis from the arcades of the Ritz.

I reported next door.

Two young officers stared at me. One was tall and dark and clean-shaven. Captain Bentley. The other was short and fat with an adolescent moustache. Major West. There was nothing exceptional to be noted about them until they stood up. They had only two legs between them. Bentley's had been shot off above the knee, West's below it.

Immediate guilt complex on the part of Second Lieutenant J. B. Nichols. Here was I with both legs, having been no nearer to France than Marble Arch, and here were these young heroes who had been through hell. And I was presuming to join them as an equal. It made me hot with shame.

There was a brief interrogation by Major West, who quickly established that I was a useless dud.

'What shall we do with him?' he snorted.

Captain Bentley regarded me with an appraising eye. 'We might put him in charge of the files.'

'Haven't got any files.'

'We could start some. Anyway, we can indent for a filing cabinet.' Then, addressing me again . . . 'By the way, do you know anything about filing?'

'No, sir.'

'Splendid!'

So they got a filing cabinet, and I was given control of it, to my considerable puzzlement, for nobody ever gave me anything to put in it, and I would not have known what to do with it if they had. Eventually I evolved my own technique. From time to time envelopes used to be delivered to the office marked 'Top Secret', and I soon discovered that they were not secret at all. They were churned out in the basement by some underling, distributed round the building and promptly thrown into the wastepaper basket. Most of them began with such legends as 'Agent 627 BQ reports considerable activity behind the lines on PQ 25 section Map 43A.' The information that followed, when it was not sheer gibberish, was so out of date that it had already been published weeks before in the British press. However, I had to file something, so this was what I filed. Though it could have had no possible bearing on the current hostilities it might one day have some archaic interest for the historian.

We now come to the story of the overcoat.

I was young, I was bored, I was ardent, and I had a great deal of time to myself. I soon lost my sense of shame and guilt because none of this fiasco was my fault. If somebody had said, 'Go somewhere and do something and have your legs shot off' I would have obeyed. But nobody gave any orders, so I began to take advantage of the situation, leaving the office earlier every day and sometimes never going there at all.

One day, exploring London, I drifted into Hanover Square, and found myself passing the window of a very grand tailor's shop called Lesley and Roberts. Normally I should not have dreamed of entering it because it was the sort of place that catered exclusively for dukes. But my eye was caught by a flash of scarlet, which came from the lining of an officer's overcoat, arranged with elegance over a Sheraton settee.

I took a deep breath and went inside. The carpets were soft, the atmosphere was warm and luxurious, there was a comforting feeling of riches. For none of these delights had life prepared me, but I decided that I deserved them.

'The overcoat in the window?'

The attendant was obsequious, but he was summing me up, through narrowed eyes. Second Lieutenant, under the age of consent, enquiring about overcoats in the window, very expensive overcoats. How should he react? He gave me the benefit of the doubt. Perhaps my father was an earl.

'Of course, sir. Would you care to try it on?'

'If you please.' And then . . . 'I assume that it is regulation wear for a second lieutenant?'

'Certainly, sir—all ranks. All regiments. By the way sir, what *is* the regiment?'

Nothing would have induced me to inform him that I was in the Labour Corps. It would have been like applying for membership at White's Club and telling the secretary that one had been educated at Borstal. So I casually murmured the words 'Secret Service' and strolled into the fitting-room.

The overcoat was rapturous, particularly when one undid the two top buttons, revealing the scarlet silk in all its glory. That was how I would have liked to wear it, flaunting its challenge in the face of the higher ranks. But that might have led to trouble. So I did it up, and regarded myself in the triple mirror with undisguised approval. I still looked like a page-boy at the Ritz, but I was now a page-boy de luxe, on the way to higher things.

I paid by cheque. It was staggeringly expensive, but the dollars from my articles in the American *Outlook* would provide just enough to foot the bill. I walked home in it all the way to Bryanston Street, and when the *canaille* of the lower ranks encountered me, all the way from Bond Street to Marble Arch, they saluted as smartly as though they had suddenly been confronted by Lord Kitchener. For once in a way I could return their salutes with a clear conscience. After all, I had earned the damned thing.

That night I wore it to the Café Royal.

In those days, the last and bloodiest of the First World War, the Café Royal was the final rallying point of the intelligentsia. Ever since the nineties it had been the capital of London's Bohemia, for whose members it formed an ideal background, with the glitter of the mirrors, the rows of marble-topped tables on which many famous artists had scribbled their casual caricatures—and the gleam of gold from the plaster Caryatides ranged round the walls. It was at the Cafe Royal that Oscar Wilde had played some of the more tragic and ludicrous scenes which littered his path to destruction.

And it was also in the Café Royal, at a later date, that I was to have the doubtful pleasure of lunching with Lord Alfred Douglas at the very table where he had sat with Wilde at one of their last meetings before the débâcle. Douglas had attacked me in a transient sheet which he was editing, called 'Plain English'; I was very angry about it and wrote to tell him so. In his reply he asked me to lunch, and of course I accepted. How could any inquisitive young man have rejected such an opportunity? It would have been like declining an invitation to have cocktails with Alcibiades. I wish that I had made notes of the encounter. All I can remember is a blotched and bloated face, glaring across the table, vividly recalling the hideous image on the last page of *The Picture of Dorian Gray*. And a spatter of spiteful recollections, in which he insisted that it was *he*, Lord Alfred, who had been the inspiration for Wilde's *Salomé* and that it was *he* who had first coined most of the immortal epigrams in *The Importance of Being Earnest*.

But it was in no ninetyish mood that I made my début at the Café Royal, flashing the scarlet lining of the questionable overcoat. My aesthetic period was over and done with. I was now a 'modern', or so I earnestly persuaded myself. I had been swept in by the compulsion of Picasso's Blue Period, via the early Medici prints. I had devoured the offerings of Ezra Pound, which nowadays induce only cerebral indigestion.

So I walked into the Café, noticed a face that I recognised, belonging to an artist called Augustus John, walked over to his table, and diffidently enquired if he could provide me with a match. He provided it. There were two other faces at the table. One of them was pale, morose and early Hanoverian, attached to the person of Osbert Sitwell. The other face was also pale, but it was far from morose and decidedly Jewish. It was easy to recognise for it belonged to the sculptor Jacob Epstein who had been the target for a great deal of vitriolic caricature in the popular press.

All three faces smiled at me and I was invited to sit down and join the party.

There are times when the social hurdles of life seem insurmountable, when nobody wants to know one and when every door slams in one's face. There are other times when everything is absurdly easy, when all the doors swing wide open. That night was one of those other times. In the space of a couple of minutes, by the simple process of asking for a match, I gained *entrée* into a magic circle. On this occasion, I did make notes. Osbert was the conversational star of the evening and I can recall two of his remarks which still sparkle. A very silly woman sat herself down with us and *à propos* of nothing, said, 'No woman ever gained anything from domesticity.' Osbert stared at her with a beady eye. 'What about Nell Gwyn?' he demanded. A stranger paused beside us and began to rebuke him for his tirades against British Imperialism. Osbert cut him short. 'If the British were turned out of India tomorrow all that would be found is a broken-down bathroom and an empty whisky bottle.' The remark was unjust and superficial, as life was to teach me, but it conveys the quality of the Sitwell mind. It also conveys the atmosphere of the Café Royal, for in no other ambience could such a remark have been made at all.

While he talked Osbert was scribbling on the menu, writing the outline of a poem which was afterwards published under the title of 'The Patriot'. He sent me a copy inscribed 'For Beverley, in memory of the Café Royal, February 1918.' It is worth quoting as an example of the bitterness which corroded the intelligence of so many of his contemporaries in those torturing times:

The Patriot

I fought for Britain with my might and main
I make explosives and I gave a son.
My factory, converted for the fight
Now manufactures gas and dynamite,
Which only pays me seventy per cent;
And if I had ten other sons to send
I'd make them serve my country to lend.

Some of the men and women whom I met on that memorable evening were to become friends for life. When I went home I was intoxicated in more senses than one.

Had I known what lay ahead I should not have been so happy. For I had been treading in very dangerous territory. Like Oscar Wilde before me, I had been 'supping with panthers'.

Meanwhile, the rhythm of life in the 'Secret Service' continued as before. Every morning I reported at Whitehall Court, let myself into the office, dealt with the mail, went through the motion of 'filing', and tried to forget that the majority of my contemporaries were already overseas, being blinded and disembowelled.

Then the tempo of life began to quicken. Our small staff was augmented by the arrival of an aristocrat, by name Peter Spencer. Since he was later to become a close friend this may sound an odd way of describing him, but it was his innate aristocracy which made the immediate appeal, maybe because I had not met so many aristocrats before. I looked him up in the office *Who's Who*. His father was Viscount Churchill, his mother was a daughter of the Earl of Lonsdale; he was a godson of Queen Victoria, a Prince of the Holy Roman Empire and he had been a page of honour to King Edward VII. Moreover he looked the part, very slim and elegant, with a way of wearing his uniform which made his fellow officers look uncouth. This façade was deceptive, for he had a distinguished war record and had twice been mentioned in dispatches for outstanding gallantry.

As if this were not enough, he had also won a scholarship in Sanscrit at the University of the Sorbonne and he had an impressive knowledge of medieval French poetry. I was flattered when he made me his friend, and treated me as an equal, and occasionally accompanied me to the Café Royal.

There was only one thing wrong about Peter Spencer as a companion for Second Lieutenant J. B. Nichols. He took drugs.

Before the critics attack me for libelling the dead they should be informed that the relevant facts about this very exceptional man have already been published. The most recent revelation is in a book by David Herbert.* Moreover, in after years Peter made no

* *Second Son*, the autobiography of David Herbert: Peter Owen Ltd, 1972.

secret of his addiction; indeed, he was inclined to flaunt it, through his intimacy with Jean Cocteau. There is a legend that when Cocteau stayed at the Hotel Wellcome in Villefranche, he smoked opium in such copious quantities that if he left the window open you could smell the fumes far out to sea.

I knew nothing of this side of Peter's life, and even if I had been aware of it there is little that I could have done. The only reason I bring him into the story is that he was part of the pattern—the pattern of the panthers, which was gradually forming round me, in a very ugly shape.

Night after night, in all innocence, I frequented the Café Royal, wandering from table to table, thrilled by the revolutionary fervours of the poets, the painters and the occasional politicians who came my way, and some of them were indeed revolutionary. Even if they were not enemy agents there were many, like D. H. Lawrence, whose public image was suspect. My few contacts with Lawrence were unprofitable. He was devoid of humour, his breath was unsavoury, and he never paid for a drink. Behind his working-class maquillage I suspected that he was a poseur, and in spite of his assertion of arrogant masculinity I guessed that he would not be very good in bed. Which was hardly to be wondered at, when one met his tiresome German wife.

However, the Lawrences were only obscure extras in a social chorus which I should never have joined at all. A moment's reflection, a grain of common-sense, would have warned me that as a member of the 'Secret Service', however insignificant, I was behaving with indiscretion. I should not, for example, have been seen talking to Ramsay MacDonald. Although he was later to become one of the dullest, 'safest', and most conservative Prime Ministers who have ever been foisted on the British people, he was at that time classified by the authorities as a public menace, because of his passionate pacifist activities. But I *was* seen talking to Ramsay MacDonald—not only talking to him, but taking notes. I was soon to discover that some little man in the background was also taking notes. The panthers were drawing closer.

* * *

The most dangerous of these animals was the legendary Chilean painter, Alvaro Guevara. Until recently I was under the impression that the legend had been forgotten, but it has now been revived in a remarkable biography by Diana Holman-Hunt,* and I have the feeling that 'Chile', as we all called him, is due for one of those renaissances which will soon be titillating the readers of the Sunday supplements.

I quote from the blurb of this biography.

Alvaro Guevara claimed Spanish royal blood and his family was extravagantly rich. Leaving Chile for England he turned to painting. His contemporaries at the Slade included Gerther, Carrington, Wadsworth, the Spencer and Nash brothers. His heroes were Walter Sickert, Augustus John, Roger Fry and Matthew Smith. He was also a boxer, and won the Gold Belt as champion of Chile.

Among the literary élite he became an intimate of the Sitwell brothers as well as Edith, of Ronald Firbank, Aldous Huxley, T. S. Eliot, Roy Campbell, D. H. Lawrence and Gertrude Stein. In Paris, where Picasso, Picabia and the fashionable surrealists were already his friends, he married the painter Meraud Guiness. Lady Diana Cooper, wife of our British Ambassador of the time, was a hostess for his daughter's coming-out party. Cecil Beaton designed the decorations.

That was the respectable side of Chile—there was another side, which I was to discover for myself. Another quote from *Latin Among the Lions*.

One night Chile was sitting alone at the Café when an exceptionally attractive-looking young man came in unaccompanied, wearing an apparently new and very elegant greatcoat, such as might be worn by a musical comedy Field-Marshal. Alvaro beckoned to his waiter and dispatched a note to the stranger's table, suggesting that he join him for a drink.

The young man succumbed to a tempting adventure. When he sat down he said that Alvaro had drawn his portrait in pencil on the marble-topped table. The head was a remarkable likeness, the figure too; but the

* *Latin Among the Lions: Alvaro Guevara* by Diana Holman-Hunt. Michael Joseph Ltd, 1974.

greatcoat was omitted; his host had drawn him in the nude. He introduced himself as Beverley Nichols and the result of this encounter is described by him in retrospect. 'I went to stay with him at his studio,' recalls Mr Nichols. 'It was a revealing experience, some of which is printable and some of which is not. On several occasions during our brief and stormy relationship he threatened to strangle me . . .'

For a fuller account of this affair the reader should turn to the pages of Diana Holman-Hunt. I shall spare a moment to fill in the gaps, not because they are unprintable, but because they have never been printed. And because, in their way, they are typical of the curious and sometimes sinister mix-ups of my whole life.

While I was staying with Chile he painted my portrait. Not in the nude but in the greatcoat. The recollection of this experience after more than half a century, emerges as a sort of surrealist adaptation of *La Bohème*, with a stridently homosexual orchestration. The studio was in a squalid side-street off the Fulham Road. It was always in an appalling muddle, with tubes of paint in the bathroom, and half-finished canvases propped round the walls. There was never anything to eat and I had to go out and buy things at the grocer's. But there was always an abundance of drink, and the place was littered with empty brandy bottles. This, of course, seemed to me quite normal; since the age of seven my 'home-life', if it can be so described, had been played out against a background of empty brandy bottles.

But I was no longer seven. I was all of nineteen. And I was having my portrait painted. That made up for everything. To be painted by Chile was a rare distinction; he was regarded by some of the critics as a more exciting painter than John; and some of his portraits, notably that of Edith Sitwell, has already caused a sensation. This picture now hangs in the National Portrait Gallery. Sometimes I go to look at it, and when I do, I get chills in the spine; it arouses so many disturbing memories—the cluttered studio, the weird régime with night turning into day and the dark, powerful figure of the madman prowling round me, staring at me for hours on end. With the spine-chilling comes a feeling of anger, prompted by what I must call the ironies of fate. For though Chile's portrait of Edith was a masterpiece, his portrait of me was a finer work. When Ronald Firbank saw it he described it as 'charged with exquisite menace', which was a very Firbankian remark. Chile had painted me as a boy against blue skies, a boy in uniform. But in the skies there were hints of thunder clouds, and in the uniform, by a magical alchemy of painting, there was a touch of tragedy. That is why I am angered by the aforesaid ironies. Edith's picture hangs for all time in the National Portrait Gallery, a lasting memorial to Chile and to herself. But mine has gone with the wind.

Here, from the wings, steps the figure of my father, who cannot be exorcised from our story. Because I had nowhere to hang it, the picture went into store. It needed room to breathe; it would have overwhelmed any of the small rooms which in those days were all that I could afford. Then my father, with his usual lunatic disregard for economics, moved into a large house in the millionaire quarter of Cambridge Square, partly because my brother Paul, through some complex arrangement with the ecclesiastic commissioners, was entitled to use it as a 'vicarage'. So Chile's picture was brought out of store and hung up at the top of the staircase. Although Paul did not like it and my mother was rather frightened by it, they accepted my word that it was a work of importance. Not so my father. From the first moment he set eyes on it he began to smoulder with anger. It was a 'bloody mess'. It was 'indecent'. Every time he staggered up and down the staircase, clutching the banisters, he paused to stare at it with bloodshot eyes, searching for new adjectives to express his righteous indignation. Then, during a bout of *delirium tremens*, the smouldering burst into flames. So did the picture. He tore it from the wall, took it out into the courtyard, and set fire to it.

Thus ended the portrait of Second Lieutenant J. B. Nichols, by the late Alvaro Guevara.

I sometimes think the portrait of Dorian Gray had a kindlier fate. At least Mr Gray had some fun for his money.

The operative word of this section is 'panthers'. Prowling, sniffing, searching, drawing ever closer. As a cat-lover I should be the last to say a word against panthers; indeed the only panther I ever met, which was introduced to me in India, was a most endearing creature. It belonged to the late Maharaja of Mysore; it had a rich fruity purr, and permitted itself to be stroked.

But panthers, in times of natural crisis, are not suitable companions for nineteen-year-old second lieutenants in dubious uniforms.

The storm broke on the night that I said goodbye to Chile. The portrait was finished and I was only too thankful to get back to the peace of the little rooms in Bryanston Street. It was after midnight, but Mrs Williams was waiting up. She was in a state of great distress and she had been crying.

'I'm sorry, Mr Nichols, but I'm afraid I must ask you to leave.'

'But why?'

'The police have been. Asking about you.'

During my absence two men in plain clothes had arrived to search my rooms. They had shown their credentials. She had been too confused to check them, but they were evidently in some way connected with the Secret Service. They had gone through the rooms with a thin comb, opening drawers, reading letters, examining books and pamphlets. They had also searched the bathroom, opening jars and bottles and sniffing them. All the time they were doing these things, they were making notes.

When the search was completed, they had put her through a rigorous cross-examination. What sort of hours did I keep? What sort of people came to visit me? Were they men or women? Were they ever in uniform, and if so what sort of uniform? Did they ever stay the night?

And then, most sinister of all . . . in no circumstances was she to mention their visit, either to me or to anybody else. Whereupon they took their departure.

'But of course, Mr Nichols, I *had* to tell you.'

'I'm very grateful.'

'I can't think what it's all about. It must be some silly mistake. Mustn't it?'

'Yes.'

'All the same . . . I do hope you'll understand?'

'Of course.'

I went upstairs to bed, but not to sleep.

It is not difficult to guess the reason for the visit of these two agents. They had several grounds for suspicion and they were all associated with the Café Royal. They come under three headings.

1. PACIFISM. I had been seen in conversation with a number of C.O.s (C.O. was a contemptuous abbreviation for 'conscientious objector'). I never had the courage to be a C.O. myself, but I had not tried to disguise my sympathy for them. Most of the C.O.s were frightened, rather mixed-up young men of no importance. But what about men like Ramsay MacDonald, the arch-priest of pacifism? How had an underling like myself ever come into contact with such a man at all?

2. DRUGS. The drug problems of the first war were negligible in comparison with those of the second. The word marijuana was unknown, and so were a great many other ugly words, connected with drugs, which now besmirch our vocabulary. The lethal tentacles of the Mafia were still quiescent; the world war had not yet begun to poison itself.

But drugs were taken, usually in the form of cocaine, which was handed round quite openly by some of the more brazen habitués of the Café. Nobody ever offered any to me, presumably because— on the evidence of early photographs—I still looked like a cherub who might have posed for Botticelli. Indeed, the only time when drugs ever came my way was at a dinner in Paris with Gertrude Stein and Alice Toklas. Our host was a lamentable American dramatist called Avery Hopwood and at the end of dinner he produced a little gold box containing a white powder. This did not appeal to me at all. I grabbed the box, emptied the stuff on the floor, paid the bill and took the ladies home. One does not associate Gertrude Stein with the trembling of an Autumn leaf but that is the impression I retain of her on this occasion, a very frightened and uncharacteristically feminine old American lady, hunched up and shaking in the corner of a taxi, as though she were scared by some evil spirit which she had unconsciously evoked.

Chile, unknown to myself, was a drug-addict.

3. MORALS. This was the area of the agent's enquiries which gave me most concern. What sort of people had come to visit me? Had any of them ever stayed the night? The answer was that quite a number of people had come to visit me, of both sexes, and that some of them had indeed stayed the night. If such questions had been asked in this day and age, I might have added . . . 'And a good time was had by all.' I might even have quoted a very apposite remark which Noël Coward once made about sex when we were lunching together at the St James's Club. He was infuriated because the Lord Chamberlain had just censored a play of his called *Ritz Bar*. (Oddly enough, I do not recall any reference to this work among the voluminous records of the Life of the Master.) It was not a very good play but the censor's objections were moral rather than artistic. *Ritz Bar* suggested that young gentlemen sometimes did things which they ought not to have done with other young gentlemen, and that young ladies sometimes did things which they ought not to have done with other young ladies, unto the third and fourth generation, and it was all an abomination in the eye of the Lord, and of the Lord Chamberlain. To which Noël had exploded . . . 'I cannot agree that it is within the province of the Lord Chamberlain, or of anybody else, to concern himself with what I happen to do with my thighs.'

But, for me, in this moment of crisis, there was no temptation to flippancy. I was very frightened. 'Some of the people who had come to visit me had stayed the night.' The contemporary comment would be . . . 'So what?' But all this, remember, was happening in the year 1918, when sexually we were still living in the Dark Ages. And this was a crisis that I had to face alone, with no guidelines, no family background, no codes of conduct except the twisted taboos of a public school and the casual encounters of a café in which life was reflected in golden mirrors through a haze of tobacco smoke.

I was in the most lamentable mess, and there was nobody to help me. Even Chopin, for once in a way, had nothing to say.

If I had had a crystal ball, and could have looked only a few weeks into the future, I might not have felt so depressed. For in the crystal I should have seen my image over the water, walking up the steps of the White House, on the way to luncheon with the President of the United States.

Did I mention that I had a rather peculiar sort of war?

CHAPTER V

❀❀❀❀❀❀

INTO BATTLE

We switch abruptly to the door of a room in Jesus College, Cambridge. The door is closed, and I am too scared to open it.

The authenticity of an autobiography is to be measured not only by what the author remembers but by what he forgets. Sometimes, in order to bring his story to life, the author extends his 'memory' to such inordinate lengths that one ceases to believe him. The arch-offender in this respect was probably Frank Harris, whose memoirs of Oscar Wilde were so diffuse, so inflated, and often so nearly fictional, that the final picture of poor Oscar emerges as an emasculated identikit.

I will not attempt to 'remember' what happened in the immediate period following the end of our last chapter. Presumably, something did happen, and it was almost certainly unpleasant, but what it was I do not know. There must have been some form of dismissal, for I *was* dismissed and sent packing, very abruptly. This is a matter of record. But whether it came in the form of a minute from the War Office, or in a telling-off from the detestable Major Darcy, or a reprimand from the mysterious 'M', I cannot say. I was in a state of shock.

All I can remember is that hideous door.

It was painted dark green and bore the words 'Officers Only', indicating that it was the entrance to the officers' mess of the X Regiment. The 'X' is psychologically significant. In every man's life there are areas so painful that his mind rejects them, covering the cerebral scars with an anonymous protective tissue that he can

62

never penetrate, however deeply he may probe. To this day I have no recollection of the identity of the 'X Regiment', nor indeed if it was a 'regiment' at all. If anybody cared to search the dusty files of the First World War, he could presumably establish its identity, and discover the devious routes by which I came to join it, but this would be a futile exercise. As far as our story is concerned the 'X' regiment was only a sound behind a door, a sinister sound that rose and fell, a muffled chorus of aggressively masculine voices, punctuated by the clink of glasses.

I had to open that door, and go inside, and take a drink.

I had to go into battle.

For now, incredible as it may seem, I was a member of this community—this mysterious, growling, menacing chorus of men with a capital M. Even more incredible, there were now two pips on my shoulder. I can still see them, if I look sideways through the mists of time. Two brass pips, indicating that Second Lieutenant J. B. Nichols had been promoted to First Lieutenant. By whom? And why? God alone knows. Here the embers of memory begin to flicker. In my pocket was a crumpled sheet of buff-coloured paper informing me that I should be required to instruct 'other ranks' in various military techniques with a view to preparing them for commissions. This is the sort of situation that is normally encountered only in very bad dreams. To expect me to instruct anybody in any sort of military activity was like requiring me to preside over the chorus of a ballet class and school them in the intricacies of *Swan Lake*. Indeed, such an assignment would have been comparatively simple; at least I could have gone to the piano and played them the score.

But this was no dream. It was a very ugly reality. And it all centred on that door.

(Here I recall one of the last remarks ever made by Somerset Maugham when he was tottering round the garden of the Villa Mauresque on the arm of his faithful secretary, Alan Searle. 'I am standing at d-d-death's door, Alan. And I am af-af-afraid to knock.')

I opened the door and stepped inside.

*   *   *

There was an immediate silence.

Twenty pairs of eyes turned towards me. Twenty elbows remained poised and rigid, holding their drinks before them. Twenty officers and gentlemen stared at me, as though I were a stray puppy that had crawled in from the street. I tried to smile, without success. The atmosphere of hostility was as thick and acrid as the fumes of smoke from their cheap cigarettes.

Somebody, evidently, had alerted them to my arrival. And they suspected that I was not the sort of person who would be welcome in their company.

As though obeying a secret signal, they turned away and resumed their conversation. Since I could not remain poised in the doorway I walked over to a table and picked up a magazine. Nobody joined me; nobody introduced himself. I was left to stand alone till luncheon was announced by an orderly. Whereupon they all trooped downstairs while I followed at a distance, and took my place next to a captain who had been promoted from the ranks. He had three wound-stripes on his sleeve. As soon as I sat down, he turned his back. Then he leant forward and addressed a red-headed major sitting immediately opposite.

'Talking of buggery,' he said.

The major grinned. 'What about it?'

'I've never been able to understand . . .' he paused, to make sure that he had the ear of the table . . . 'I've never been able to understand why . . . if a chap wants to go in for buggery . . . why he doesn't bugger a *woman*.'

There was loud laughter. He leant back, very pleased with himself, and gulped a glass of beer.

It has taken fifty years, and over fifty books, to bring myself to report a sentence such as this, which to this day, in spite of all the literary filth in which one has been obliged to wallow, strikes me as the ultimate in obscenity. Perhaps this is making a great fuss about nothing; if so, I must plead the excuse of antiquity. Elderly gentlemen who refuse to put down their pens should not complain if they lay themselves open to ridicule.

'Why doesn't he bugger a woman?'

Six words, echoing over the years, with an increasing cacophony.

Why report them? Because as I have suggested more than once, every autobiography is to some extent a spiritual autobiography, and those words, in that context and at that moment of time, were in the nature of a spiritual assault. Today, no doubt, they would not have so violent an impact; over the years one's sensibilities have been so numbed and blurred by violence that one is no longer shocked—at any rate in public—by things which, in one's heart, one knows to be loathsome and degrading.

Even so, the words cannot be ignored because of the context in which they were delivered. They were obviously spoken for my special benefit. A tough and aggressively masculine captain—he might have been the prototype for Hobbes' 'brutal and licentious soldiery'—a captain who had been promoted from the ranks, wearing on his sleeve the wound-stripes which proved that he was still smarting from the stings of battle, was suddenly confronted by a schoolboy lieutenant who was neither tough nor particularly masculine, who had no right to have been commissioned at all. He reacted accordingly.

The agony of the situation was intensified by the fact that I understood his point of view, indeed, I sympathised with him, and with his fellow-officers. All of the men at that table had been through hell, and most of them, in varying degrees, were shell-shocked. How could they fail to see in me a legitimate target for persecution?

All the same I still think that some of them, just one of them, might also have shown a little sympathy for myself. After all, it was not the schoolboy's fault.

The leader of the persecution pack quickly revealed himself as the commanding officer, Lieutenant Colonel Gilbert Cradock. He did not look the part. He was a pale flimsy creature with a feeble sandy moustache. He had been relieved from active service because he had been partially blinded in the retreat from Mons. But he still saw clearly enough through his thick spectacles, particularly when he was looking at myself. And what he saw he did not like at all.

His first remark, when I reported to his office after luncheon, was typical of his attitude.

'Nichols, I believe? And when shall we have the pleasure of seeing you properly dressed?'

This question needs explanation. Among my various physical troubles at this period—and there were quite a number of them—was some sort of bone disorder in the left knee, which had never been properly diagnosed. My reason for mentioning this unattractive disability is because it precluded me from wearing the regulation puttees and breeches. I was obliged to parade in slacks.

'Not setting a very good example, is it, strolling about in slacks?'

I began to stammer something about the instructions of the last medical board but he cut me short.

'You seem to be very fond of medical boards,' he barked. 'Do you want to spend your whole life going from one medical board to another? Is that your idea of soldiering?'

The questions, and their insulting implications, were unanswerable. He looked down at papers on his desk.

'You will read your orders on the notice-board. You may dismiss.'

I saluted and did a smart about-turn, a manœuvre which was not made any easier by the knee.

Then I went downstairs to study the notice-board. What I read was worse, far worse, than I had imagined. There were various postings of officers to other regiments, several lectures on such subjects as map-reading and rear-guard strategy, particulars of a new physical training scheme, and then at the bottom . . .

C. Company. General drill and bayonet practice. Assemble 9 a.m. King's Common. Instructing officer Lieutenant J. B. Nichols.

My immediate reaction to this appalling announcement was one of panic. I wanted to run away, to get out of uniform and escape to some remote retreat where I could hide until they came to arrest me. How could I conceivably 'instruct' these hardened warriors in bayonet practice of all things? I had only once taken part in this exercise at school, before sickness exempted me, and my knowledge was confined to a nightmare memory of racing across a field, stumbling towards a sack and digging it frantically until the sawdust spilled out, while a hoarse sergeant bellowed obscenities behind me. 'Get on with it—twist his bloody guts out—get him in the bloody balls!' That was how one taught men to use the bayonet, and I was physically and mentally incapable of it.

I left the notice-board, found the way to my small sitting-room, and sat down on the narrow bed to think. Here was a crisis that had obviously been contrived by the C.O. to hold me up to ridicule and contempt and I had not the faintest idea how to cope with it.

The following day. King's Common. A sullen morning with a sharp East wind. So far so good—or at any rate, no actual disaster. The fifty men of C. Company are standing at ease for a short break after an hour's drill which seems to have gone off quite creditably. I have marched them up and down, and made them present arms and shoulder arms and slope arms and right wheel and left wheel and about turn and anything else that I could remember about such things, and nobody had laughed or mutinied or given any sign that he saw anything odd. But the ultimate ordeal lay ahead, in the shape of a row of sacks hanging at the other end of the common. In a few minutes I should have to march the company up to those sacks and 'instruct' them—yell at them, inspire them with synthetic hatred, and presumably prod the horrible things myself as an example of how it should be done. How indeed!

At this point an angel dropped from the skies. His name was Lewis Cohen and he had been assigned—evidently by God—to act as sergeant for the day. From the first moment that our eyes had met, on our march to the common, I had felt a kinship. He was a dark, wiry little chap in his early thirties and his tunic sported an impressive row of ribbons for gallantry which were sewn on casually, slightly awry. What appealed to me was the sense that he was subtly caricaturing the whole military set-up. No man could have been smarter or more efficient, but in the tilt of his cap and the flourish of his salute there was an unmistakable hint of Charlie Chaplin.

67

He sprang to attention.

'Permission to speak, sah?'

'Yes, sergeant?'

'Would you like me to take over, sah?' He glanced at the slacks. 'Your leg, sah. Might be a bit awkward.'

'Thank you, sergeant. It would.'

'Very good, sah.'

He saluted, and as he did so he winked. There was a world of understanding in that wink. Sergeant Cohen had 'got' the whole situation.

Everything sprang to life. With a resounding bark he lined the men up before him and gave the order to fix bayonets. Then, striding up and down the ranks he proceeded to inspire them with the required spirit of bellicosity interlarding his exhortations with a generous spice of sanguinary oaths. Finally, he fixed his own bayonet and hurled himself at the nearest of the sacks, jabbing and slicing it with such brilliantly simulated hatred that one felt that at any moment the sawdust might turn to real blood.

It was a superb performance but it was brought to a swift conclusion.

'Mr Nichols!' I turned and saw the Colonel striding towards me. 'You will stand your men at ease.'

He was so angry that he was short of breath. 'May I ask the meaning of this exhibition? Have you read your orders?'

'Yes, sir.'

'What were they?'

'To give instruction in the use of the bayonet, sir.'

'And why are you not doing so?'

As he was shouting I shouted back. I wanted the men to hear my answer.

'Because sir, I have not yet been instructed in the use of the bayonet myself.'

Silence. Tomorrow, obviously, I should be shot at dawn. But as it happened, there could not possibly have been a more effective reply. It took the Colonel off his guard. He knew that I was speaking the truth and he knew that if blame was to be attached to anybody it was to himself. He must also have been aware that the men knew it too.

So there was no shooting at dawn. There were a few snarling references to general slovenliness, and a further reference to the slacks. Whereupon, with a final order to Cohen ... 'Carry on sergeant!' ... he took his leave.

As Cohen carried on he gave me another wink.

This was only the first episode in a campaign which never let up. I was treated as a criminal for the sole reason that I had been classified as unfit for service abroad.

And then, at a stroke, the scene was transformed.

'History repeats itself; historians repeat one another.'

This may apply to history but it should not apply to autobiography. And yet, at this stage, I am obliged to repeat myself, for everything that had happened to me on my previous assignment to Cambridge began to happen again, on a somewhat larger scale, and at a swifter tempo.

The reader who has followed these lamentations may remember that my earlier problems at Cambridge had been greatly eased by A. C. Benson, the Master of Magdalene. And he may wonder why, in these present discontents, I did not approach Benson, if not for help, at least for consolation. The reason is sad and simple. Benson was no longer there; he was in the throes of one of the many bouts of acute melancholia which tortured the later days of his life. Moreover, although only a few months had elapsed, the whole Cambridge scene had changed and darkened, as though the smoke from the mounting fury of the battles in Flanders were drifting across the Channel, filling the skies with menace. The life of the University still flickered on and some of the Colleges were still open, but they seemed to be tenanted by ghosts.

Meanwhile, I had a good deal of time to myself. After the fiasco of the bayonet practice the Colonel seemed reconciled to leaving me alone. He had not the authority to ship me over to France and his small brain seemed unable to devise any tortures which would not have made him look as ridiculous as I should have looked myself. So I decided to make the best of things. After all, I still had eyes in my head and there was beauty all around me. There were long vistas by the river where the willows were dancing, and secret courtyards, hushed and withdrawn, where one could forget the world. I began to explore the University and to learn something of its history.

One of my first ports of call was Christ's College, because of its associations with Milton. During my last term at Marlborough there had been a brief but passionate period in which I read Milton to the exclusion of almost all other poets. (I can still recite 'Lycidas', and many of the other shorter works by heart.) I wanted to pay a belated homage to him and in particular to visit the mulberry tree in whose shade he was reputed to have composed some of his earliest verses.

I found the tree in an inner courtyard and was gazing at it with suitable emotions when there was a voice behind me.

'Are you by any chance a Miltonian?'

He was a short plump figure in a shabby scholar's gown. He was about sixty and everything about him was soft and round and gentle, even his voice. He emanated benignity.

'Yes, sir. I certainly am.'

'Then there is no need for me to instruct you in the history of our celebrated tree.'

I will remain faithful to my rule against inventing dialogue. But when certain scenes remain clearly in the memory I think it is legitimate to suggest, however sketchily, the words that must have accompanied them, even if they were not spoken into a tape-recorder. We continued to talk, and as we talked we walked, until we came to the door of the Master's Lodge. My newly-found friend opened it and gestured me inside.

'Isn't this the Master's Lodge, sir?'

'It is, but since I happen to be Master of Christ's and also Vice-Chancellor of the University, there is no cause for alarm.'

I followed him, scarcely able to believe my good fortune. Here was an encounter that promised even richer rewards than the association with A. C. Benson. In this topsy-turvy situation of the war, part military and part academic, the Vice-Chancellor—whose name was Sir Arthur Shipley—had precedence over the entire military establishment. His wishes had the force of law. If, for example, he had decided that any of the colleges should be exempted from military occupation, nobody could have questioned his decision.

I must make the most of this situation. I must exploit it for all it was worth. If this implied that I was prepared to play the role of a youthful gold-digger, I should be the last to deny it. Why not? I was very near the end of my tether. I was being treated as a pariah by a horde of illiterate louts. I was being kicked from pillar to post. If I had anything to offer—and the Café Royal, a million miles away, had suggested that I had—now was the moment to get to work.

We had tea in an enormous room which subtly alerted me to my host's personality. There was a Tudor ceiling of delicate plaster-work. Most academics would have left it alone, to gather the dust. Sir Arthur had picked it out in gold-leaf. I congratulated him on this, and he purred with pleasure. We had China tea from exquisite Meissen cups, and out of the jackdaw attic of my mind I fished the word 'Meissen', and used it, and he purred again. There was a total rapport between us. For the first time in my nineteen years I realised, with a stab of pain, what life might have been like if one had had a father—what vistas might have been opened, what talents might have been developed.

The clocks of Cambridge—every English university marks the passage of time with the mystic music of horology—were striking five when he led me to the door.

'I notice that you are limping. Have you been wounded?'

'I'm afraid not, sir. I have never seen active service. I have not been wounded.'

I began to stammer out some sort of apology but he cut me short. 'That can scarcely be regarded as your fault. Nor your mis-fortune, in view of the latest news from France.' And then, abruptly—'Would you care to dine with me?'

'I should be honoured, sir.'

71

'Tonight?'

'I should have to ask the Colonel, sir.'

'If you inform him that you have been invited . . . or shall we say commanded? . . . to dine with the Vice-Chancellor, I think we may assume that he will give his consent.'

An hour later. The Colonel's office.

'Permission to dine out, sir.'

'When?'

'Tonight, sir.'

'Rather short notice, isn't it?' A pause. The famous sneer. 'Well, I imagine that for one night we can dispense with your company in the mess.'

'Thank you, sir.' I clicked my heels, saluted, and turned to go.

'Just a moment. You are aware that certain restaurants are out of bounds. *Where* will you be dining?'

'At Christ's College, sir.'

'With a fellow-officer?'

'No, sir.' And this time it was I who contrived the pause. 'With the Vice-Chancellor, sir.'

The effect was electric. If I had told him that I was dining with the entire royal family he could not have been more astonished.

'Sir Arthur Shipley? Is he a friend of yours?'

'I hope so, Sir.'

'What is that supposed to mean? How long have you known him?'

'About an hour, sir.'

I was beginning to enjoy this dialogue. And I am *not* inventing it.

'You have known Sir Arthur for an hour? And you get yourself invited to dinner? Where did you meet him?'

'In the courtyard, sir.'

'On what grounds did you approach him?'

'I did not approach him, sir. He approached me.'

'He approached *you*? Why?'

72

There could have been several answers to that question, but all of them would have sounded impertinent, so I said nothing.

There was a moment's silence, in which the Colonel was obviously struggling to control himself. At length he growled . . .

'You realise, of course, that this is a considerable honour. I trust you will do nothing to make Sir Arthur regret his invitation. Permission granted. You may dismiss.'

Here we must cut a long story short. The dinner was a resounding success. Sir Arthur's invitation was repeated again, and yet again. And after every dinner at Christ's the hostility of my fellow-officers was markedly relaxed. They began to include me in their conversations. One of them even asked me to join him in a drink.

But the Colonel had not finished yet. The petty humiliations continued and he never tired of his sneering references to the offending slacks. His hatred of me was pathological. Today, with a greater understanding of abnormal psychology. I realise that he had an advanced inferiority complex.

Since he could not interrupt my growing friendship with the Vice-Chancellor, he had to contrive some other method of attack. He found it in a curious institution which for some reason never explained was called Course K. This was the brain-child of a retired general at the War Office, one of the large number of distinguished ex-officers who had been dragged from obscurity at the beginning of the war and had been cluttering up the corridors ever since. The object of the Course was to instruct senior officers in the general strategy of European warfare.

The Colonel decided to send me on Course K.

The idea was quite mad, and was motivated solely by his determination to expose me to the final disgrace. If the powers that be had heard about it he would have been severely reprimanded. As it was, nobody heard about it, with the exception of the Vice-Chancellor. When I told him, his reaction was unexpected. 'My dear Beverley,'—(we were now on Christian name terms)—'I have no doubt that you will do extremely well.'

'But I know nothing of warfare. As for Europe, I have never even crossed the Channel. I shall have nothing to say.'

'You will think of something.'

Thanks to his quiet confidence I thought of a great deal. In the latter period of my Marlborough career the Sixth Form had studied the Italian campaigns of Napoleon as a subject for the end-of-term essay prize. I had decided to win it, and had done so. When the day of the examination came I knew every twist and turn of the River Po, every mountain pass and—which is more important—every mood in the Napoleonic mind. And they were still very clear in my memory.

Very well. The officers of Course K would be instructed in the campaigns of Napoleon, which would be cunningly related to the current manœuvres in Flanders. What is more they would like it.

And they did. I came out top of the lot and returned to Cambridge with a recommendation that I should repeat the performance for the benefit of Colonel Cradock's own battalion.

This must surely be one of the most lunatic episodes in a war that had long lost any contact with reality. It confirmed my conviction—which was later to be developed in *Cry Havoc*—that in all wars the first condition for success is that the vast majority of the population must be driven insane.

We are nearing the climax of this curious saga.

The scene is again Christ's College, and I am again dining with the Vice-Chancellor. By now, the father–son relationship was firmly established and it is difficult to explain to the average reader, coming from a normal home, how much this meant to me. Until this time 'father' had been a dirty word; it had even tainted the Lord's Prayer. How could one bring oneself to mouth such phrases as 'Our Father, which art in heaven' when one's father was the epitome of the Devil?

After dinner we went into the main hall, to sit under the gilded ceiling and drink coffee from the Meissen cups. We were so content in each other's company that we often relaxed in silence while Sir Arthur smoked his cigar. But tonight he was preoccupied. I asked him if anything was wrong. He smiled and shook his head. 'On the contrary.'

He went to his desk and returned with a letter which he handed to me. 'I think you should see this before I post it.'

I read the letter and even before I had finished it I realised that it was destined to change my whole life, not only in the present but in all the years that lay ahead. It was addressed to Colonel Ian Hay, who may still be remembered by older readers as the most popular best-selling novelist of the First World War. Ian Hay was now His Majesty's Minister of Information. The letter was a request, which was tantamount to a command, that Lieutenant J. B. Nichols should be released from his 'duties' (!) in order to act as secretary to a group of distinguished academics who were shortly sailing on a mission to the United States. Lieutenant J. B. Nichols, so the Minister was assured, was ideally fitted for such a delicate role, (which was news to Lieutenant J. B. Nichols, who had no conception of what secretaries were supposed to do). The letter ended with a sentence expressing the Vice-Chancellor's pleasure, on behalf of the delegation, in accepting President Wilson's invitation to luncheon at the White House.

Repeat. 'The authenticity of an autobiography is to be measured not only by what the author remembers but by what he forgets.' All I can remember is that when I walked back to Jesus College that night I was weeping. The façade of the King's Parade was misted and the portico of Jesus College was blurred. Tears, as we all learn in our passage through life, come in all varieties—hot, cold, sour, sweet. One of the most lamentable songs that echoed over the British Isles in those days was entitled 'Tears', and it was bellowed by countless full-bosomed contraltos to thousands of eager young recruits, who were being dispatched to the abattoirs of Flanders. Why not? It comforted the troops and it profited the contraltos.

All the same, I shall not attempt a psychological analysis of my own tears, as I walked back that night, by the light of the silvery moon. They may have been tears of triumph.

The next few weeks go blank. This need not worry the literary historian, for the whole story is still to be read in *Twenty-Five*, my first autobiography.*

The trip to London, the interview with Ian Hay, the embarkation to America, the lunch with the President, the whole astonishing panorama of adventure—they are all recorded in these pages. Perhaps they may still be read with amusement if only as an example of what happens when a lively youth, precipitated into the centre of great events in stirring times, takes the trouble to make notes.

What I did not record in *Twenty-Five* was the reaction of the Officer's Mess when they learned the news. The loathsome Colonel Cradock was literally struck dumb; he was deprived of speech. There were papers to be signed, passports to be counter-signed, travel documents to be stamped. The papers were signed in silence, and when he handed them to me he averted his eyes.

On my last dinner in the Officers' Mess they were all there, waiting for me. The whole snarling, smouldering, bitter gang of men with a capital M. It was like entering a cage of dangerous animals, and I deliberately taunted the animals by appearing in a full-dress evening uniform of navy blue, with touches of gold braid, tailored at great expense by the same establishment that had provided the notorious overcoat. It would have been the ideal costume for the juvenile lead in a Ruritanian romance, and it was almost more than they could endure. But there was nothing that they could do about it.

The last thing I remember as I drove away on the following morning, en route for the New World, was a white face staring from an upper window. It was the face of the Captain who had taken the first bite at me on the day of my arrival, the man who had used the filthy words about buggering a woman. I thought it would be appropriate to give him the gesture of the V-sign—arm extended, first and second fingers of the right hand spread apart.

For this had been a battle, and a battle which I had won.

Postscript. The first thing I did on my arrival in New York was to buy a brightly coloured picture postcard of the Statue of Liberty

* *Twenty-Five:* Jonathan Cape Ltd, 1926.

and address it to Colonel Cradock, care of the Officer's Mess, Jesus College, Cambridge, England. On the back of it I wrote a message which was short but—to me—very sweet.

Having wonderful time. Wish you were here.
J. B. Nichols.
Lieutenant.

CHAPTER VI

🙞🙞🙞🙞🙞

THE STAR
SPANGLED MANNER*

If I were to be born again, which God forbid, I would choose to be born an American. Not for the power nor the glory nor the glittering prizes; not for the wealth nor the width of the blue horizons; not even for the weather. I would choose to be born an American because only in America, as our century hurtles towards its crazy conclusion, can one still find the established virtues and the ancient graces which were once the heritage of England.

I dimly sensed this very soon after my arrival in the States. Indeed, in Chicago, I nearly went completely off the rails and applied for American citizenship. Sir Arthur briskly put a stop to that, on one of the few occasions when he found it necessary to assert his authority. He pointed out that apart from running the risk of being court-martialled as a deserter I was destined for a career at Oxford as soon as the war was over, as it nearly was. And he reminded me that it might not be a bad idea if I began to acquire some sort of education.

'The established virtues and the ancient graces.' Here I must flash forward. In later years I had some success on the American lecture platform, in most of the major cities from coast to coast, visiting every state in the union with the exception of Washington.

---

* *The Star Spangled Manner* (Doubleday Doran, New York, 1928) was the title of the first of two books which I have written about the United States. Over twenty years were to elapse before the publication of the second, which was a rather more serious assessment (*Uncle Samson*, Doubleday Doran, New York, 1950).

78

(Not the Washington that everybody knows, which is not of course a state at all, but the one in the top left-hand corner of the map. I hope that Washingtonians will not resent this somewhat cursory description of their state.) On my first visit I was booked to speak at Newport, Rhode Island, but in spite of the substantial fee I was not looking forward to it. Newport's reputation was brash and brassy; it was the country of the dollar princesses. It was Scott Fitzgerald territory and I did not greatly care for Scott Fitzgerald either as a writer or as a man. Whenever I met him he was so drunk that he was not funny.

(Note on Scott Fitzgerald. The legendary Lady Mendl once described him, in her raucous twang, as 'a social parvenoo—not real society—only café society'. This was a case of the pot calling the kettle black, for if ever there was a 'parvenoo', who epitomised café society, it was dear old Elsie Mendl. Née Elsie de Woolf she had made an immense fortune as the first internationally successful interior decorator, selling dubious Louis Seize commodes to Chicago meat-packers. In Paris she met a man called Sir Charles Mendl, and a marriage was arranged, of exceptional convenience to both parties. He was established in comfort, and she was now 'her ladyship', which added fifty percent to the cost of the commodes. They became great friends of the Windsors, with whom they evidently had a spiritual rapport.)

We were talking of Newport, the Scott Fitzgerald country, which has become smeared through the medium of Hollywood, with the patina of American 'vulgarity'. I went there fearing the worst, I discovered the best. I discovered another Newport—not the Newport of the Vanderbilts and the bogus 'châteaux' flaunting themselves along the Atlantic coastline—but a Newport that was modest, withdrawn, and altogether enchanting. After the lecture a member of the audience asked me if I should like to see it. As we got into her car she said, 'Of course it is ridiculous for me, an American, to take you on this sort of expedition when you have such riches at home.'

We went on our tour and as we meandered through the winding streets my eyes opened wider and wider. For an Englishman, coming from a country that was being bulldozed and vulgarised beyond recognition, the old Newport was—and still is—a revelation. Every house, every street-sign, every little garden was exquisitely tended and preserved. Even the garages, by a miracle of the landscaper's art, were blended into the picture behind neatly clipped hedges of yew and box. It was like stepping back into the eighteenth century. Moreover, there was no suggestion of 'restoration', no feeling that one was being asked to admire a period filmset. Newport had preserved its elegance because the Americans had loved and cherished it. This applies not only to Newport, not only to the whole exquisite tapestry of New England, but throughout many parts of the United States, particularly in the South.

Any Englishman with a nostalgia for his country's past, any Englishman who is sickened by the spectacle of his market towns being massacred to make way for supermarkets and his stately homes being transformed into zoos should take ship for America. I rather like the phrase 'take ship'. It reminds me of the Queen Mary, and the Mauretania, and the Aquitania and the Île de France, and all the other proud vessels, though some of them were not so proud, in which I have circumnavigated this planet. To 'take ship' is to travel like a gentleman and to enrich one's life, even if one is travelling steerage, as has sometimes been my experience. To fly is to be shuttled about like a robot, to be cut off from life, to be anaesthetised from all the pleasures of the passing hour.

Of all the innovations of this century the habit of flying must surely be regarded as the greatest waste of time.

We are in the autumn of 1918, a few weeks before the end of the First World War. I am nineteen, rising twenty, a formidable age. I have sailed past the Statue of Liberty; and although I have never heard a shot fired in anger I am disguised in the uniform of a first lieutenant in the British army, a uniform to which I have added a few glittering improvements of my own invention. And although I have not the remotest pretensions to scholarship I am 'in charge' of one of the most distinguished scholastic deputations ever to visit America, scientists and professors of international repute who spoke a language that I did not even begin to understand. It only goes to show what can happen if one meets the right people, wears the right clothes, and puts on the right expression. And if one knows how to *listen*. That was perhaps my greatest asset. All those intellectual giants were so absorbed by their own subjects that they could talk of nothing else. For instance there was a darling old man called Sir Henry Jones who was the world's greatest expert on early Byzantine mosaics, and a not so darling old man called Professor Joly who was the world's greatest expert on the Martian canals. They were constantly in conflict, because they would not listen to one another. I listened to them both, like mad, and soothed them down, gazing at them with suitable veneration. I also found things for them. Sir Henry had only one tooth which he was constantly losing. My job was to retrieve it. Professor Joly had quantities of boots, which he insisted on leaving outside his hotel bedroom. I tried to explain to him that in America one does not leave boots outside one's bedroom door, but he froze me with a look of Martian disdain. I had to waste a great deal of energy in tracking down the Professor's boots. Obviously, I had my uses.

The American adventure is recorded in *Twenty-Five*, so I will not repeat it in these pages. But there were some things about it which I could not have printed fifty years ago. Today I can take the risk.

We were thrown in at the deep end. Only a few days after our arrival we were being conducted through the winding corridors of the White House, where we stepped into the presence of the world's most important figure—President Wilson. The informality of it, in these days, seems incredible. We were not asked for any credentials, we were not required to sign any papers, and we were not 'frisked'. I have visited the White House on several occasions. (The most memorable was when the British ambassador arranged for me to interview President Coolidge who apparently was not properly appreciative of the hardships which the British people were enduring at the time. Why I should have been chosen to instruct the President in these matters I have no idea, but the interview was a success. Within half an hour I had him near to tears and on the following morning there was a headline in one of the Washington papers ... 'Beverley Nichols, the Man who made Coolidge cry.')

The White House was as informal, as wide-open in the Coolidge days as in the Wilson era. Things are different today. On my last visit, after Kennedy's assassination, there was an armed sentry at the gate and a great deal of very searching interrogation.

The passage of time constantly modifies the pictures engraved on the memory, erasing some, bringing others into sharp relief. Today my most vivid memory of Wilson is his use of the word 'Hohenzollern' to summarise the forces ranged against America. 'America is not going to leave the Hohenzollerns in power,' he proclaimed. 'It would mean leaving a running sore in the heart of Europe.' He never mentioned the German army or the German navy or the character of the German people. Everything was summed up in the person of the Kaiser. It was the same when he spoke of the British Empire. He seemed to see it only in terms of the monarchy—for whom he expressed his admiration—as though our war effort were being personally conducted from Buckingham Palace. His whole view of world affairs showed an exaggerated estimate of the power of princes—a tradition which still colours American opinion. I was to learn the strength and persistence of this tradition in later years, when I visited Chicago during the régime of one of the weirdest characters who ever stepped onto the stage of American history, Mayor Thompson of Chicago. Thompson was a small-time Middle-Western crook who came into power by the use of a single lunatic slogan—'Keep King George out of Chicago'. He really did persuade millions of eager trusting citizens in the vast Chicago complex that dear, sweet King George, trying to cope with the domestic problems of Buckingham Palace, was engaged in a hellish plot to invade Chicago. I tackled Thompson about this personally, in the sleazy down-town hotel which was his campaign headquarters, and wrote an interview which infuriated him so much that I was advised to keep out of Chicago till the campaign was over.

All this, however, was in the future. On this first trip, described in *Twenty-Five*, I was so busy taking verbal snapshots and pasting them in my mental album that I had no time to look below the surface. Today, what stands out with shocking clarity is the quite astonishing ignorance of the mass of the American people of the nature of the war that they were fighting and the reasons for which they were fighting it. The whole swirling maelstrom of horror was simplified and tinted in crude primitive colours, as though Walt Disney had been commissioned to produce a series of cartoons on the crucifixion. They had some excuse, of course; they were far from the sound of battle, they had never seen the enemy in the skies nor the wounded in the streets. All the same, their ignorance was almost incredible. We visited all the great American universities and even in such seats of learning as Harvard and Yale and Princeton I found myself talking to professors who would not have passed the most elementary examination in European history. To them, Europe was a fairy tale in which kings and princes still jousted in ancient tournaments.

It is arguable that American ignorance of world affairs, in the past fifty years, has been responsible for most of the greatest disasters of the twentieth century. Well . . . they have learned, and are still learning. But they have learned in a very hard school.

Here is one example of the astonishing mentality of the American people during the First World War. We arrived in Chicago on November 8th, 1918, to discover that the war was over. The peace treaty had been signed while we were still in the train. We entered a city that had gone mad. Snowstorms of paper fluttered down from the skyscrapers as the telephone books were torn to pieces. Bells clanged from every church. All the taxi-drivers were drunk and the pavements were littered with prostrate figures. When we reached the club where we were staying we had to step over recumbent bodies while our bags remained in the hall.

But the war was not over. The armies were still locked in bloody conflict. It was all an invention of William Randolph Hearst, the almost omnipotent newspaper proprietor. He had decided that the American people had had enough of this foreign nonsense. So he called a halt, and signed the peace treaties, and rang the bells of peace.

Could this have happened in any other country? Could the life of one of the greatest cities in the world have been totally disrupted by the whim of a multi-millionaire? I doubt it. And even if the millionaire had succeeded, would he not have been sharply reprimanded by the powers that be? Would there not have been public pronouncements, radio proclamations, Presidential denials, calling Chicago back to its senses? If there were, we heard nothing of them. The chaos continued for nearly three days until the armistice was actually signed, on November 11th, 1918.

I made the most of those three days. As all our official engagements were cancelled I was left to roam the city by myself, picking people up and being picked up in return. My British uniform opened every door. If I paused outside a theatre, wondering whether I could afford the price of a seat in the upper circle, I was grabbed by the arm and rushed into the stalls with a pocketful of cigars. One of these theatres was starring an enchanting actress called Laurette Taylor in a piece of classic schmaltz called *Peg o' my Heart*. When the play was over Miss Taylor took me out to supper and gave me my first avocado pear, which went to my head in more senses than one. She was convinced that I was a hero, hot from the fields of Flanders, and I saw no reason to disillusion her.

There were many of these encounters and most of them were as fleeting and transitory as the flecks of paper that ceaselessly fluttered through the cavernous streets of the windy city as the inhabitants continued to tear up the telephone books. But one of them was not so casual.

If you do not believe in luck I should very much like to know what you do believe in. It is a commonplace little word but it carries awesome echoes of fate and leads to the ultimate philosophical labyrinths of predestination in which men wander until they lose their reason.

In Chicago, during the final lunatic hours of Mr Hearst's bogus armistice, I decided to spend my last few dollars on buying a drink in one of the city's grandest hotels which had a bar on the roof. So I pushed through the swing doors, walked through the crowded hall, and stepped into an elevator which was occupied by a lady in a black dress.

In doing so I also stepped into a palazzo in Venice, a mansion in New York's Washington Square, a villa in the South of France and a great many other delectable retreats. Most important of all, I stepped into a little English cottage which was to change my life and make my fortune, the cottage which turned me into a gardener and gave me the background for a book called *Down the Garden Path*.

I closed the door of the elevator; the lady smiled and pressed the button, the lift shot up with the usual alarming American ferocity. Suddenly there was an explosion and we came to a shuddering halt.

I stared at her in dismay. 'What has happened?'

She continued to smile. 'We seem to be stuck.'

'Did I do anything wrong?'

'Certainly not.' She pressed the button again. Nothing happened.

'Is there anything we can do?'

'We can sit down and wait for something to happen. It usually does. What are you doing in our crazy city?'

Here it came again, this damnable situation. In spite of the constant stimulus of the American adventure, and although I was having some social success, I could never feel at ease. I was haunted by the sense of sailing under false colours. My British uniform stamped me in American eyes as a war hero and I had done nothing in the least heroic. Perhaps it was foolish to be so concerned about something for which I was in no way to blame, but my temperament and my background had given me a lamentable and probably contemptible habit for taking the blame when things went wrong. Nothing *had* gone wrong; indeed, I think that I could claim to have had my share in contributing to the success of our bizarre expedition. It was not only a question of finding Sir Henry Jones's single tooth and retrieving Professor Joly's boots; it was a question of being young and alert and anxious to please and knowing when to say the right thing. I had these talents and I knew how to use them. In short, I had 'charm'. It is a fatal gift to be born with. No self-respecting fairy godmother should include 'charm' among the qualities with which she endows her offspring. It is a talisman which opens every door, and then ensures that the doors are slammed in one's face.

Should I use this 'charm' on the lady with whom I was stuck in the lift? No. Very definitely not. Something told me that she was going to be important in my life. Something also told me that she was not the sort of woman who would be impressed by false pretensions. So in answer to her question 'What are you doing in our crazy city?' I told her the whole improbable story and made no attempt to conceal my feelings of shame and guilt, which were deeper than I suspected, for I had been bottling them up ever since we left England. By the time I had finished I was very near to tears. But I also know that I had made a friend for life.

Meet Emily Borie Ryerson. A stoutish woman in late middle-age, very simply dressed in black, leaning back on the bench of the elevator, with one hand on an ebony cane and the other playing with a long string of pearls. Not a figure of beauty or elegance, but if I ever had to write an essay on 'The Most Remarkable Woman in my Life', she would come very high on the list. Hugh Walpole, who adored her, once said that if Aeschylus had ever known her he would have made her the heroine of a great tragedy.

I learned one of the themes of her tragedy on the same evening that we met. After we were rescued from the elevator she whisked me off to her home in Riverside Drive, which was Chicago's Millionaire's Row. In the hall an old butler was waiting whom she greeted in excellent French. His name was Dominique. I wandered into a salon which was pure Louis Seize—not 'decorator's' Louis Seize but the sort of furniture one finds in modest *châteaux* on the Loire. There was a Bechstein piano and on the wall a magnificent tapestry. I wandered over to the mantelpiece. Judging from her collection of photographs Emily Ryerson had some distinguished friends. There was a snapshot of Clemenceau, affectionately inscribed, and another of Venizelos. There were English royals, and Henry James, and the young Toscanini and a lovely sketch of Eleanor Dusé. There was President Wilson himself. And there was a man in a yachting cap, leaning against a ship's railing, smiling gaily and waving a cigar. I was standing opposite it when she came back to the room.

'That was my husband. Shortly before his death.'

86

I was not prepared for this bleak statement. I muttered something about being sorry and then, because the silence was embarrassing, I said, 'Was that your yacht?'

'No. It was not a yacht. It was the *Titanic.*'

Our eyes met. There was a long pause and then she nodded. That nod told me the whole story. Not that the whole story of Emily Ryerson's connection with the *Titanic* has ever been told, or ever will be, because the only person who could tell it is myself, and I am too ancient and too fatigued.

One day I may write more about Emily. I have only to close my eyes to see her against an endless variety of backgrounds. In Venice, standing on the steps of her palazzo in the early light of dawn, holding out her stick to help me as I stepped out of the gondola. In Washington Square, New York, where she threw open her house for my sole occupation, and left me to my own devices, after opening a bottle of champagne. In Paris, in the Rue de Lille, in London at Covent Garden. In the villa at Cap Ferrat.

To give some idea of her quality I may mention that in the last years of her life, when she was very frail and when her eyes were failing, Somerset Maugham would often walk down from his own villa, which was only a few minutes away, in order to sit by her bed and read her his stories. This, from Maugham, was an exceptional tribute. He had his moments of generosity but he was not in the habit of making this sort of gesture. He was very easily bored and when he read from a book he stammered even more painfully than when he was conversing. And yet, out of affection and respect, he gave her many hours of his time, which was already running short. It says a great deal for him, and it says even more for her.

Emily always wore the same black dress, which she ordered by the dozen, always with the same black stick and the same ropes of pearls which—very characteristically—were imitation, because she did not wish to be bothered by baubles that she had to worry about. She must have been immensely rich, but one never had any feeling of opulence, only of generosity and warmth and a fierce lust for life. One of her endearing habits was to begin sentences with the words, 'The greatest thing about life is . . .' And then she would pronounce her verdict about what the greatest thing in life was. It might be courage, it might be tolerance, it might be a capacity for self-criticism; in lighter moments it might be the climate, or a jar of caviar.

But my clearest memory of her is walking down the garden path of the little cottage in Huntingdonshire. It had belonged to her brother, John Borie, who is buried in the churchyard under a simple stone of granite for which she chose the inscription, 'An American who loved England'. She came across to settle his affairs and summoned me for the weekend. There she was, a little stouter, a little greyer, in the inevitable black dress, her arms full of roses. I held her in my arms for a moment; she had become very dear to me. And as I looked over her shoulder, towards the thatched roof and the porch with its clustering honeysuckle I knew that I had found a home. The first home that I had ever known. This was it.

Not long afterwards I was able to buy it from her. No doubt she would have given it to me. But no. This had to be something I had earned by my own efforts, with my own talents, every stick and stone of it, every flower and every tree and every blade of grass. Only thus could it be wholly mine.

All through being stuck in a lift!

Here I shall draw the curtain on the American adventure because after Chicago everything seemed an anti-climax. It is time that we took ship and sailed for home.

I cannot recall the name of the ship we sailed in. All I remember is standing on deck in a state of mental and physical exhaustion. I have seen the members of the delegation to their respective quarters. Sir Arthur Jones, clutching his one tooth, Professor Joly, about to lose his boots and all the rest of them, including darling old Sir Arthur, with whom I share a cabin. Soon I shall have to go below and tuck him up, gently but firmly, because he has a habit of rolling out of bed.

Fortunately, the ship's lights are glimmering again, because the war at last is over and there will be no danger from submarines.

Even more fortunately, from my point of view, none of my flock will get lost in the darkness, obliging me to retrieve them by the light of a torch. It has not been an easy assignment. But as I stand on deck, listening to the gentle throbbing of the engines, I feel that I need not be ashamed of the part I have played in it.

I stare at the receding Statue of Liberty, silhouetted in the light of a crystalline December moon. The most awesome moment in this world. Second-rate in its design and shady in its conception. But because of the waves of emotion that have swirled round it over the years, because of the passions of the millions to whom it has been a symbol of deliverance, it is invested with an aura of majesty which lifts it high above all other human monuments.

I sum up, staring at the receding statue, which has dwindled to a midget. We are heading for the open sea. Sitting alone on deck I decide that I am a very mixed-up kid. In the past few weeks I have been thrown into social and political circles which would have dizzied the heads of men twice my age. I was quite unprepared for the experience. True, I had got myself a sort of education and had gone through the motions of becoming an officer and had learned that I had a facility for extricating myself from awkward situations. But what had it all been in aid of?

Why did I feel so lost and desolate? I suppose it was because I lacked the one essential which gives purpose and stability to a young man's career. I had not the background of a stable home, however humble, to which I could return, or a normal family, however undistinguished, from whom I might gain comfort. True, I had a 'home', but it was haunted by an evil ghost, my father. True, I had a mother whom I loved, but the love was distorted by the agony of her tribulations. I had brothers—and for one of them I had an enduring affection. But I did not really know either of them. We spoke a different language.

And where did I stand sexually? I had no idea. Here was the greatest mix-up of all. Experience had shown me, all too clearly, that sex was available at the drop of a hat. I had the sort of face and body which people wanted to take to bed. The trouble was that I did not *want* to get into bed . . . at any rate, not that often. What I wanted, always did want, and always shall want, was to sit bolt upright at a piano practising arpeggios and then, when my fingers were aching with this exquisite torture, to allow them to drift into a tune, and to have the technique to transform that tune into a work of art. That was how Chopin did it.

But one cannot practise sex with one hand and play arpeggios with the other—not both at once. This was one thing that life had taught me. I doubt whether it has taught me much else.

The statue has faded. We are in the open sea. There is a tune in my head. I tear out a slip of paper from my diary, draw five lines, and scribble the tempo sign . . . six/eight . . . and the key signature . . . five flats. I write the first twelve bars. Then I scrumple it in my fist and throw it overboard. What the hell. Nobody will ever hear it or play it or sing it, unless it happens to drift into the lap of some amiable mermaid and even she will only glance at it, hum the first few bars and then throw it back into the deep water.

Time for bed. Time to go down to the cabin and deal with darling Sir Arthur who, of course, has fallen out of his bunk. He is very heavy; he needs a lot of propping up; and the seas are rising. There are storms ahead.

CHAPTER VII

🌹🌹🌹🌹🌹🌹

DREAMING SPIRES

It would be false modesty to deny that my Oxford career was exceptional, particularly as I had to cram everything into eighteen months, which is half the time allotted to the average under-graduate. In the middle of it all, on the crest of the wave, my father, in an alcoholic spasm, withdrew all financial support. If I had been given a few months' notice I might have scraped through; I might have scribbled something, or sold something, such as the gold cigarette case which I had acquired in America, or prostituted myself in some way or other. But he gave me no notice. He just said 'enough is enough', put his cheque book in his desk and locked the drawer. Why? To answer that question one would have to try to comprehend the labyrinths of the alcoholic mind, which would be an unprofitable exercise.

Only eighteen months. But in this crowded interlude, I made my mark.

1. I became President of the Union. Whether this office has any significance in modern England I would not know. But in the times which I am recording, to be President of the Oxford Union meant that one was a potential Prime Minister or Lord Chancellor.

2. I was editor of the *Isis*, which was regarded as the voice of contemporary Oxford opinion. Again, I have no idea what this means to the modern generation. In those days it meant a lot. It

was the first step on the difficult and dangerous ladder to the commanding heights of Fleet Street.

3. I was founder, editor, and financier of my own literary period-ical, *The Oxford Outlook*. The financing was the most difficult part; I had to go about rattling collecting boxes for shillings and half-crowns. *The Outlook* was the only 'quality' magazine of its nature which had a fairly long life, and it was indeed a 'quality' production, with contributions from many of the leading figures of the day. What is more, it actually made money.

4. I recreated the defunct Liberal Club, and contrived a mass meeting at the Town Hall which was addressed by all the stars of the Liberal Party, from Mr Asquith downwards.

5. I published my first novel *Prelude*, to which we have already referred.

6. I made my début as a concert pianist at one of the musical evenings in Balliol College, which were of a very high standard. This was not an unmitigated success. I chose to play Chopin's Second Scherzo, which is not a beginner's piece. All was well till the last sixteen bars, when my mind went blank. So I ended with a few crashing chords, improvised on the spur of the moment. This finale came as a shock to the other concert pianists present, but nobody else seemed to notice that anything had gone wrong. This was one of many occasions when life taught me that one can get away with anything so long as one keeps one's nerve.

All this feverish activity, which included getting a degree* and leading a hectic social life, by no means devoid of romantic inter-ludes . . . all this in the short space of five terms, suggests an almost

---

* 'Getting a degree'. Owing to my father's decision to stop my career in mid-stream I was unable to go through the normal academic routine. I had to take a shortened course specially devised for ex-officers which, though it entitled one to the letters M.A., carried no academic distinction.

daemonic energy. And indeed, I was being driven by a demon. For always, in the background, was my home, Cleave Court, 'the institution for the criminally insane' to which I was compelled to return during the vacation. The horror of this home could never be forgotten, even late at night, when I returned to my rooms, which were always bright with flowers. At all costs I must contrive escape routes when Oxford was over and when the time came to face the outside world. For this I needed money and in order to make the money I must first make a name, and make it quickly.

What I made of that name is another story, and not, perhaps, a very inspiring one. All that matters, in the present record, is that from the age of twenty-one, whenever I entered a room, it was necessary for me to introduce myself.

On the infrequent occasions when I have revisited Oxford in recent years to speak at the Union, I have been unimpressed. Most of the speeches sounded as if they had been compiled by computers and they were badly delivered, in a dreary monotone. None of the speakers knew what to do with his arms or his legs. I soon discovered what to do with mine. Nothing at all. Very few Englishmen can make oratorical gestures without looking ridiculous. Worst of all, many of the speeches were actually *read*, and even if they were not read in their entirety, there was a constant reference to notes. This surely was inexcusable. I have never used a note in my life. A speaker should walk out onto the platform with empty hands and nothing up his sleeve. To speak with notes is as deplorable as to play the piano with a score, turning the page in the middle of a melodic line. The musical simile is apposite, as I hope to prove.

The reader must now be prepared for a rather lengthy diversion, but it is justified. The art of oratory has played a major role in history—a role which no serious historian has yet endeavoured to assess. (It would form a fruitful theme for the explosive genius of Professor A. L. Rowse.) As long as men inhabit this planet they will continue to jump onto platforms and make speeches, exhorting their fellows to follow them down paths which may lead to triumph or disaster or—as in most cases—to nowhere at all.

Here are a few notes for those who are inclined to jump onto platforms.

We might begin with a little history. It is very British history but it has also an American connotation.

One of the greater orators of the Victorian age was Mr Gladstone, Queen Victoria's least favourite prime minister, and one of the most frequently quoted catchwords of the late Victorian political scene after his death was ... 'Oh for an hour of Gladstone!' This was a plaintive plea from millions of liberals who felt lost without their leader.

I had always suspected that Gladstone was a phoney. This is not an historical appellation but it applies, more crisply than any conventional classification, to much of his conduct in public and in private. One day my suspicion was confirmed—here comes the promised diversion—by no less a person than Mr Frank Sinatra. You may think that it is a long step from Gladstone to Sinatra; not at all; it is precisely half a mile. When young Mr Sinatra came to London in the thirties a newspaper syndicate suggested that I should write a 'profile' of him. It was an agreeable commission. In those days Sinatra was as slim as a straw; he had eyes of a very dangerous shade of blue; and there were strange echoes in his singing voice which appealed to me. I asked this phenomenon to lunch at the Ritz, and it was a great success. But after lunch I could not think what to do with him. (How many people still alive could truthfully assert that they could not think what to do with Frank Sinatra after lunch?) I could not ask him to sit in the hall, so I rang up the B.B.C. and got onto the historical record department.

'This is Beverley Nichols. I have an exciting young American singer with me. I want to bring him round to hear some records. His name is Frank Sinatra.'

'Never heard of him.'

'You will. Can we say in half an hour?'

'What records do you want?'

'Caruso. Patti. Anything. So long as it's antique.'

'See you in half an hour.'

This was typical of my interviewing technique in those days. I used to place my victims in incongruous surroundings and record their reactions. One of the most successful examples of this method was provided by Sam Goldwyn. Everybody else used to portray him on a film set or in the suite of an opulent hotel. I took him to the Garrick Club, which is among the most tranquil and elegant clubs of London, and sat him down under a portrait of David Garrick. The result was as vivid as a sketch by Sargent.

I wanted to do the same sort of thing with Frank Sinatra. The voice of the present, young, vibrant, exquisitely attuned to the echoes of the present, blended by a sort of verbal counterpoint with the voice of the past. Caruso had seemed the obvious choice, but when we got to the B.B.C. they offered something much better. They offered Gladstone, of whom young Frank had never heard. But he had certainly heard of the man to whom Gladstone was speaking on the record. Thomas Edison. (The Gladstone–Edison interview is one of the first occasions on which history steps from the past into the present, and I cannot understand why no contemporary historian has yet had the intelligence to realise its significance.)

The record coughed and scratched to its conclusion. There was a moment's silence. Young Mr Sinatra switched his turquoise million-dollar eyes in my direction.

'Gladstone,' he said. And then . . . 'That man was a phoney.'

'Why do you say that? What do you know about him?'

'Nothing. But he was a phoney. It's all in the voice.'

To have one's convictions confirmed from such an unexpected source was gratifying. For it was indeed 'all in the voice'. Gladstone had the voice of a ham actor—pompous, unctuous, oily, totally bogus. Today he would be laughed off the stage.

I could write more about Frank Sinatra on that occasion, to show that he was by no means the simpleton whom the press were presenting to an enraptured public. He had a lively intelligence and he was no ignoramus. For example, we played him a record that Florence Nightingale had made shortly before her death. The frail voice flickered through a buzz of echoes and scratches and distortions. She was speaking of her comrades in the Crimean War and she mentioned a name that none of us could decipher. We played the record again and yet again. The name still eluded us. Then Frank Sinatra sat up and grinned.

'Got it!' he cried. 'Balaclava!'

The diversion continues, though we still have a tenuous link with the art of oratory, inspired by my memories of the Oxford Union.

'It's all in the voice,' Frank Sinatra had said. In other words it is all a question of music, the touchstone of all the arts. This is the cue for the entrance of Adolf Hitler. Hitler was the supreme example of the fact that the art of oratory was nothing to do with the intellect, and even less with the moral sense. Hitler had the brain of an evil adolescent, his arguments were beneath contempt, but he knew how to deliver incantations which held the multitudes in thrall. He had the magic, and it is indeed a magic, even if it is a very black magic. On the weekend after the Sinatra interview I went to stay with old Mrs Ronnie Greville, who used to feel *déclassée* if there were not at least two ambassadors in her weekend parties. On this occasion Jan Masaryk—the tragic envoy of Czechoslovakia, whom the Nazis murdered, though his death was recorded as suicide—was a fellow-guest. We were sitting together, reading the Sunday newspapers, when he suddenly got up and turned on the radio. Hitler's voice flooded the room, shrill, raucous, with the authentic timbre of insanity. For a moment he stood there, staring at the set in horror. Then he switched it off. His hand was shaking and the colour had drained from his cheeks.

'Five minutes of that,' he muttered, 'and I should be physically sick.'

'What was he saying?'

'Something about the Jews. But what he was saying does not matter. It was the sound, the actual voice. It is really a question of music.'

Which was another way of saying what Sinatra had said only a few days before. Masaryk was an intensely musical man, whose mother had been a pupil of Liszt.

One day, perhaps, somebody will invent a truth machine with

the power to analyse the credibility of an orator through the vibrations of the vocal chords. When that day comes a great deal of history will have to be rewritten.

I made my first speech at the Union in a debate on the reform of the divorce laws, and when I sat down I knew that before long I should be sitting in the Presidential chair.

I learned the speech by heart. Not only did I learn it by heart, but I learned it musically, making full use of the art of alliteration. I can still see it in my memory, with the consonants in capitals. For example: 'Such Conduct, on such an oCCasion, is not only beneath Contempt, it is beyond Comprehension.' If oratory is an art, and a musical art, as I believed in those days and still do, one must understand the orchestration of the words, and one must also appreciate that certain words, in any speech, have the same colour and quality as certain instruments in an orchestra. Conduct, Occasion, Contempt, Comprehension ... these are words of percussion, and they were used in a percussive context.

I learned not one speech but three speeches, all by heart, capable of being adapted to any of the volatile moods of the moment. I learned them forwards, backwards, and inside out, taking the manuscript out on long lonely walks by the towpath of the Oxford Canal. On one occasion I was so absorbed that I forgot where I was and walked over the edge of the towpath and fell into the canal. All this effort, for a single ten-minute appearance in an undergraduate debate! It may not have been a proof of genius, but it certainly showed that when the occasion demanded I had an infinite capacity for taking pains.

The choice of divorce as a subject for my début as a debater was deliberate but dangerous. (I seem to be drifting into a momentary alliterative spasm ... Divorce, Début, Debater, Deliberate, Dangerous!) I chose divorce because at that time it was very much on my mind. The increasing tensions of my home life and the mounting agonies of my mother were more and more difficult to endure, and on the previous vacation, when my father was upstairs in his bedroom, vomiting with such violence that he could be

97

heard all over the house, I had called a family conference to discuss what could be done about it. Something had to be done; the situation was desperate. But what? In spite of the cruelty of it all, cruelty was not grounds for a divorce. Nor was drunkenness. The law was only interested in adultery, which seemed to me then and seems to me today the most flimsy and senseless of all excuses for breaking up a marriage. Very well, I argued, if the law wanted evidence of adultery, why could we not provide it? I would undertake to provide it myself. I would go out into the streets of Torquay and find some woman, bribe her, and bring her back to the bedroom, and shut her up with my father and then disturb him in *flagrante delicto*. I would also undertake to go into the witness box and lie my head off in order to incriminate him. The suggestion was ludicrous, but the fact that I made it in deadly earnest shows how near we all were to breaking point. Needless to say, every effort to deal with the tragedy was defeated by my mother's stony resistance. She was tense, she was terrified, her life was an unending nightmare, but she had taken this monster for better or for worse, and no power of heaven or of earth would persuade her to break her marriage vows.

For most people—people who have come from a normal background—the marriage service is a moving and beautiful experience; even if they have no religious convictions it has something of the quality of great music. But I am not 'most people', and I cannot attend a marriage service. I cannot hear the music; I can only hear the clank of chains.

That is why I described the choice of divorce for my first speech as not only deliberate but 'dangerous'. Undergraduates do not care for earnestness in their speaking. As a rule they will only tolerate sincerity when it is expressed in the form of an epigram. A good epigram—at any rate in the Oxford of my time—was jealously guarded and reserved for special occasions. The most glittering epigrammatist of the twenties was the historian Philip Guedalla, who taught me several tricks of the trade. A typical example of his wit was provided by his description of a very unimaginative Tory politician as 'an invented Micawber waiting for something to turn down'. This was in the authentic tradition of Oscar Wilde, but Wilde's epigrams were more than mere puns; they often had a solid core of philosophical truth, even when he turned the truth upside down. 'Nothing succeeds like success' might have been spoken by Aristotle, standing on his head.

Fortunately for the reader I cannot remember my own epigrams, but I knew how to produce them, and I delivered them in the approved Oxford manner. After which, without warning, I let them have the real thing. I painted the tragedy of a drunkard's home and the cruelty of the law which enslaves his wife and his children. I did not of course name my father, but I left nobody in any doubt that it was of him that I was speaking.

This was one of the rare occasions when I allowed myself to wear my heart on my sleeve. Life had already taught me that this was a dangerous habit. Since then, I have often wondered whether it would not be safer to have no heart at all.

This diversion has so many side-tracks and culs-de-sac that our story line has been completely lost. My excuse for lingering a little longer is the importance of the subject. A great speaker, for good or for worse, can change the course of history. The late G. K. Chesterton, commenting on the growing power of broadcasting, noted the irony of the fact that scientists had contrived a device whereby one man could address the entire world at the precise moment in time when nobody had anything to say. This was a typical Chestertonian paradox, and like most of his paradoxes it was not true. There has never been a time when nobody has had anything to say. But there have been all too many times when nobody knew how to say it.

This applies with particular force to British history. The worst speaker of recent times, and I suspect of several centuries, was a man whom I greatly admire—Sir Anthony Eden. If he had been even reasonably articulate, the whole lamentable concatenation of events which led to the disaster of Suez need never have occurred. But he was not articulate. After hearing one of his speeches Winston Churchill, who was a loyal friend and colleague, observed,

'Dear Anthony delivered himself of every commonplace in the English language, with one exception.' When asked to name the exception Winston replied, 'You will find it written up in all places of public convenience. It is, "Kindly adjust your dress before leaving."' These are hardly the words to inspire a great nation in times of mortal danger.

The mention of Winston reminds me of one of the rare occasions when I met him, shortly after the war, and when he did me the honour of paying me a compliment. An American newspaper was compiling a syndicate in which various European authors were asked to give their opinions of Churchill's greatest service to the Allied cause. We were offered a dollar a word, which is not to be sneezed at, even though we were limited to five hundred words. I gave my own opinion in a sentence of only five words, but they put it top of the list and paid five hundred dollars for it. The five words were . . .

'He mobilised the English language.'

The phrase had come to Winston's attention; he had remembered it; and when we met he quoted it back to me, twirling a balloon glass of brandy in his powerful podgy hands. Why not? The words were true; they went to the heart of the matter. They dated from the days of Dunkirk and I scribbled them on a dark and lonely night in a deserted cottage near the south coast. On the previous day I had been touring the coast in a jeep, which was a depressing experience. Against the armed might of Germany we seemed to have nothing but a few strands of chicken wire, hastily erected on the cliffs, and a clutter of ancient contrivances masquerading as 'anti-aircraft artillery' manned by a rabble of youths who had no idea how to use them. I motored back to the cottage through narrow lanes from which all the signposts had been removed, driving very slowly because the use of headlights was forbidden. I went in, drew the black-out curtains and lit a couple of candles— the only form of lighting available after the destruction of the local power station. Then I turned on the radio. Through the room echoed Winston's voice, in one of the classic speeches of the war. (I cannot be sure but I think it was the one about 'fighting on the beaches'.) It was not a beautiful voice, and certainly not a golden voice, it was a voice of brass. But trumpets are fashioned from brass and his words had the flourish of trumpets, calling the whole free world to battle.

Oratorical Curiosa. The most effective speech I ever heard— effective in the sense that it electrified the audience—was written by myself. (If one does not sometimes blow one's own trumpet nobody else is likely to do so.) I would not make this boast if it could not be verified, or at least, put to the test. The speech can be heard to this day on the gramophone record which was made 'live' at Covent Garden during Melba's farewell performance. This was probably the most moving operatic occasion within living memory, though the word 'living' is perhaps inappropriate, since most of the people who heard it must now be dead.

The speech was an example of what can be done with a single word, if it is properly spoken, in the right context. On the day before the performance I went round to see Melba in the beautiful house in Mansfield Street which was her last London home. She was in a terrible state, pacing up and down the Aubusson carpet in the music room. 'This speech is driving me mad,' she cried. 'Look at all the people I have to thank!' She thrust a sheaf of papers at me. It was scribbled all over with 'majesties' and 'royal highness' and 'excellencies' and heaven knows what. Then more notes about thanking the conductor and the orchestra and the stage hands. On and on. Then a single name . . . Austin.

'Who is Austin?'

'The stage-door keeper. He's been there for forty years. And he's always seen me into my carriage.'

(The nostalgia of that word 'carriage'!)

Whereupon, greatly daring, I scrumpled the notes and threw them into the fire-place. 'You can forget all that,' I said. 'You can curtsey to the royals, and say something nice about the orchestra, but after that, you only mention Austin. In precisely the words you've just spoken.'

There was a scene, of course. She twisted her pearl necklace—always a bad sign—and snorted (even her snorts had an angelic timbre)—and told me that I was impossible, and that I need not stay to luncheon. But when I left I was smiling. I knew that I had won.

You can hear it all now, after forty years. I have never much cared for gramophones, largely because I never seem to be able to work them properly. But I know how to play this record and when I do the whole occasion comes to life, including the garden scene from *Faust*, the fourth act of *Otello*, and the whole of the final *addio* sequence from *La Bohème*, nearly three hours of magical singing, of a beauty that has vanished from this world. I can see the curtain falling, rising again on a stage that had been transformed into an immense bouquet of flowers ... Melba stepping forward, curtseying to the royals, a little unsteadily, for she was physically exhausted, thanking the orchestra, thanking the stage-hands, pausing. Then she said what I had told her to say ... and thank God she remembered it. She said:

'And finally I should like to thank my dear old friend ... Austin ... who has been at the stage door for forty years ... who has always, always seen me into my carriage ... and has always ...'

And that was as far as the audience would let her go. There was a roar of applause that seemed to shake the old opera house to its foundations. There was nothing more to be said, it was the farewell to end all farewells. I sometimes wonder what happened to old Austin, and if she left him anything in her will.

I will end this all too lengthy diversion with a few notes which may be of service to the future historian. (On reflection I suspect that the reason why the importance of oratory as an historical force has not been recognised is because it has to be seen and heard. The history of the future will not be written in the library, it will be written from the radio and television screen.)

As a general rule the worst speakers are the intellectuals. If they are not actually struck dumb they are inaudible. In America people used to walk out of H. G. Wells's lectures; even when he was hugging the microphone he could not make his squeaky little voice carry to the back of the hall. Osbert Sitwell, whom I loved and admired for many years, was so bad that I once had a row with him by imploring him not to give a public performance of *Façade* in New York. Neither he nor his sister Edith had the faintest idea how to use their voices; they were both completely devoid of a theatrical sense; and though *Façade* was an amusing trifle, which was well enough for a matinée in Mayfair where the Sitwells were social and literary celebrities, it was lunacy to present it in New York where, at that time, they were neither. And so it proved to be; indeed it was even worse than I had feared. Something went wrong with the microphone, Edith had to recite her little jingles from the background and when Osbert tried to walk on he got mixed up with the curtain behind the stage and plunged about like a captive elephant.

Actors, if possible, are even worse than intellectuals. Noël Coward realised this and usually refused to speak at all. It is a pity that his friends never learned to follow his example. At Noël's memorial service Lord Olivier, whose abundant genius certainly needs no recommendation from myself, was chosen to make the principal address. What could be more fitting? A great actor paying tribute to a great man of the theatre, who was also a devoted friend. The result was very embarrassing. Larry—evidently speaking from a full heart—regaled us with a terrible little story about a French baker and then proceeded to recite one of the few really bad lyrics that Noël ever wrote, something on the lines of 'Do let's be kind to Auntie Mabel.' All this from the pulpit, with deep sincerity, to a congregation near to tears. It confirmed me in my belief that it needs a supreme genius to make a supreme gaffe.

The title of this chapter is 'Dreaming Spires', which was used by Compton Mackenzie to describe the Oxford interludes in his *Sinister Street*, with which my own *Prelude* had been compared.

Compton Mackenzie's Oxford was very different from mine, but then we were different kinds of people. Compared with him I was an intellectual lightweight, my scholarship was scrappy, and my enthusiasms were often transient and ephemeral. All the same, I cannot have been a total nitwit if only because of the number and the quality of the distinguished men, during this period, who gave me their friendship, such as John Masefield. In those days Masefield still had some of the aura of his swashbuckling youth. Incredible as it may seem *The Everlasting Mercy*, which first brought him into the public eye, was regarded as faintly improper; very few people guessed that the day would come when he would be clad in the respectable mantle of Poet Laureate. I met him by the simple procedure of writing to ask him if he would contribute a few sentences to the first number of *The Oxford Outlook*. I never expected him to reply. Why should he bother with an unknown undergraduate pestering him to contribute to an unknown magazine? But he replied by return of post, and he sent me not merely 'a few sentences' but two of the finest sonnets he ever wrote ... 'On Growing Old'. They have since been published in many anthologies.

> Be with me Beauty, for the fire is dying
> My dog and I are old, too old for roving
> Man, whose young passion sets the spindrift flying
> Is soon too lame to march, too cold for loving.

After this I saw a good deal of John Masefield, who used to ask me up to his little red house on Boar's Hill. Although he had been tamed by his devoted but extremely conventional wife, who had smoothed away the rough edges, I had the feeling that he was still a rover at heart, and that he missed the sea, which he had known in every mood of its beauty and terror. He found relief through his hands, making models of ships, exquisitely carved and contrived in all their intricate detail. Once, when he was showing me his latest creation, a model of an old sailing vessel of the eighteenth century, he stared at it for so long that I told him he looked as though he wanted to sail away in her. 'Sometimes,' he said, 'I do.'

Another Boar's Hill personality was the reigning Poet Laureate, Robert Bridges, who was also kind to me. He was rather an alarming man, majestic, leonine, with a snowy beard and silvery locks, flowing with just that touch of abandon which made one wonder whether, perhaps, Nature had not been improved upon. The two poets did not care much for one another, though I doubt the authenticity of a story which has often been quoted about them. When Bridges was asked what he thought of Masefield's poetry he is alleged to have replied: 'Masefield's sonnets? Very nice. Pure Shakespeare. Masefield's *Reynard the Fox*? Very nice too. Pure Chaucer. Masefield's *The Everlasting Mercy*? Mm. Yes, pure Masefield.'

Then there was W. B. Yeats, whom I came to know rather better than some of the critics who have been cashing in on their memoirs of him for the past forty years. This was an accidental relationship. When I left my college rooms I went to a charming old house looking out onto one of the most elegant backcloths in Oxford, the Sheldonian Library. Suddenly Yeats arrived as a lodger, complete with wife and baby. He became part of our communal life, and we often took meals together. I came to know him *en pantoufles*; bits of him I liked, other bits I did not. He was discourteous to his wife and when he noticed the baby, which was seldom, he looked at it as though it were a bundle which somebody had left on the doorstep. All the same, he had reserves of charm, which were always available when he was flattered.

One day I set 'Had the Heavens embroidered cloths' to music and he was so pleased that he inscribed a volume of his poems to me with the extraordinary inscription 'From One Irishman to Another'. This was presumably the highest compliment that he could pay to any Englishman, but I had done nothing to deserve it. I have many Irish friends, and have delighted in their company. (The best conversation in the world, conversation which brings the same delight as musical improvisation, has always been in Dublin.) But in the end I have always had to face the fact that Irishmen are so busy being Irish that they have not much time to be anything else. There have been exceptions, like George Moore and Oscar

Wilde, but they are few and far between. As a general rule Irishmen have Ireland on the brain; they are intellectual imperialists who see the map of the globe in shades of green. Yeats was no exception. Even when he was discussing Wagner he somehow managed to bring in Ireland, as though he were complaining that Wagner had omitted to give Brünnhilde an aria on the theme of the Londonderry Air. I have only one 'quote' of his conversation. (Its authenticity is guaranteed by the fact that it was published, without contradiction, during his life-time.)

Why can't the English understand that the Irish people are *Irish*? Why can't they realise that they're dealing with a race of peasants who believe in fairies, and are quite right to do so? I myself have seen the saucers of milk which Irish peasants have put outside their doors for the pixies to drink. *If the English could only learn to believe in fairies, there wouldn't ever have been any Irish problem.*

These words of Yeats should be remembered. They seemed endearing nonsense at the time, but rather less endearing nonsense today. Very few fairies of my acquaintance have devoted so much of their energy to the invention of lethal devices for blowing up old ladies in tube stations and contriving the random destruction of maternity hospitals. 'Had I the Heavens embroidered cloths'! It was a magical phrase and I set it in the manner of Debussy. Today I should change the words and set them for the percussion section of the orchestra.

From the aggressively Irish to the aggressively English—G. K. Chesterton. (What a busy little boy I seem to have been!) He came to speak at the Union but what he said in the debate was less interesting than what he said to me afterwards in private. I wrote it down and got him to check it so it can be quoted verbatim.

Somebody said in the debate that I am the slave of symbols, that I believed in magic, that in a ceremony or an institution or a faith I merely examined what was on the surface and took it all quite literally, like a peasant in the Middle Ages.

But it isn't I who am the slave of symbols. It is you, and your friends who believe in the superstition of divorce. I venerate the idea which lies behind the symbol. You only venerate the empty shell. Take the case of monarchy. Somebody remarked tonight that we had taken away half the duties and prerogatives of the king and that the monarchy still remained. They went on to say that we could take away half the duties and prerogatives of marriage and that marriage would still remain. Perhaps it will, but what will be the use of it?

Because I bow down to the sceptre and because I take the words 'honour and obey' quite literally, you say that I am the slave of the symbol. But I bow down to the sceptre because I believe in the power that lies behind it. I keep to the smallest details of the marriage service because I believe in marriage. If you believe neither in the sceptre nor in the service, and yet bow down to them, then you are the slave of the symbol. A time will come—very soon—when you will find that you want this ideal of marriage. You will want it as something hard and solid to cling to in a fast dissolving society. You will want it even more than you seem to want divorce today.

Although the years have diminished G.K.C.'s stature as an intellectual force, there were times when he could hit a nail on the head. But then he was not married to an alcoholic.

CHAPTER VIII

⊛⊛⊛⊛⊛⊛

THE OLDEST
PROFESSION IN THE WORLD

I left Oxford at the end of 1920 and returned to Cleave Court, Torquay, because I had nowhere else to go. The contrast was bitter. After eighteen months of hectic activity, of gaiety and laughter and youthful triumphs, I was again a prisoner in this cold, shabby, shambles of a house, in which there was no laughter and certainly no music, only the sound of my father's footsteps shuffling down the rambling corridors, or, in the more dramatic moments, crashing down the staircase.

I was broke—worse than broke, for I had a sheaf of unpaid bills from tailors, florists and wine-merchants, poignantly reminding me of my pathetic efforts to join the ranks of the *jeunesse dorée*. The royalties from *Prelude* were quite inadequate to meet these obligations, and though the book was still selling, my scanty earnings were swallowed up by my father's incessant consumption of whisky. And I had to help out with the housekeeping.

Nowhere else to go? This is not quite true. I could have gone to Paris, or Cannes, or New York, with all expenses paid, and the odd gold cigarette case as a bonus, because I was still good to look at. That was the trouble. These glamorous invitations had strings attached; if I accepted them I should be expected to pop into bed with people and I had an unfortunate and unprofitable aversion to popping into bed with anybody, male or female, by whom I was not physically attracted. If I had my time over again I hope that I should have conquered this aversion. A great deal of nonsense has been talked and written about prostitution, which, by and large, has been a beneficent influence in the history of the world.

The theme of the Balliol essay which had won me a sort of scholarship was . . .

'Compromise is the grave of the soul.'

'Only the highest ends are gained by compromise.'

We were asked to comment on these two opinions and I passionately upheld the thesis that compromise *was* the grave of the soul. Today this seems high-faluting nonsense. Without intelligent compromise no progress of any sort is possible, whether personal, political, social, or economic. Even Christ recognised the need for compromise when he enjoined us to render unto Caesar the things that are Caesar's. It is open to question whether He would have given the same advice if He had lived in the days of the Welfare State.

What is true about compromise is even truer about prostitution, and I only wish that in those days there had been somebody, some older and wiser man or woman, who could have discussed the matter with me and put the whole problem in its proper perspective —somebody who would have pointed out to me that what one did with one's body was of the smallest importance provided that one preserved the integrity of one's mind and spirit. On the whole I managed to do so, but life would have been much easier if I had done more popping into bed. After all one could have shut one's eyes and played Bach fugues in one's head until the physical exercises were over. There was one occasion when I had the whole thing lined up—a flat in Mayfair, a settlement of a thousand a year and most important of all, a Steinway piano. When it came to the crunch I decided to turn the proposition down, and this was a decision which I have never ceased to regret. It was in no way to be commended; it was due to a misguided code of morals and a morbid physical fastidiousness. If I had accepted these immoral earnings they would not, in fact, have been immoral at all, for they would have enabled me to devote my life to music, which was wha Nature had created me for. God evidently had other plans.

Speaking of prostitutes, with whom I seem to have a natural affinity, the most lovable member of the profession who ever came into my life was called Babette Gamble. The name was so ludicrously appropriate that I once accused her of inventing it. Not at all. Her father, a merchant seaman, was called George Henry Gamble, and when she was christened, in somewhat alcoholic circumstances, he had chosen 'Babette' on the spur of the moment. I found Babette very alluring and sometimes, when I was in Paris, I stayed with her at Claridge's Hotel in the Champs-Élysées, where she had a suite which was paid for by a Chilean millionaire. Claridge's in Paris has not the *cachet* of Claridge's in London, but it was good enough for me. And I, apparently, was good enough for Babette. When we went out to dine at Maxim's together she always stuffed a wad of francs in my pocket and refused to let me give her any change. Babette was in the grand tradition of ladies of pleasure; in an earlier generation she could have competed with La Belle Otero. Her extravagances were fantastic; she had, for example, 365 pairs of shoes. A whole wall of her suite had been transformed into a cupboard for these shoes and when one opened the sliding doors one was confronted with a glittering of myriad sparkles, for many of the shoes were studded with precious stones. Inevitably she came to a sticky end; on her fortieth birthday she threw herself off the roof of an hotel—not Claridge's, because she could no longer afford it. When they lifted her into the ambulance the wind lifted the sheet from her mangled body and there was a momentary sparkle of diamonds. She kept her shoes even when she stepped into the arms of death.

Meanwhile, banished to the shabby grandeur of Cleave Court, Torquay, I was busily prostituting myself in a more respectable fashion, by writing another novel.

I had no urge to write a novel, but what else was there to do? How was I to get a job, any sort of job that would keep body and soul together? To the younger reader this question may seem rather odd. Any young graduate in these days who leaves a university with a respectable record can be reasonably certain of finding employment; and even if he does not find employment he can count on some sort of assistance from the state. I had not a 'respectable' record; I had a brilliant record. Moreover, I had quite a number of rich and influential friends. But nobody, literally nobody, came forward with any practical ideas. I put advertisements in *The Times*. I went up to London, and trudged round the agencies. The only place where I nearly succeeded was in a shady advertising concern, but the things they wanted me to do—visiting ladies of title to persuade them to endorse cosmetics—were so degrading that even I could not bring myself to do them. Here we are confronted by another character deficiency. I have never known how to ask for favours, never acquired the technique of borrowing money, or seeking invitations, or applying for free seats at the theatre. This is not to be interpreted as a sign of virtue; it is sheer stupidity and I have always had more than my fair share of it.

So I sat down and wrote a novel with Oxford as a background. I had no idea how it was going to shape, so before writing the words 'Chapter I'—which are the only words any novelist can write with conviction—I went to the little arty-craft shop on the King's Parade, bought a box of paints, sat down and designed the cover. It never occurred to me that the cover would not be accepted, as it was, that the novel would not be accepted, as it was, that it would not be brilliantly reviewed, as it was—and that it would not be finished in precisely four months, which was the time I had set myself. This is an example of what is known as professional authorship, and I loathed every moment of it.

Patchwork has long been out of print and the quality of life it celebrated has vanished beyond recall. But it might still offer fruitful material for the student of morbid psychology. Seldom can a young soul have been stripped so bare, revealed in such detailed nudity. Although there is not a sentence that could bring a blush to the cheek of the most fastidious, there are hidden depths of horror and passages which—to a mind instructed by Freud and Krafft-Ebing—are casebooks of perversity.

The most shocking feature of this ostensibly innocuous work comes towards the end when I killed my mother. What would Freud have made of *that*? In the book, under the name of 'Lady Sheldon', I gave her everything that I would have loved to give her, if I had been able. I made her beautiful. She was not beautiful. Life with my father had destroyed the beauty of the face which had once enchanted him. I made her rich. She was not rich, she was on the poverty line. I made her elegant. She had no elegance. I sent her travelling round the world, I suggested that she had known the sparkle of Paris and the allurements of the Riviera.

But she had known none of these delights, and so in the last chapter I killed her. It was a mercy killing, and though it only happened on paper—sheaves of paper scribbled over and over in my shabby bedroom—it was very real to me. I *wanted* her to die, in comfort, with grace, with the scent of flowers about her. Life set the stage very differently. God still had twenty years' torture up His sleeve.

Patchwork earned me an advance of a hundred pounds and I decided to use this to finance an onslaught on London society. This was yet another example of character deficiency. If I had been a tough young genius I should have tried to grow a beard and got on a ship and sailed for the open seas; if I had been a musician of integrity I should have retired to an attic in Paris and studied composition. But I had been corrupted. The American adventure and the Oxford successes had given me a false sense of values and I cherished the illusion that I had the sort of charm that could open every door.

To some extent this must have been true, because on arriving in London my first address was St James's Palace. Even the opportunity to cross the threshold of this ancient edifice is not given to the average citizen. I not only crossed it but resided in it for a week. At a dinner party in Oxford I had casually met a nice old man called Sir Sidney Greville who was comptroller to the Prince of Wales and an intimate friend of Queen Mary. It would have been foolish not to have made oneself agreeable to such a person and at the end of the evening he asked me to stay at the Palace when I next came to London. There was nothing suspect about the invitation; from first to last he was the quintessence of avuncularity. I seemed to be able to make him laugh and accepted the role of Court Jester. It might lead to something; and at least, I reflected, it would be 'experience'.

Experience it certainly was. The grey gloomy fortress of a building at the end of St James's Street, the sentries strutting up and down in their scarlet tunics, and me, arriving in an exceptionally decrepit taxi, wishing that I had bought a new suitcase and wondering how much to tip the driver. Then sweeping into the courtyard, pressing the bell of the private apartments. The door flung open by Sir Sidney's manservant, a gigantic ex-Life Guardsman whom I immediately recognised as an enemy. His function was to protect his master from 'hangers-on', and he had obviously concluded that I had arrived with the intention of hanging on to everything in sight. And dear old Sidney advancing with his arms held out in welcome and an expression on his face that demanded, almost plaintively, that I should make him laugh.

This was difficult because of the fretful, nagging, pervasive presence of the Prince of Wales. Although he never appeared in person—I have no idea whether he was even in England at the time—the telephone was constantly busy with his problems, most of which seemed to be of a singularly petty nature. Could H.R.H. wear a dinner-jacket or must he appear in tails? Was it necessary for him to have a hat if he was travelling in an open car? The most awkward questions seemed to be concerned with the seating of the guests at his own parties—the mystic rites which the French call *placement*. H.R.H. seemed quite unable to grasp the importance of *placement*. He would compose lists in which nonentities were seated on his right, in the place of honour, while ambassadors were relegated to the bottom of the table, below the salt. There were plenty of other people who could have advised him about these matters—which in any case he should have been able to settle for himself—but for some reason or other they always seemed to end up on Sir Sidney's lap. 'One day,' he sighed, 'there will be a diplomatic incident and I shall get the blame.'

As the days went by I grew more and more bored. Staying in a palace, I decided, was overrated. I wrote a great many letters on royal writing-paper, with the intention of sending them to friends who would be impressed, but I never posted them. I toyed with the idea of swaggering through the gloomy archway, up St James's

Street and into Jermyn Street, which boasted the grandest men's shops in the world. Silk pyjamas I would buy, and shirts made-to-measure, and monogrammed dressing-gowns and suede shoes, and hankerchiefs of the finest linen. If one were to give one's address as care of the Honourable Sir Sidney Greville, St James's Palace, all these extravagances would be dispatched without question, and there would be no hurry to pay the bill. But though I pressed my nose against the windows of these elegant establishments, which all bore the words 'By Royal Appointment' over the doorways, I never went inside. Once again, character deficiency. All the decent instincts of a prostitute, but never the courage to see it through. I knew all too well that when the accounts were rendered I should pay them myself.

The palatial interlude was made all the more difficult because Queen Mary had a habit of dropping in at unexpected hours, and whenever she appeared I had to be spirited away, hidden in the background until she had gone. Why? I asked Sidney this question, in some indignation, after one of her visits. Why could I not meet Queen Mary? He looked at me with obvious embarrassment and then said, 'You might be rather difficult to explain.' This bewildered me. Why should I be difficult to 'explain'? I spoke the King's English; I had on my best double-breasted suit; I was a rising young author though I had not as yet risen very far. What was there to 'explain'?

I repeated the question. I shall never forget the answer.

He came over to me and put his arms on my shoulders. He smiled. He was the essence of avuncularity.

'My dear Beverley,' he said, 'don't you ever look in the glass?'

I left the Palace on the following day in a state of some disgruntlement and headed for 107B Pimlico Road, the residence of my brother Paul, who was then an impoverished curate in St Peter's, Eaton Square. 'From the Palace to Pimlico Road' sounds like a phrase from a Betjeman poem, and it sums up very accurately the social and spiritual seesaws on which I was balancing. I was always being thrown from one extremity to another, from rags to riches, from the glitter of the spotlights to the depths of obscurity. 107B was a hateful little slum over a repairing garage that clanked all day and night to the sound of hammers. When I arrived Paul handed me a letter which had been forwarded from Cleave Court. I opened it and read:

The Duchess of Marlborough
At Home

The address was Carlton House Terrace. Then there was the word 'Dancing'. And in the left hand corner the word 'Decorations'. It was a word that rather intimidated me because it indicated that royalty was to be present. I could not imagine why I had been asked. Then I remembered that the Duchess was the mother of Lord Ivor Churchill with whom I had enjoyed riotous evenings at Oxford, so I decided to go along.

I am about to describe an episode of total triviality, but sometimes the trivia of life leave scars that time cannot eradicate. This is one of them. There is no need to expand it into a three-act tragedy so we will use a staccato technique. Arrival at Carlton House Terrace in a taxi so shabby that it looks as though it has just emerged from a knacker's yard. Alight from taxi. Specks of rain. Place right hand over white tie. Walk up steps and ring bell. Long pause. Ring bell again. Have I got the wrong date? Door swings open revealing major-domo, who registers surprise. Alarming vista through doorway. Footmen in the scarlet Marlborough livery scurrying through the hall to take up their positions.

The doors of the drawing-room are flung open, revealing all the Marlborough grandeur. The sort of furniture that a Hollywood producer would hire for a super-de-luxe production. And in the room, only women. I had arrived so early that dinner was still in progress. The men were finishing their port in the dining-room. They had not 'joined the ladies'.

The voice of the major-domo. 'Mr Beverley Nichols.'

A flurried duchess advancing to greet me. Various other women getting up. They were so festooned with jewels and ribbons that they looked like Christmas trees in a high wind. Lunatic figments of dialogue. Nobody knew who I was though I muttered something about 'Ivor', which gave the duchess a vague clue. (Ivor, as it happened, was ill.) Then the men began to trickle in. Beribboned, clanking with medals. Stopping short when they saw me. Who was this person? Had he climbed in through the window?

I was on the rack for about an hour. At ten o'clock the first guests began to trickle in, the guests who knew the social ropes, who were aware that one did not arrive on time for a duchess's dance. Then there were sounds of music and the footmen began to serve champagne. I found myself standing next to a very beautiful young woman who did not seem to expect me to explain myself. She smiled at me and we danced together. She was perhaps the most beautiful person I have ever seen or ever shall see. Lady Diana Manners.

But even the magic of Diana was not enough to lift me out of my misery and when the music stopped I escaped. I was the first to leave just as I had been the first to arrive. I walked all the way home, in the rain, back to 107B Pimlico Road. Paul, fortunately, was already asleep, and there was no need to invent an account of social triumphs. That could wait till breakfast.

Why has this ridiculous episode left so indelible an impression on me—an impression that is stamped more deeply than any of the wounds of peace or war that lay ahead? Why does it still chill my spine? Why does the fear persist? God knows, and perhaps one should apply to God for an explanation. But one really cannot go running to God every time one's brain is bruised. Or can one?

Every autobiography, as we have already suggested, must be to a large extent a spiritual autobiography. If we accept this premise I am not emerging with much credit from this self-revelation. Hundreds of words about a social solecism at a duchess's dance and an open admission that this ludicrous incident has left a lasting scar on my soul! What sort of soul can it be that bruises so easily? That is what I am trying to find out.

Obviously, from the facts so far recorded, I emerge as an appalling snob. I shall cling to that word 'snob'. It is an important word. One cannot form a character analysis without a serious assessment of the extent to which snobbery has influenced a man's conduct. It may also help me to give some shape to this random narrative.

I am writing of a period in which snobbery, in its most primitive sense, was more blatantly exhibited and exploited than at any other time in British history. Here, once again, I must confess to a certain moral unorthodoxy. Just as I believe that prostitution, by and large, has been a beneficent influence in the story of mankind, so I believe that snobbery, in one form or another, has been a beneficent influence in the story of civilisation. In the pre-war years the thinking of the British public was greatly influenced by the pronouncement of a popular philosopher called Professor C. E. M. Joad. He constantly hit the headlines with outrageous statements on the radio. I rather liked Joad, though he was admittedly ridiculous. He used to play Bach every morning on an odd sort of pianola contrivance not because he was particularly enamoured of the fugues but because the exercise of pedalling was good for his constipation. But though his body was sluggish his brain was alert. He subjected every problem to a simple test. Again and again he would say, 'It depends on what you *mean* by . . .' whatever it might be. His technique was sharply illustrated during a discussion with a rather tiresome young poet who quoted Keat's well-worn couplet:

> Beauty is truth, truth beauty—that is all
> Ye know on earth, and all ye need to know.

Admittedly this is one of the most idiotic assertions that can ever have fallen from the lips of a genius but it needed a man like Joad to expose its idiocy. He turned on the young ass and tore him to pieces. 'What do you mean by "truth"? What do you *mean* by "beauty"?' A debate on this theme might form the basis for a stimulating parlour game.

What do I mean by 'snobbery'? I will give some examples which may throw light on the social background of the period.

The power of snobbery as a social phenomenon and as an

economic impulse can best be studied through the immense appara-
tus of advertising. Concentrate, for a moment, on the eternal force
of feminine beauty. It may not be literally true that the face of Helen
of Troy launched a thousand ships, but it is an historical fact that
the faces of American women, in the present century, have set in
motion commercial enterprises of a magnitude that rivals the
armament industry. (At some point in this scatter-brained volume I
really must write my reminiscences of Helena Rubenstein who was
a glorious old warrior in the Battle of Beauty. I established a certain
rapport with her in New York because I discovered one of her most
cherished secrets, and she was afraid that I might disclose it. It was
a combination of creams and lotions which I will call 'X' and I
happened to become aware of the ingenious manner in which she
had learned about it. The process had been perfected by a remarkable genius called Doctor Oreste, whose headquarters were in
Sloane Street. The theme song of Doctor Oreste was '*il faut souffrir
pour être belle*' and he invented a cream which induced so fierce a
sensation of scorching that it could only be used in front of an
electric fan. As it happened, in spite of the agony, the cream was
quite harmless and was lavishly employed by Lady Cunard, which
may explain why she was often so late for her own luncheons in
Grosvenor Square. End of diversion.)

The power of snobbery in those days was most strikingly
illustrated by the face of the Countess of Oxford and Asquith. It
was not a pretty face and Margot Oxford, as far as I knew her, was
not a very pretty personality. In spite of her reputation for intelligence she had the brain of an agitated gnat, always darting about,
stinging people. When one lunched with her at The Wharf the
cocktails were lukewarm and she was rude to the servants. But
Lady Oxford, because of her social position, was suddenly presented to the British public as an established beauty. Why? Because
'*she used Pond's Cold Cream*'. She had a silhouette like Punch and
even when she was photographed by Cecil Beaton the result was
rather scarifying. The best account of her face was provided by
herself when, in an unguarded moment, she admitted that she had
not got a face at all but only 'two profiles stuck together'. She made

this remark to myself, at a luncheon party in Bedford Square, and I was foolish enough to agree with her, because I thought that the remark was witty and endearing. This led to a coolness between us. One should never agree with women when they tell the truth about themselves.

The most stupendous snob I ever knew was the late Sir Henry Channon, M.P., who was one of the most prominent figures in London Society for over forty years. And not only in London but throughout Europe, for wherever minor royalties were apt to congregate, with their accompanying retinues of the international aristocracy, Chips was to be seen fluttering in the background.

The rise of 'Chips' Channon is a classic example of what can be achieved by a young man fanatically obsessed by a single ambition and prepared to devote his entire life to achieving it. Chips was determined to climb high up the social ladder, and though at first the odds seemed heavily weighted against him he climbed to the topmost rungs and stayed there. I first met him at a ball in Lansdown House, where he cunningly annexed my partner, not because she was one of the prettiest girls in the room but because she was the daughter of an earl. However, there were no hard feelings and since his rooms were close to mine we walked home together in the small hours of the morning. I asked him in for a final drink. When he looked round my very modest apartment he said:

'I should have thought that with your looks you could have done better than this.'

'Perhaps I could, but as you observe, I haven't. What are you proposing to do with yours?' (His features were quite agreeable but by no stretch of the imagination could he have been described as handsome.)

Then he told me in all seriousness, lying back in my shabby armchair, and ticking off his future conquests with his fingers as though he were compiling a catalogue. (A) He was going to find a girl with a great deal of money and marry her. (B) She would be a member of the British aristocracy. (C) He was going to have a large estate in the country. (D) He would also have a house in Belgrave Square, or Eaton Square; that would be good enough; but Belgrave

Square was better. (E) He was going into politics. He would find a safe Tory constituency, to which he would be elected by a large majority. (F) After serving so many years as a member of Parliament, he would be given a knighthood. He would be Sir Henry Channon, M.P., of Belgrave Square, where he would devote the latter part of his life to entertaining the great ones of the earth.

Each and every one of these ambitions he achieved. He married the daughter of the immensely rich Earl of Iveagh. He acquired the house in the country and the mansion in the square, and through the Iveagh influence he stood for a constituency so overwhelmingly conservative that unless the Tory candidate was in the last stages of Parkinson's disease, he could not possibly fail to get in. In due course he received his knighthood.

Why? How? The secret of life is not to be found in the answer to these questions, but they have their interest for the observer of the social scene. Chips Channon came from a respectable Chicago background, but—to use a rather obvious pun—he had very few chips to play with when he arrived in England on his campaign of social conquest. How did he manage it?

I can give a very personal answer to this question. In the years that followed I saw little of Chips. Apart from a weekend at his country house and the occasional dinner in London our paths seldom crossed. But he never took me out of his address book because he suspected that the day might come when he would have a use for me. The day came. I was then living at a house called Merry Hall, working very hard and seeing few people. My only fixed engagement was with my old governess Miss Hazlitt, who used to come to lunch on the first Monday of every month. We would have something simple to eat and go for a drive in the country and pick wild flowers and come back for tea, when she would open her heart and tell me, at great length, how wonderful God was being to her and how she was overflowing with gratitude to Him. As it happened, God, in my opinion, was being rather beastly to her. He had given her acute arthritis and swollen ankles and established her in a gloomy home for retired governesses on a very inadequate income. However, one thing God had done, with my co-operation. He had arranged these little Monday outings, which were the only bright interludes in her lonely life. They meant everything to her, and they meant a great deal to me. Who am I to argue with God, who had ordained them?

Then, one Sunday, towards midnight, Chips rang up.

'Beverley . . . at last! I've been trying to get you all day. I want you to come to lunch tomorrow.'

'I'm terribly sorry, but I have to lunch with my governess.'

'Wait a minute. Queen Helen of Rumania is coming. She specially wants to see you.'

'I'm terribly sorry, but my governess is coming.'

'QUEEN HELEN OF RUMANIA.'

'I heard you the first time. And please give her my love. But I can't come to lunch.' Crackle, crackle. 'I must lunch with my governess.'

'This line is terrible. You keep on saying something that sounds like governess.' Crackle, crackle.

'I did say governess. And I'm . . .' crackle crackle '. . . lunching with her.'

My 'anti-dialogue-invention' rule has certainly broken down here, but this lunatic conversation really did take place. Chips was very disgruntled when I rang off.

Perhaps in this fleeting recollection I have discovered my own definition of snobbery. I am unquestionably a snob about governesses. Particularly when they are living in lonely rooms, in desolate homes for old ladies, with arthritis and swollen ankles, and nothing to look forward to except a modest luncheon once a month, and a bunch of faded buttercups at the end of it all.

CHAPTER IX

❀❀❀❀❀❀

THE GLORY
THAT WAS GREECE

The lunatic conversation with the late Sir Henry Channon, M.P., in which I declined his invitation to lunch with Queen Helen of Rumania, jogs us back to reality and offers a chance to impose some pattern on the story.

Helen of Rumania takes us back to the twenties. She was one of the characters in what I will call The Greek Adventure, which was the next landmark in the story of my life. Of all the episodes which we have been recalling it was the most unexpected and the most bizarre.

The story begins, not in Athens but in a shabby lodging house in a back street of Portsmouth. This shift of scenery demands an explanation. Once a year Cleave Court had to be let furnished, for a period of about ten weeks, in order to supplement my father's rapidly diminishing income. These 'lettings' were a period of agony for my mother, not only because she hated leaving her home and her garden but also because all the work devolved upon herself. One might write a black comedy about it. The bargaining with the prospective tenants. Could we ask for fifteen pounds a week, or would that frighten them off? Would they be willing to take on the maids? (We still had three servants!) Most important of all, would my mother be able to disguise the fact that the whole place was falling to bits? The urgency of this question can be illustrated by the figure of my mother in the drawing-room, dragging a basket of logs across the carpet in order to conceal a burned patch which was a memento of one of the occasions when my father had fallen into the fireplace.

So we found ourselves in Portsmouth for ten weeks. Ten weeks is a long time when one is young and frustrated, with no job and no prospect of getting one. What was I to do about it? The only thing seemed to be to write another novel. So I went to the little stationer's behind the pub opposite my bedroom window, bought a packet of paper, carried it back to my rickety desk, sat down and wrote the word 'Self'. This, I decided, would be the title. In the circumstances it was an odd word to choose because I had also decided that the novel must be in no way autobiographical. There had been quite enough autobiography in *Prelude* and *Patchwork*. This new work must be all out of my own head. I had not the faintest idea what it would be about, nor what sort of people would be in it, nor what they would do nor why. But the word 'Self' could be made to apply to practically anything.

I have been making so many claims to brains and brightness that it is a relief to be able to confess that *Self* was one of the worst novels that can ever have been written, let alone published. It was a blatant crib of *Vanity Fair*, which probably owed its inspiration to my partiality for prostitutes. The characters were wooden, the story was hackneyed, the dialogue was trite, and it contained not a grain of humour. The whole thing was so ghastly and I hated it so much that I finished it, not in ten weeks, but in five, lugged it back to the stationer's shop, who had it typed, and posted it to my publishers, Messrs Chatto & Windus. I could not even bear to correct the typescript.

Now comes a mystery. Chatto & Windus were, and are, a very distinguished firm, with a star-studded list of novelists, headed, in those days, by the young Aldous Huxley. They immediately accepted my load of trash and gave it the same treatment as they gave to Aldous. A greater mystery follows. The first edition sold out and they wrote to tell me that they would like to reprint. Here, for one of the very few occasions in my life, I showed a glimmer of artistic integrity. I informed Messrs Chatto & Windus that if they insisted on reprinting *Self* they must also let me write a foreword stating that in my opinion it was muck, that I was ashamed of it, and that anybody who bought it would be justified in asking for his money back. To my surprise they agreed to this condition; the new edition appeared with this foreword, and eventually *Self* sank into oblivion. A second-hand copy today might be worth quite a lot of money.

Three weeks after finishing *Self*, in a back street of Portsmouth, I was clicking my heels in a gilded salon in the royal palace at Athens, bending over the hand of Queen Sophie of Greece.

I have asked the printer to leave a space of two lines in order to stress, topographically, the contrast between these two periods of my life. Once again we have a variation on the rags-to-riches theme. If all the world's a stage I seemed destined to sit either in the royal box or at the back of the gallery.

The Greek adventure was more than usually inexplicable because I never discovered, from start to finish, why I was chosen to go to Greece at all. This time it certainly had nothing to do with the curly hair; there was no suggestion of anything homosexual or hetero-sexual or even vaguely romantic; it was a simple business proposi-tion. But why *me*? The assignment called for a tough, hard-bitten war correspondent, at least twice my age, experienced in intrigue and handy with a gun. There were all the ingredients for a James Bond thriller.

Here, stripped of its inessentials, was the scenario. Greece was on the verge of yet another revolution. The country was in the direst distress, ruled by a monarch—King Constantine—who was not recognised by the Allies, who had already been exiled once and who, unless drastic measures were taken, would be exiled again. The national exchequer was almost empty, the national spirit almost broken, and the national manhood almost exhausted by the war against Turkey, which had already lasted, on and off, for seven years.

The only way in which Greece could be saved was by the recogni-tion of King Constantine by the Allies. Such an event was, at the moment, out of the question, since Constantine was regarded in France and England and America as an arch-traitor. After all, he was married to the Kaiser's sister, Queen Sophie. He must be a sort of miniature Kaiser himself, who by his double-dealing and his treachery had imperilled our cause throughout the whole of the Near East.

But that legend of Constantine, it was now alleged, was false. It had been built up, during the war, by interested agents on a fabric of falsehoods. The astounding nature of these falsehoods was contained in a collection of documents which was being carefully guarded. In those documents was material for a book which would cause a sensation throughout Europe as soon as it was published.

Would I go to Athens, under the special protection of the Greek Government, examine the documents, and write that book? Would I avert the revolution and save the tottering throne?

I would indeed. At least it would be better than churning out trash in a back street of Portsmouth.

I shall not write at length about this interlude because the whole scenario, today, would sound as dated as the plot of a Ruritanian operetta. Who wants to read about the intrigues of Balkan politics, fifty years ago? Who cares whether King Constantine was right or wrong, or whether Venizelos, who played so spectacular a role at the treaty of Versailles, was a great patriot or an unscrupulous intriguer? If it comes to that, who cares about Greece at all? Certainly not the average commentators in the contemporary press. They see Greece only as a pawn in the game of power politics—a pawn with whom the Western powers might well dispense, if the occasion should arise. In this I happen to think that they are tragically mistaken. After all, the greatest miracle in the history of the Western world was wrought in Greece; it was here that the flame of civilisation first flickered. I refuse to believe that it has died out. Wait for the next full moon, walk up to the Acropolis, and decide for yourself.

But this is the story of a small person, who must content himself with small matters, such as the hand of Queen Sophie, over which I am bending, in a rather clumsy attempt to kiss it.

I have switched to the present tense, because memory at this point revives with startling clarity. The whole situation is totally ridiculous and more than somewhat alarming. Here I am in Athens, in a suite at the Grande Bretagne hotel, standing in front of the looking-glass, surveying myself. All seems well. No physical complaints. On the contrary. Bright eyes, clear skin, slim as a straw. But what about the clothes? I have designed, for the occasioni a sort of semi-morning-coat, which has just been delivered by the valet, who has lingered so long that I have been obliged to give him a tip. The tip has come from a fat wad of 100-drachma notes presented to me, at the royal palace on the previous day, by the Lord Chamberlain, whose name was Count Mercati.

Here, I had thought, stuffing the notes into my pocket, was what I had always hankered after—prostitution. Prostitution with a capital P. But it was prostitution of the most elegant variety, and all as clean as a whistle. Nobody had suggested popping into bed. Indeed, nobody had suggested anything at all. That was the main cause of anxiety.

For after handing over the notes in his very Ruritanian office— lots of gilt chairs and bogus baroque commodes—Count Mercati had produced a dossier of documents which, so he claimed, con- tained the sensational material for the book which was to rehabili- tate the image of King Constantine. On returning to the hotel, where I made straight for the bar, it needed only a couple of dry Martinis to convince me that the 'documents' were a load of rub- bish. Most of them were composed, in very bad French, by 'agents' who obviously did not know their business. There were a number of tattered maps and plans, and sheaves of yellowing press-cuttings, which were Greek to me in the most literal sense of the word, for they were written in the modern vernacular. And though I had acquired a smattering of classical Greek at Marlborough it was scarcely adequate to translate the colloquialisms of contemporary Athenian journalism. (It is interesting for the student of languages to note how much classical Greek does, in fact, survive, and how subtly it has been modified by the passage of time. At school we learned that the Greek for the word 'King', in English script, is 'Basileus', and it is still, but the letter 'B' has been softened into a

'V', and the 'u' has become 'f', so that one now pronounces the word as 'Vasilefs'. This makes me think of the letters of the Greek alphabet as pebbles of the beach on an infinite shore, over which the waters of twenty centuries have rolled, smoothing away the harsh oral impact of the words themselves, while retaining their essential significance.)

But this was not the moment for such reflections; there were graver problems to be faced, of which the most important was ... should I, or should I not, kiss the hand of Queen Sophie, who was not only a queen in her own right, but the sister of the Kaiser and the granddaughter of Queen Victoria?

'There's a divinity doth hedge a King.'

Was Shakespeare a snob? Or is there indeed a mystique about the institution of royalty which cannot be explained in terms of its political significance?

I am inclined to think that there is. During the next six months I was to establish a close relationship not only with members of the Greek royal family but also with their numerous European connections, such as the spectacular Queen Marie of Rumania. And though my temperament was naturally attracted by the fairy-tale atmosphere of a royal court, I always felt that there was a reality of power behind the fairy tale and that on the whole it was a beneficent power. Perhaps it was this conviction that gave so much importance to the small formality of kissing Queen Sophie's hand.

I had to be at the palace at eleven, and at fifteen minutes before that hour I hailed a rickety 'amaxa' drawn by two horses and trundled over the bumpy streets towards my destination. Life suddenly became a symphony in blue and white. There was a deep blue sky above and a faint breeze drifting in from the sea. In the distance the Acropolis shone like a white rose on a blue canvas. Under the pepper trees the flower stalls sparkled with the first blue gentians from the mountains, and outside the palace the sentries wore white kilts and tight-fitting blue jackets with rows of golden buttons. They sprang to attention as we swept through the gates and when the doors were opened the Lord Chamberlain was standing in a blue uniform; he led the way down corridors carpeted in blue, into a long room where the Queen was waiting. She was all in black and she had one of the saddest faces I have ever seen.

But her first words were anything but sad. (We have at last arrived at the hand-kissing episode.) I stood there hesitating. Heels together, sketching a bow. Now or never. Our eyes met. She must have been psychic. She broke into a rippling laugh.

'I believe I know what you're thinking. Whether to kiss my hand.'

'Yes, ma'am. Should I?'

For answer she gave me a very British handshake.

'Some Englishmen think they must, and then always look embarrassed. Except, of course, Captain A. Have you met Captain A yet?'

'No, ma'am.'

'You will. And then you will see what I mean.'

So our friendship began, on a family joke. Captain A was a British officer attached to the Embassy and vaguely in liaison with the Greek Court. Nobody seemed to know what he did, or why, but he was always popping in and out of the palace on the flimsiest of excuses, and he was tolerated not only because he was *plus royaliste que le roi* but also because he was such a nice little creature who might easily have been offended. His passion was hand-kissing. If he noticed even the most obscure princess wandering about at the bottom of the garden he would scurry out to pay his respects and kiss her hand. Some of the younger royals used to tantalise him, and keep their arms behind their backs, so that he was left hovering around, like a dog sniffing a bone, waiting for a chance to seize a hand and kiss it.

Queen Sophie, though she saw the joke, did not approve of these tactics and on one occasion I heard her reprimand a rather hoydenish young lady—not Greek—for her behaviour. 'Captain A,' she said, 'is an English gentleman and he has a complex.' And when the hoydenish young lady waited for an explanation she added, 'Kissing hands. Like kissing shoes. It is a complex,' and she left it at that.

What would her grandmother, Queen Victoria, have thought of it all?

*　　*　　*

The next six months passed in a dream. This is hardly orthodox autobiography but it is the best I can manage, because the whole Greek episode was divorced from reality.

What was I supposed to be *doing*? It was the same question that I had asked at the age of nineteen—only three years ago—when I had been propelled into the Secret Service, disguised as a British officer. The same question that I had asked a few months later when I was swept off to the United States. But now the question presented itself more urgently than ever, because as the days went by and lengthened into weeks it became glaringly apparent that there was nothing that anybody *could* do.

God alone knows that I tried. I followed up the clues in the dossier of 'documents' provided by Count Mercati, but without exception they led to nowhere. Most of them, incredible as it may seem today, centred round the colourful personality of Compton Mackenzie, who had been head of the Anglo-French police in Athens in 1915. According to the dossier he had bribed one of the Evsons of the bodyguard to put arsenic in King Constantine's wine, and when this nefarious plot miscarried he had hired a collection of thugs to set fire to the royal palace at Tatoy. I did a good deal of painstaking detective work on these stories, interviewing scurrilous characters in shady cafés along the waterfront of the Piraeus, and I was soon convinced that the whole thing was bogus. Years later, during the Second World War, I went up to stay with Compton Mackenzie on his island of Burra in the Hebrides, and we had an enjoyable weekend comparing our Athenian reminiscences, sitting in the kitchen, he with a bottle of malt whisky and I with a bottle of vintage port, under the jewel-eyed scrutiny of three elderly Siamese cats who were disposed on top of the stove which—they had decided—was the most sensible place from which to contemplate the follies of the world.

Back to Athens. As we were saying, I tried my damnedest to earn the wads of drachma notes that arrived every week from the office of Count Mercati. I wrote a number of interviews with King Constantine, which were factual, impartial, and readable. They were rejected by the London *Times*, the *New York Times*, and all the other leading journals who condescended to consider them. There was a hoodoo on Greece, and on everybody and everything connected with Greece. In despair, I returned to flippancy, and wrote a fluttering series for the London *Daily News*, under the title 'From an Attic Window'. These articles were gobbled up, and more were demanded. More were supplied. My little London bank balance began to assume respectable proportions. Prostitution was paying But why must it always be prostitution? Why did nobody ever listen when one had anything to say that was of real importance?

Did Greece give me anything at all, apart from the Lord Chamberlain's drachmas?

Yes, it gave me a great deal.

It was in Greece, for example, that I first became aware of flowers—'aware' in the sense that I realised that flowers were going to be very important in my life, more important, perhaps, than people.

Among the few companions of my own age with whom I formed a friendship was Queen Sophie's nephew, an agreeable young man called Prince Philip of Hesse, who afterwards married a daughter of the King of Italy. He was bored with the stuffy formalities of court procedure and he persuaded King Constantine to lend us one of his motor-cars so that we could drive out into the country and bathe from the cliffs. There were only three royal motor-cars, and though they were all on the point of collapse they were impressive vehicles because they all had large crowns on the back. Our own crown was painted in blue and gold on an enamel plate attached to the boot by string, and it was always falling off with a loud clatter.

'Do we *have* to have this bloody thing?' demanded Prince Philip on our first expedition after it had fallen off for the third time.

I thought not, because when you are driving a motor-car in the capital of a small monarchy and your crown falls off and rolls into the gutter it is apt to cause a sensation and even to arouse the suspicion of the police. So we put the crown in the boot.

It was on one of these picnics that I first had this almost mystical experience with flowers—an experience even more intense than the early encounter with the buttercups which had inspired the school-boy sonnet. I had finished bathing and had clambered up the cliff to open the picnic basket and uncork a bottle of Retsina, when I looked down and saw at my feet a pool of blue . . . a clean, exquisite blue, that seemed like a bouquet from the gods, tossed from the clouds for my especial benefit. It must have been a cluster of wild irises. Reticulata? Stylosa? Unguicularis? Today I should know the name, but on that enchanted morning my mind was uncluttered by horticultural nomenclature; the flowers came like the first chord of music on a blank manuscript, a chord that was to drift into an infinite series of modulations as time went by. This has been one of the abiding consolations in an otherwise pointless life. I may not have made the music that I might have made on the concert platform, but I have made it with flowers in the garden, in many gardens. After all, when you are making a garden, all you are doing is setting Nature to music.

Why didn't I take notes? It was Spring, we were in the Mediterranean, and though Greece is no paradise for the botanist, and in summer is largely scorched and arid, there were many treasures hiding among the rocks if I had only known where to look for them. Drifts of early lythospermum, clusters of sedums and numerous varieties of the gentians that were sold from the flower-stalls in Constitution Square. In every garden I have ever made there have been echoes of Greece. Even to this day, outside the gate of my garden near Richmond Park, you will see a cluster of the rare Sternbergea lutea, which very few people seem able to grow in the British Isles. I first discovered it in the island of Corfu, tumbling over the rocks in a golden cascade. It flowers for me in late Autumn, not in a cascade, but in a few brave blossoms gleaming through the November mists, like the memories of his youth in the heart of a very elderly gentleman.

That is one thing that Greece did for me. It lit the first flame of a passion for flowers that has burned brightly ever since.

Another thing that Greece did—and here we are on a more mundane level—was to give me a feeling of social assurance that I might otherwise have never known. The years ahead were to include numerous periods of financial and professional uncertainty; through my own stupidities I was to be subjected to many humiliations and constantly faced by all the moral problems immortalised in Kipling's 'If'—a great poem, whatever the intellectual snobs may say about it. I was compelled to 'meet with triumph and disaster and treat those two imposters just the same'. The Greek adventure helped me to do so. It made me unsnubbable. If at a very early age you have been received as an equal by princes you are not likely to be intimidated by peers, even if the peers are very rich and very important, and even if you have a reporter's notebook in your hand. I remember going to interview Lord Curzon, as part of a journalistic job. The butler kept me waiting in the hall as though I had come to tune the piano. (Lord Curzon bore a marked resemblance to his butler, though the butler had more breeding.) Lord Curzon tried to snub me. He was pompous and arrogant and he did not even ask me to sit down. But I remembered Kipling. 'If you can talk with kings and keep your virtue and mix with crowds nor lose the common touch.' Well I had talked with kings. And I had not 'lost the common touch', which is more than can be said for Lord Curzon, who was really a very common little man, even though he had been Viceroy of India. So I sat down, unsnubbed, and the interview was never published.

Finally, apart from what Greece did for me, what did I do for Greece? Here we return to the prostitution motif. The answer is that like all honest prostitutes I did what I was paid for. I had been commissioned by Chatto & Windus to write a book that would save the tottering throne of Greece, so I sat down and wrote it. Against all the odds, in spite of a total absence of material—and in spite of all the tempestuous emotions of a highly-sexed young man in a passionately romantic country—I shut myself up in the suite at the Grande Bretagne, day after day, night after night, and produced eighty thousand words of a book to which I gave the title of *The Athenians*. On the last day of my sojourn in Athens I hurried down to the Central Post Office and dispatched it to London. I had to hurry because Queen Sophie was giving a farewell dinner party to meet Queen Marie of Rumania.

Now comes another proof of the theory that 'the authenticity of an autobiography is to be measured not only by what the author remembers but by what he forgets'. I have no recollection of what *The Athenians* was about. I have a dim suspicion that it must have been a novel; but what sort of novel? This can be of some small interest for the student of abnormal psychology. In the years to come I was to write over fifty books, all of which were profitably published, and though I leave them to gather dust on the bookshelves, for it would be excessively tedious to read them again, I have at least some idea of what is in them. But of *The Athenians* I can remember nothing at all. Perhaps this is because it is the only book of mine that was not published. I probably felt insulted, and burned the typescript in a moment of pique. It is humiliating for a young man of twenty-two to write eighty thousand words and to have them thrown back in his face. All those sweaty nights bent over a desk in the Grande Bretagne when I might have been rolling about on beds of violets, or misbehaving on the waterfront of Piraeus or —best of all—practising arpeggios on a cracked piano. Yes, it was humiliating. My mind refused to accept the humiliation, and shut up like a clam. That was the root of the matter. To have a book rejected, this was not the sort of treatment that I was prepared to tolerate, and I vowed that it would never happen again. And in a lifetime of scribbling, it never did.

But though I burned the typescript I did not burn the manuscript. It turned up in an old tin trunk about twenty years ago. I had not the heart to read it, or even to flick through the pages, and I was about to take it out to the incinerator when I had second thoughts. Christmas was approaching and I had yet to think of a present for perhaps the most remarkable woman in my life, who shall be known as Dorothy. (Not that there ever *have* been any women like her.) Apart from her beauty, and her own brains and bravery, she had everything, from rubies to Rembrandts. Then I looked at the bundle of yellowing manuscript. This at least was something that nobody else could have given her, and if it were properly bound she might find a place for it on an obscure shelf of her library, as a sort of literary curiosity. So I took it round to Asprey's and had it bound in white leather, with golden lettering, and sent it to her, and I think she was pleased with it. But whenever she has tried to discuss it with me, I have changed the subject.

Very peculiar things happen to writers after their death. Some quickly vanish into the waters of Lethe; others refuse to sink, and are washed back to shore by the shifting tides of public taste, and resuscitated by literary beachcombers. In case I should come into the latter category *The Athenians* might be an interesting piece of literary driftwood. Eighty thousand unpublished words, bound in white leather, on a back shelf of a library in a villa by the sea. It ought to be worth a fiver, if only for the binding.

CHAPTER X

❧❧❧❧❧❧

WOMEN IN MY LIFE

I got into *Who's Who* at a very early age and I shall probably not get into 'Who Was Who' at all, a prospect which can be viewed with equanimity. *Who's Who* is a fascinating volume. The title is a stroke of genius and must have made a large fortune for Messrs A. and C. Black Ltd, who direct its publication from very gentlemanly and old-fashioned offices in London's Soho Square. Once, scenting a story, I went along to ask them the principles which guided them in their selection of candidates for inclusion. Were bribes ever offered? Were some people ever cross because they were not put in? Messrs A. and C. Black Ltd were too gentlemanly and old-fashioned to supply such information.

Who's Who? It is the sort of question which Gertrude Stein might have posed in one of her more lunatic moments of inspiration. 'A rose is a rose is a rose,' she proclaimed. From which it must follow that 'a who is a who is a who'. But what *is* a who?

I turn to my own entry for the year 1930, taking an autobiographical leap of five years, because I want to get on with the story. I seem to have been quite busy. By 1925 I have earned the right to call myself an author, with a bestseller to my credit. The tempo quickens so swiftly that in terms of music it would be scored Presto Agitato. This is the record.

1926 saw the publication of a second bestseller—*Twenty-Five*. In 1927 there were two more books—a novel about Mayfair called *Crazy Pavements*, which created quite a stir, and a collection of forty 'Profiles' called *Are They the Same at Home?* 1928 saw the publication

135

of my first book about America and also a controversial volume called *Women and Children Last*. 1929 saw my first London play, which was a flop, and my first London revue, which was not. I was called 'Cochran's 1930 Revue'. It was responsible for most of the book and some of the music, and it ran for over a year.

In the history of the theatre Cochran's revues deserve a chapter to themselves. He was an impresario who combined the flair of a Barnum with the discernment of a Diaghilev—a theatrical pirate who ransacked the world for any riches that might take his fancy. He would hear a tune—such as Cole Porter's 'Wake Up and Dream —and create a whole evening of magic around it. He would glimpse a girl in Paris, such as the enchanting Alice Delysia, capture her like a butterfly in a net and transport her to London and to stardom. The greatest designers, the most brilliant lyricists and the finest choreographers were at his beck and call.

To be chosen to create a revue for Cochran was an accolade that I had not expected. Although I was billed as the principal composer the most important part of the score was in fact written by a young genius called Vivian Ellis who inspired the whole production from the prelude to the finale. Vivian is a composer who ranks with Lehar and Johann Strauss, and occasionally—as in the operettas which he wrote with A. P. Herbert—he has received the acclaim that he deserves. Then, after a while, he drifted out of the spotlight, and though he is certainly not forgotten he is overshadowed by 'composers' who are not fit to button his boots. Why? Is it because the exquisite fabric of his *œuvre* is too delicate to withstand the uproarious onslaughts of the 'pop' age? I do not know. But I do know that songs like his 'Wind in the Willows' will still be whispering round the world long after the animal snarls and grunts of the 'pop' groups have been forgotten.

Yes—I was certainly busy in those distant days. Apart from the books and the plays there was a perpetual stream of popular journalism, to which was added the role of dramatic critic. There was a stint as London correspondent of *The New Yorker*. There were three American lecture tours. There was a trip round the world, arising from my association with history's greatest prima donna, Nellie Melba. This resulted in yet another book, which I wrote under Melba's name. It was called *Melodies and Memories* and numerous critics, biographers, and film producers have been cribbing it for the last forty years, without acknowledgement.

Riveting reading? Hardly. The end product of all this scribbling, which must often have amounted to ten thousand words a week, is unlikely to arouse the interest of posterity. But it is apposite autobiography because I must still have been possessed by the aforementioned demon—a demon urging me to make more and more money. But it cannot have been an entirely malevolent demon, because my desire to make money was, as always, inspired by an abiding passion to make music, to sail away to a remote island and sit in a hut, and play and play in solitude, torturing my fingers till I fell off the piano stool in an ecstasy of agony. I once read a story about Schumann who developed a hatred for the little finger of his right hand because it would not do what his mind was telling it to do. So one night, when he went to bed, he tied it to the bed-post, twisting it upwards with a piece of string. The results, apparently, were unfortunate. Whether this story is factual or false is unimportant for the moral is of eternal significance; it crystallises the resolution of the true artist to crucify himself in the cause of his art. I was not a true artist. I used to stare at my hands, and speak to them, and curse them. Then I would go to the mirror, and use my fingers to arrange a white tie for wearing to a dinner party.

Money! With the exception of Anthony Trollope few authors have told the truth about the part that it has played in their lives. Either they have boasted of having too little—particularly if they have risen from the ranks of the 'workers'—or they have boasted of having too much. I had both. I had too much to live the life of an artist, and too little to live the life of a young-man-about-town, which in those days I was doing in quite a big way.

I had an elegant little house in Westminster. That is one of the things which *Who's Who* does not mention. Over the mantelpiece hung two superb Guardis.

The mention of the Guardis reminds me of the title of this chapter, for they were given to me by Melba. (They were later snatched away again in a moment of pique, as I shall recall in another chapter.) And Melba, in one way or another, was certainly among the most important 'women in my life', for even from my schooldays the echo of her voice gave me my first assurance of a heaven in this world and the possibility of a paradise in the next.

It might be thought that I have already written enough about the late Dame Nellie Melba to preclude me from writing any more. After her death I produced a novel about her which was not only a *succès d'estime* but a *succès de scandale*, whereupon I turned it into a play, in which Edith Evans gave one of the greatest performances of her career. When the play had been running for nearly a year, they turned it into a film—(whoever 'they' may have been)—and though the film has long been forgotten, it is worth recalling in this volume, if only to stress my total lack of integrity as an artist.

I was lecturing in America when the film was being made and if I had been a 'serious' writer—a Priestley or a Pinter—I should have flown back to England to see what was going on. After all, I had put a lot into *Evensong*.* Apart from the authenticity of the central character I had contrived a strong story, but it was not the sort of story that would be easy to put on the screen; although it was written in the convention of comedy, it was essentially a tragedy of an ageing prima donna who finds that the gold in her voice is tarnished, that the world is slipping from her grasp. It would need a great actress to do justice to the role, and a director of genius. I did not know the name of the actress who had been chosen, nor the name of the director, and I did not even bother to find out.

Why? Because old Mrs W. K. Vanderbilt was giving a little fancy-dress party and I did not want to miss it. This is a deliberate over-statement, but I shall 'stet' it, if only to emphasise my lamentable lack of any sense of proportion. Gracie Vanderbilt was an agreeable monster who presided over a mansion in what is now the unfashionable part of Fifth Avenue. It really was a 'mansion', a word that has always seemed to me rather vulgar except in the

---

* *Evensong:* Jonathan Cape Ltd, 1932.

'many manions' context of The New Testament. When you crossed the threshold, from the uproar of Fifth Avenue, you stepped into another world, a world which enshrined the aristocracy of Europe. The men-servants were parodies of the real thing. Copies of *The Times* were neatly disposed on Chippendale desks. There were, of course, no cocktail cabinets but there was always an English butler ready with a whisky and soda, which Gracie pronounced 'sodah'. Gracie would not have understood what one meant by a Scotch on the rocks. And there were innumerable photographs, in silver frames, propped up all over the place—photographs of royalties and semi-royalties, on yachts and against the balustrades of stately homes.

I went to Gracie's little party disguised as Lord Byron. It was an appropriate choice, not only because I looked rather like him (before his profile disintegrated) but because it invested me with the necessary aura of British nobility. It was not a very good party, and it went on so long and there was so much champagne that I did not get home till the small hours. 'Home', by the way, was an extravagant apartment in East 42nd Street, which in those days had a certain *cachet*. When I staggered through the front door, there was a Western Union telegram on the mat. Did I mention that I had—and still have—a 'thing' about telegrams? This 'thing' dates from my boyhood, when a telegram inevitably implied some disaster connected with my father. Standing there, not too steadily, I recalled that in the past few days there had been quite a number of telegrams, none of which I had opened, partly because of the 'thing' and partly because I had been so busy dressing up as Lord Byron for the delectation of Gracie Vanderbilt. I opened the telegram. It informed me that the film première of my *magnum opus* was imminent and that I must return to England with all speed.

Prepare for farce. Switch to London, a few nights later, to the something-or-other cinema in the Strand. To the eminently forgettable première of the totally undistinguished film *Evensong*. It should have been a great moment in my life. My name in bright lights, the motor-cars discharging the usual hordes of celebrities, the lovely ladies crowding on me to wish me good luck, the flashing of the photographers, the curious feeling of atmospheric tension which is generated by these occasions—the same feeling that one has when there is thunder in the air. The tocsin clang of the alarum bells, the increasing urgency in the voices of the ushers telling us to go to our seats. The final press photograph, of myself at the bottom of the staircase leading to the dress-circle, surrounded by a cluster of starlets.

This was *la vie en rose* and I had no doubt that it would go on for ever. And it was all because I had written a story about an old lady who had lost her voice. Here, for a moment, there was a flicker of artistic integrity. If *Evensong* had been a conventional glamour story of life behind the scenes it would have been nothing to boast about. But it was not. It was a tragedy of age, and though this brilliant and glittering audience might be surprised that it had come from my pen, I hoped and believed that they would be impressed.

I took my seat, the house lights dimmed, the music sang out, and the screen came to life. And I began to blink. I found myself gazing at a scene which was, to say the least of it, unexpected. The scene was a convent in Ireland and Melba, aged eighteen, was escaping from an upstairs window. As far as I was aware she had never been to Ireland, nor entered a convent, let alone escaped from one. However, perhaps this was only a momentary example of poetic licence before they got on with my story. But more startling revelations were in store. The scene switched to Venice—which was never mentioned in the book—or the play—and Melba, who had now attained the age of twenty-five, was shown having an affair with a gondolier. I had never credited her with any affairs at all, because the whole point and the whole tragedy of the story was that she was past the age for having them. And so it went on. Episode followed episode, increasingly grotesque and further and further removed from the original work. Only five minutes before the end of the film did the heroine reluctantly put on a white wig and sing the *addio* from *La Bohème*. End of film, lukewarm applause, and exit author to the nearest pub for a strong ale. I had planned a celebration party at the Savoy. But there was nothing to celebrate.

*   *   *

The title 'Women in my Life' suggests a promise of revelations that I do not propose to fulfil. Women, as it happens, have played a greater part in my life than men, in moments of delight or in moments of despair, but I shall not dwell on the intimate aspects of any of these relationships. 'Sex' in the pages of a novel, on the stage of the theatre, or the screen of the film, has always bored me and always will. Why? I suppose it is because the act itself is clumsy and uncouth. Let me put it like this . . . copulation in the ballet of life is not a theme which lends itself to choreography. The mystical impulses that draw men to women—or men to men or women to women—these can be set to music of ravishing beauty and excitement, but when it comes to the climax I do not think that they can be put into words. If the young critics of today disagree, let me offer them a very simple challenge. Let them give me the name of a single major dramatist, poet, novelist, or artist who has created any work of lasting significance through recording the details of the physical orgasm. Just one, from Shakespeare onwards. It cannot be done, not in words, though a great many highly-esteemed novelists and dramatists are in fact trying to do it. All in the name of art. Bang, bang, bang. Jerk, jerk, jerk. Pant, pant, pant. And if the bangs and jerks and pants are loud enough and graphic enough the man who records them may make a fortune but he will not be numbered among the immortals.

Sex in the raw, from the frescoes of Pompeii to the lavatory scribblings of D. H. Lawrence, is not, or should not be, presented to the public to be judged in terms of artistic achievement. We have all been titillated by sexual revelations but the arts should have a higher aim than titillation. The most obvious example, in terms of autobiography, is Pepys. For the Pepysian scholar it is no doubt interesting to note the numerous occasions on which he took down his trousers for improper purposes, but for me it is a bore. When writers take down their trousers I turn the page. When artists start to scribble on the walls of lavatories I leave them to it. One of the most exquisite draughtsmen of the nineteenth century— still underrated—was Aubrey Beardsley. A drawing like 'The Wagnerians' has the compelling force of Goya at his most fiercely inspired. But when Beardsley took to pornography his pen faltered and his eyes betrayed him. I still remember the melancholy which pervaded me when I first saw these tragic scrawls. They used to be sold under the counter, or passed round at literary cocktail parties. In the present climate of opinion we may presumably look forward to the day when they will be printed, at the taxpayer's expense, and placarded on the walls of London's underground railways.

The mention of 'The Wagnerians' suggests that music is the exception to the theories that I have been trying to formulate; music is the only medium through which the physical orgasm can be transformed into a work of art. The overture to *Tristan* is one long sustained orgasm, so explicit that towards the climax one feels that the composer is exposing his body even more brutally than he is exposing his soul.

The women in my life. Where to begin?

I think I shall begin with Dorothy Hart in the long gallery of a very beautiful house on the Sussex hills. We are finishing dinner—Dorothy and her sister-in-law, whose name is Nini. I am lucky to be dining with two such ladies; they both have more than their fair share of attraction, but it is of Dorothy that I wish to write.

Looking at her—the year is 1945 and she is still in her thirties—you would not guess that on many occasions her small and deceptively fragile body had been subjected to physical tortures that would have driven some women insane. I will not go into the gruesome details, but I will give one example, because it is a story in itself.

At the end of the war Dorothy went to America for a very drastic operation, and she went alone. She had a host of friends, but in moments of crisis Dorothy has always fought her own battles. The reason for the operation is yet another story. When she was expecting her first child her husband took her for a drive in his new Isotta-Fraschini. (That is a 'period' name if ever there was one.) Her husband's name was Geoffrey Hart, and he is still remembered as a legend in the city of London. Geoffrey was a genius, head boy at Harrow, senior classical scholar at King's College, Cambridge, a millionaire at the age of twenty-five. There was only one thing wrong with Geoffrey. He did everything at top speed. A phrase of his drifts back to me over the years. He once took me out in the Isotta and as we gathered momentum I asked, rather tremulously, what speed we were doing. 'This car,' he replied, 'is becalmed at ninety.'

The time came when Geoffrey drove too fast. There was a serious accident in which Dorothy lost her unborn child. More than that, she lost her hearing. She was almost totally deaf. I am cutting this story short to reach the pay-off line. She walks into a specialist's consulting room in New York. He is the only man in the world who can perform this operation and she is warned that it is very dangerous. With her medical history, how will she stand up to it? She is very near the end of her tether but she does not show it. Her voice is still calm and gentle when she replies, as though she were thinking aloud . . . 'I shall stand up to it as the British stood up at Dunkirk before America came into the war.'

And she did.

Back to the long gallery. In the candlelight she looks like a school-girl. Her eyes are untroubled, she might not have a care in the world. As it happens, she has a great many cares. When Geoffrey died he was engaged, as always, in a whirl of financial activities some of which were highly speculative. Though I did not realise it at the time, she was caught in a financial maelstrom. But I sensed that she was lonely, and I knew that she was in pain. Apart from her other physical troubles there was some disorder in the spine. So I thought that perhaps she might like me to stay on for an extra day to keep her company, extending the weekend till Tuesday morning.

Here I shall break my rule about recalling dialogue.

Dorothy   I'm terribly sorry, but I have to go to Newcastle on Tuesday.

B.N.   But that's nearly four hundred miles and it's beginning to snow. Which car are you taking?

Dorothy   I'm not going by car. I'm going by train. My chauffeur's wife is expecting a baby and I wouldn't like him to be anxious.

B.N.   But this is insane. The whole British railway system is in a mess. It's a ghastly journey in any case. Even after London you'll have to change trains at least twice. And what about your poor back? *Why* do you have to go to Newcastle?

Nini (*in sepulchral tones*)   Dorothy has bought a battleship.

B.N.   She's bought a *what*?

Nini   A battleship.

Dorothy Nini darling, you exaggerate. It's a minesweeper.

B.N.   How on earth did you get hold of a minesweeper?

Dorothy I've been negotiating with the Greek government.

B.N.   But what do you want it *for*?

Dorothy I want it for the engines.

B.N.   What are you going to do with them?

Dorothy I shall need them in South America.

Telling this story in dialogue makes it sound even more Alice in Wonderland than it was, though it was certainly fantastic enough. Among the more daring ventures in which Geoffrey was involved at his death was a highly-imaginative project for supplying power and light to a South American republic. I am totally unqualified to explain it; all I can say with assurance is that it was the sort of scheme that demanded a brilliant financial brain and an exceptional knowledge of intricate international economic detail. Even the most hardened operators in the city would have been daunted by its complexities.

Dorothy calmly decided to go ahead with it. I think that one of the reasons which impelled her was her loyalty to Geoffrey's memory. She had loved him very much, she had respected his genius. She would see it through.

Very well, I would try to help her. I would drive her up to Newcastle.

The early hours of Tuesday morning. Pitch dark, with driving snow and sleet. I am at the wheel of a Jaguar, which I have never driven before. I am extremely alarmed, because I know nothing about motor-cars. Even in a country lane, trundling along in an old Ford at forty miles an hour, I am apprehensive. Never mind. In for a penny in for a million pounds, which was roughly what was involved in this operation.

We reach London at dawn and breakfast in a café where Dorothy meets a man with whom she has a highly complex technical conversation about the engines. Off again, heading for the North. The snow thickens and suddenly the windscreen wiper gives up the ghost. In those days there were few garage facilities, and we have to drive the next two hundred miles with the window open, while I scrape away the snow with a frozen hand. Round about seven o'clock Dorothy says to me, 'Beverley, you must be tired.' We stop for dinner. Dorothy scans the wine list. Among her unexpected gifts is an encyclopaedic knowledge of wine. She chooses a nectar which sustains us till we reach Newcastle. In the hall of the hotel she bids me goodnight. She is, I suspect, in considerable pain from her spine, and her single good ear is not working too well. But she still looks like a schoolgirl and there is still a sparkle of laughter in her eyes.

'Beverley, you must be *very* tired. Have breakfast in bed and we'll meet for lunch.'

'But what about you?'

'I have to be at the docks at eight.'

'Then I shall come with you.'

Somebody should make a film about the following morning. Dorothy, in silver mink, walking up the gangway of what seems to me to be a very large and menacing vessel. The crew lining the railing, barely concealing their grins. There are wolf-whistles in the air. The captain salutes, and suggests a cup of coffee in his stateroom. He is obviously *épris* by this charming little lady. Dorothy has other ideas. 'Thank you,' she says, 'but I think we should go straight to the engine-rooms. We have a great deal to discuss.'

I wait in a cabin. Nearly two hours pass before they return. Dorothy is her usual sweet and tranquil self but the captain looks distinctly shaken, and so does his chief engineer. There is a brief conversation which I do not understand, though it seems that Dorothy is issuing some sort of ultimatum, with a time-limit attached. When we leave the ship there is no longer any hint of wolf-whistles. The crew look as if they had been struck by a bomb, as indeed they had—a bomb wrapped in silver mink.

Driving back to the hotel in the Jaguar I ask Dorothy what the hell had been going on. All I got was ... 'Beverley darling, you are not mechanically minded. And I do not think you have much head for business.'

What happened to the ship? What happened to the engines? What happened to the South American republic for which they were destined, to supply the power that would light their streets? I have no idea. But I do know the name of the company in the city of London through which these operations were conducted. And I hope and believe that Dorothy, who was a majority shareholder, did not lose any money out of it.

I could write a book about her; indeed, I have already done so.* I shall mention only one side of her extraordinary personality, because it is autobiographically to the point. At the beginning of these reminiscences, I asserted that nobody had ever taught me anything. Dorothy is one of the very few exceptions to this rule. Dorothy has taught me a great deal—perhaps all I really know—about art. The Hart collection of pictures and furniture is among the most beautiful minor collections of Europe, and there have been many Hart collections. Throughout her career, in good times and in bad, in sickness and in health, Dorothy has cherished her treasures as though they were the children that she was never destined to bear. Living among these treasures, as I have often been privileged to do, watching the manner in which they have been assembled, arranged and rearranged, has been a liberal education. If your eye has been directed towards perfection you find yourself automatically rejecting the second-rate. Dorothy has never

* The story of Dorothy and Geoffrey Hart, *mutatis mutandis*, was the inspiration for the third in my series of detective novels. It was first published in 1957 under the title of *The Rich Die Hard*, and has recently been reissued by W. H. Allen.

accepted the second-rate. Here is one example. I once found myself lunching at a country house which was only a few miles from the Hart estate. Among the guests was the Spanish Ambassador, a very charming and highly intelligent man. He had been to a London auction sale the day before and had not been impressed. There had been a picture 'by' Joachim Patinir which was a fake. How could this happen? Didn't we know about Patinir in this country? I told the Ambassador that I could introduce him to one person who knew a great deal about Patinir, as she happened to own one. After lunch I drove him over. The front door was wide open; we went inside and walked through the long gallery to the room where the Patinir was hanging, lit by the pale Autumn sunlight. The Ambassador stood before it for a moment. 'But this is fantastic!' he exclaimed. 'This is as fine as anything we have in Spain!'

A soft voice came from the doorway. 'I think it is finer.'

Dorothy had entered unobserved. She did not seem surprised to see us nor was she impressed by the status of the man who had paid this tribute to her treasure. All she cared about was that here was somebody who knew what she knew, that here was a superb masterpiece. I left them together, adoring the picture in silence.

The Patinir is in my eyes and in my brain and in my heart, setting an eternal standard of beauty and of truth.

And so is its owner.

CHAPTER XI

❦❦❦❦❦

MORE WOMEN IN MY LIFE

What would have happened if one had been born with an ugly face and an uncouth body?

If one were writing about oneself this would be an intolerable question, a monstrous conceit. But in this context I am not writing about myself. The physical body of the man I am trying to resuscitate has long since disappeared. Apart from the inevitable ravages of age, his body has been so chopped and sliced and mutilated that it can no longer give pleasure either to its owner or to anyone else. The best one can hope for is that one has not yet reached the stage when one will frighten horses in the streets.

Having said this, the speculation is inoffensive. Looking back over the years I now realise that my face was responsible for opening many doors which might otherwise have been closed. Some of them led to delight; some, with a sharp drop, to hell. That is not the point. All that matters is that when I knocked on the door, people let me in, because they liked the look of me.

The book of mine which seems destined for the longest life was called *Down the Garden Path*, and it bears the following dedication:

> To Marie Rose Antoinette Catherine de Robert
> d'Aqueria de Rochegude d'Erlanger
> whose charms are as gay
> and numerous as
> her names.

I have often wondered why Catherine d'Erlanger has received such scant attention from the social historians of the decades before the war. All the other great hostesses have been done to death.

148

Tens of thousands of readers have been led through the portals of 4 Grosvenor Square, to listen to the witticisms of Lady Cunard, as she cavorted with Sir Thomas Beecham, or demanded silence for George Moore, or paid homage—which she was bitterly to regret—to the Duke of Windsor. Hordes of literary tourists have been admitted to the drawing-room of Lady Colefax at Argyll House, which was a magnet for the intelligentsia, though that is perhaps the wrong image, for sometimes one had the feeling that she had stood outside the front door and dragged in her guests with a lasso. On a grander scale, the memoir readers have been admitted into the intimidating presence of Mrs Ronnie Greville at Polesden Lacey, and watched her wicked intrigues over the teacups in her lavishly over-gilded drawing-room. (Cream from the home-farm, cinnamon-flavoured scones for Queen Mary in case she happened to pop in, and three sorts of tea, one of which was specially brewed for Lord Reading.) And the political commentators have constantly buzzed round Lady Londonderry reporting—not too accurately—the splendours of Londonderry House, and speculating on the consequences of her somewhat incongruous flirtation with the Labour party, in the person of Ramsay MacDonald.

I knew all these old girls pretty well, and by an odd coincidence, I was in—very nearly—at all their deaths. Emerald Cunard at the Ritz—in the last days of the war—lonely, deserted by Sir Thomas, comparatively destitute, but still indomitable. Maggie Greville at the Dorchester, when the last bombs were falling, by no means alone, far from destitute, equally indomitable, and still sustained by cream from the home-farm, in spite of rationing. Sybil Colefax at my own house, her body twisted with cancer, living on God knows what. Till the very last she remained a tireless hostess, but towards the end she was in straitened circumstances. And whenever one accepted an invitation to dinner, one received, a few days later, a little bill. It was a curious device and if it had been discovered by an unscrupulous gossip writer she could have been made to look ridiculous. But her friends were loyal, and kept silent, and we always sent along our fivers, which were more than adequate for three courses and a bottle of plonk.

Perhaps the toughest of them all, particularly in her later days, was old Lady Londonderry. ('Circe' to her friends.) When I last entered Londonderry House she had only a short time to live. Most of the place had been shut up, never to be reopened, and one had the feeling that the great staircase was thronged with ghosts. We lunched upstairs in a room brimming with flowers sent over from Mount Stewart, the estate in Ireland. She was in considerable pain, with a broken hip, but she was still the life and soul of the party, which included Jack Profumo. Somebody mentioned an unfortunate member of Parliament who had been arrested in Hyde Park for indecent behaviour with a guardsman. Apparently he had led the young man into a shrubbery, where his improprieties were clearly visible to the police. This was not the sort of topic which in those days was considered suitable for discussion with octogenarian dowagers, but Circe was more than equal to the occasion.

'What a *silly* man!' she exclaimed. 'There are plenty of laurels in Hyde Park. Why did he have to choose a *deciduous* shrub?'

Catherine d'Erlanger seems to have escaped the notice of the memoir writers. Why? She was as rich as any of the others. In a scatter-brained way, she had a livelier intelligence. And unlike any of her rivals she had a radiant sexual appeal which she kept until middle-age. In a corner of her vast Piccadilly house there used to hang a full-length portrait of her as a young woman, a very revealing painting in the manner of a late Victorian Rubens. She might have been posing as a model for a Bacchante. When I first saw this picture I happened to notice the date—1898, the year that I was born. As time went by the picture was moved further and further into the shadows, and one day the date was painted over. But she never lost the Bacchante allure.

> Some enchanted evening
> Across a crowded room . . .

What an admirable song that was! A song with a haunting melodic line and a lyric that made not only poetry but sense, because it caught, in a single phrase, the rapture of a lost generation of young lovers.

It was on an enchanted evening, in a crowded room, that I first met Catherine d'Erlanger. The month was May; the chestnuts were in flower in Hyde Park; the milieu was the main salon in the Piccadilly house. I had been taken along by Diaghilev, and I went with some reluctance, because I was writing an article about him, and I wanted to get away into a quiet corner and make notes. Apart from that, he was accompanied by a very good-looking young dancer who seemed to regard me as some sort of rival. We will call him V. He was a young man who liked to have the stage to himself. So much so, that eventually he got what he wanted, and played to empty houses.

As soon as we made our entrance, Catherine left her other guests and came across to join us. The first thing she said, after we had been introduced, was 'I will paint your portrait.'

This aroused an immediate and extremely petulant reaction from V. 'But you have not yet finished your portrait of *me*.'

'*Cher enfant*, I finished it last night.'

'You have not shown it to me.'

'Then we will go and see it at this instant.'

So off we go, the flamboyant Bacchante, V, scowling behind, me, longing to get into my quiet corner to make notes, and Diaghilev bringing up the rear, polishing his monocle, looking like a large and highly civilised spider.

We climb a great many marble steps and at last we reach the top. Catherine flings open the door of her 'studio'. And I stare, in some bewilderment, at a cluttered gallery of identikits.

Why has nobody ever brought Catherine's paintings into a book of memoirs? There she was, year after year, painting away like mad, producing portraits of the great, the near-great, the notorious, and the nobodies. While she painted, she talked, and the talk was often brilliant. But nobody has ever recorded it. Nor has anybody, as far as I am aware, ever reproduced any of her pictures. This perhaps was not so surprising, because they really were, as I have suggested, identikits—sexless, ageless, and totally devoid of any expression, apart from the faintly criminal aura which one associates with the composite portraits of rapists and terrorists which are released by the police in order to 'assist them with their inquiries'.

At this period one of Catherine's most constant companions was a very beautiful young lady—we will call her Thelma—who, when she first appeared on the social scene, seemed to be connected with some sort of shop. I cannot remember what shop it was because everybody in those days seemed to be opening shops—hat shops, scent shops, flower shops, antique shops. Thelma was far too beautiful to stay in any shop for long and soon she was married to a millionaire. But not before Catherine had painted her portrait. There it hung, next to the portrait of V which we had come up to inspect. V was furious.

'You have made me look exactly like Thelma,' he protested.

'But, *mon enfant*, you are exactly like Thelma.'

V was even more furious. As a protégé of Diaghilev he was jealous of his reputation for virility. 'I am not like any woman.'

Catherine stretched out her hand to a table, picked up a brush, dipped it into a pot of black, and painted a dainty little moustache over the portrait's lips.

She turned to V with a radiant smile. 'After this, *mon enfant*, there can be no mistake.'

I do not remember how Catherine painted my portrait, nor what happened to it, but I remember the picture itself, very clearly. It was the image of Thelma, and also of V (without the moustache) and of all her other sitters. It was the identikit to end all identikits, except that, in my case, the aura of criminality seemed to be faintly enhanced.

We became friends overnight, and soon I came to look upon this vast house as a second home. The Baron d'Erlanger seldom appeared. Now I come to think of it, very few of the husbands of any of the great ladies of the period ever appeared. Did anybody ever meet Emerald Cunard's husband—or Maggie Greville's, or any of the other social giantesses? Perhaps they were all dead. The

The father of the man

My mother in the year of her marriage

The schoolboy

The dangerous overcoat

```
        B A T T A L I O N    O R D E R S
                        by
            Lt. Col. H.A. Cradock
                   Commanding
        GARRISON OFFICER CADET BATTALION
                   No. 177              Cambridge.
                                        July 27th, 1918

. . . . . . . . . . . . . . . . . . . .   . . . . . . . . . . . . . . . . . . . .

1. DETAIL.         Officer for the day Sunday - Lieut. Mann
                                 Monday - Captn. Anderson
                        Next for duty -  "   Fleming-Brown

                   Battalion Orderly Sergeant - Sergt. Dean
                                 Monday - Sergt. Crick
                        Next for duty - Sergt. Hall, H.

2. CHURCH                The Battalion will attend Divine Service in
   PARADE.         All Saints' Church, Jesus Lane at 9-30a.m.
                   All Denominations and Bugle Band to attend.

3. ANTI-GAS              The U/M Officer qualified as a Regimental
   INSTRUCTOR.     Instructor in Anti-Gas Measures at the 49th Course of
                   Instruction, held at the Command School of Instruction
                   in Anti-Gas Measures.
                        Lieut. J.B. Nichols...... Distinguished.

                                        (Signed) A.H. CHARLES,
                                             Captain, A/Adjutant,
                             Garrison Officer Cadet Battalion.
. . . . . . . . . . . . . . . . . . . .   . . . . . . . . . . . . . . . . . . . .
```

Documentary proof of the author's military prowess in World War 1. Preserved from the Battalion Orders of GOCB No. 177, whose HQ were in Cambridge in July 1918

'Mission to America' (Back row, from left to right): Professor A. E. Walter, Provost of Worcester, Oxford; myself. (Front row, from left to right): Professor John Joly, Dublin University; Sir Arthur Shipley, Vice-Chancellor, Cambridge University; Sir Henry Miers, Vice-Chancellor, Manchester University; Sir Henry Jones, Vice-Chancellor, Glasgow University

Myself with the Rt Hon. Sir Esme Howard, British Ambassador to the United States of America. The photograph was taken outside the White House in 1928

The Sacred and the Profane. Sanctity and cigarette cards

Beverley Nichols

Reading a copy of *Revue* with Frances Day

With Merle Oberon in her dressing room

Dorothy Hart

Cecil Beaton, Gladys Cooper and myself
during an evening of laughter

Cyril

'Escape 1939'

Outside St Mark's in Venice. Photograph taken by Catherine d'Erlanger

Cottage garden, 'Allways'—'A garden is the only mistress who never fades, who never fails'

After 'Allways'—Number One, Ellerdale Close

'Beverley Nichols in the Thirties' by Cecil Beaton

only husband whom one met was Sybil's Sir Arthur, and he was such an exceptional bore that if it had not been for Sybil her guests would have scattered at the very sight of him. He knew a great deal about the laws of England and also about the laws of France, and at one time he had some sort of advisory post connected with the construction of the Channel Tunnel. Once, walking home with Max Beerbohm after lunch, I asked what Sir Arthur had been talking to him about for so long. Max heaved a deep sigh. 'Surely you need not ask? He was boring the Channel Tunnel.'

With the Baron d'Erlanger, it was very different. I once had a strange insight into his relationship with Catherine. I was taking her to the ballet, and as I walked up the marble staircase I heard the sound of a man sobbing. Women's tears are distressing enough, but when a man cries it is almost unbearable—a theme I once developed in a long-forgotten book of short stories.* I stayed on the staircase wondering what to do. The sobbing continued, and with it came a tragic monologue of melancholia. It had nothing to do with me nor with Catherine; it was a dark and desolate indictment of life in general and it ended with an appeal for death, which he seemed to be addressing to her personally. 'And after death,' he sobbed, 'there will be nothing. There must be nothing. There must be total annihilation.'

When at last I entered the room Catherine was holding him in her arms. She did not seem disturbed by my arrival. She merely smiled, rather sadly, and gestured to a side-table, where there were two tickets for the ballet. 'You must take somebody else,' she said. Then she turned back to the Baron. 'Tonight,' she murmured, 'he is not himself. I would not wish him to be alone.'

But who was 'himself'? And why, with such a background, and with such a radiant companion, did he seek 'total annihilation'?

My other memories of Catherine are scored in a very different key. In spite of her riches and her proud ancestral lineage she saw herself, *au fond*, as a typical housewife of the French bourgeoisie. Sometimes she carried this attitude to extremes. I would call for

---

* *Men Do Not Weep:* Jonathan Cape Ltd, 1941.

her in the morning, never knowing quite what to expect, and she would be waiting on the doorstep in an ancient mackintosh. Under the mackintosh, there would be the sparkle of diamonds, but she seemed to think that these jewels were invisible. She would take my arm and guide me round to a side-street where the Rolls was waiting. She had evidently convinced herself that this distinguished chariot was also invisible for as we walked she would say, 'This morning, *mon enfant*, we are going to the Caledonian market and if we are going to bargain they must not think that we are rich.'

So we went to the Caledonian market, to return with an incredible collection of junk, broken vases, and mouldy tiger skins. Sometimes we went to fish shops. 'When I was a young girl,' said Catherine, 'my mother taught us how to manage a household. Did you know, *mon enfant*, that when one buys a fish one must poke it in the eye to see if it is fresh?' The fish shops were usually in very squalid streets where I fancy that the Rolls immediately sent up the prices, although Catherine remained convinced that it was invisible. After she had played her role as a French housewife, and poked a great many fish in the eye, we would return to Piccadilly and hand them over to the chef, having saved, so she persuaded herself, at least two shillings. They were usually served with a rich sauce *béarnaise*.

It was not long before Catherine was inviting herself to the *Down the Garden Path* cottage. I was apprehensive. It was primitive, I told her. There was only one small bathroom and the water had to be pumped up from the well. She would not be able to bring her maid. She scorned such hardships. If necessary she would go to the well and pump the water and pour it over herself from the bucket. Had she been obliged to do so, I am sure that she would not have complained. Although she could be as *grande dame* as the Queen of Sheba if she chose she fitted perfectly into a country cottage, and as soon as she arrived she invented a game called the Wild Flower Race which was simply a competition to pick wild flowers. You were allowed only a single example of each variety in your bunch, and the one who found the most flowers was the winner. I described this game in the book, though I attributed its invention to an anonymous character whom I called 'Princess P' because Catherine did not like publicity. I also told the charming truth about her. I quote: 'Princess P is beautiful, intelligent, and amazingly amiable. But in this game she proves herself to be entirely devoid of moral responsibility. If she suddenly notices a rare flower she will clutch one's arm and tell an outrageous story in order to distract one's attention. She will simulate fatigue, giddiness, pretend to have things in her eye, and worst of all, if she discovers an unusual clump she will pick a single flower and ruthlessly destroy all the others in order that she may be possessed of a unique specimen.'

Some of my most vivid memories of Catherine are connected with Venice, where she had a palazzo on the *Riva degli schiavoni* which has a superb view of the Grand Canal. I cannot remember the number, but it was within a stone's throw of the Hotel Danielli. On the first occasion that I went to stay there she had made a muddle about the dates and my bedroom was chock-full of Venetian chandeliers. They were in a thousand pieces, covering the bed and the floor with a glitter of multi-coloured glass. They could not possibly be moved because they would all get mixed up as, of course, they eventually did. 'Never mind,' said Catherine. 'It is of no importance. We will stay with Bertie at the Malcontenta.'

Who was Bertie, I asked. And what was the Malcontenta?

The first question was excusable, because I could hardly be expected to know that Bertie was her most constant companion. Not that she had attempted to conceal the fact, either from me or from anybody else. It would never have occurred to her to do so; she was not the sort of woman who considered it necessary to explain her friends.

But I should really have known better than to ask about the Malcontenta. 'You are an infant,' observed Catherine shortly. 'You know nothing whatever about European civilisation.' She went on to inform me that the Villa Malcontenta was one of the greatest masterpieces of Palladio. 'You will fall in love with it,' she said, 'because it is like a piece of music.' And I did.

We arrived as dusk was falling and Bertie, who was in residence, greeted us on the flight of steps that led to the main entrance. He was in workman's clothes and covered in whitewash but he did not seem at all put out by our arrival. There was some champagne, he told Catherine, and he believed that there was some pâté which we could have for dinner. This, Catherine assured him, was precisely what we wanted. Nothing more. (As it happened I should have liked a great deal more as I had not eaten since breakfast.) 'And now,' said Catherine, 'we must show him his room.'

This was the climax of the evening. We walked down long corridors under high ceilings and always there was the sense that Palladio had been singing songs in stone. When we entered the room allotted to me I had a moment of dismay because there was nothing in it but a battered iron bedstead and a chamberpot. And over the bed the plaster was crumbling.

'Show him,' demanded Catherine.

Bertie lit a candle and held it up to the crumbling plaster. There was a glimmer of blue and red. Then he handed me a small tool with a blunted edge. 'Try it yourself. Tap the plaster.' I tapped and some white dust fell to the floor. Tapped again. We peered more closely at the wall. There was a gleam of gold.

'I think,' he said, 'that we have discovered an angel.'

'We will call it Beverley's angel.'

We had indeed discovered an angel. Behind the ancient plaster of the Malcontenta's walls there were frescoes that had been hidden for centuries. When I went to bed that night I tapped till I could tap no longer. And I went to sleep under the fragment of an angel's hand that seemed to be holding a flask of gold.*

---

* The frescoes of the Villa Malcontenta are presumably familiar to the art historians. I do not know how many were revealed but I fancy that some of them were painted by Crivelli. They were certainly in the Crivelli tradition. An exact reproduction of the villa itself was later built in Kent at Mereworth, where it eventually came into the hands of Lord Rothermere. I was later to have the curious experience of staying at Mereworth in the bedroom which precisely corresponded with the one I had occupied in Venice—without, of course, the frescoes. Mereworth is now owned by an Arabian multi-millionaire and I hope that he treats it kindly.

From the sacred, once again, to the profane. The very profane. I came to know Bertie Lansberg (or was in Landsberg?) very well in some ways and not at all in others. Although I never bothered to learn to spell his name nor inquire as to the country of his origin, this did not seem to matter. He was about forty, he had money of his own, and he was physically hypnotic, like a Satyr who has strayed into the Ritz. He was also totally amoral. This adjective is often misused, and associated with wickedness. It is more aptly connoted with innocence, or perhaps ignorance. He really did not know the difference between what society regards as permissible or impermissible, and it never occurred to him to find out. He had his own standard of values.

For me his most attractive attribute was his erudition. As we wandered about Venice together he knew the name of every painter, every sculptor, every architect, every plasterer, and of all the patrons who had inspired and financed them. He also seemed to be familiar with all the details of their sex lives. I remember pausing to admire a small and exquisitely delicate ivory crucifix which hung in a dark corner of one of the most obscure chapels in the city, where very few tourists ever ventured. Bertie approved my taste, and immediately supplied the relevant names and dates. Then he added, *en passant* ... 'It is interesting that such a man could produce a work of such spiritual ecstasy. Why? Because he had an insatiable passion for elderly gondoliers. Very elderly gondoliers.' He was surprised that I was not acquainted with such an elementary detail of artistic history. Then he said something very characteristic. 'Most historians of art begin with the œuvre and then, if they are interested enough, go on to discuss the sexual implications. El Greco is the most obvious example of this. A great deal of nonsense has been written about El Greco's sexual inclinations which should be obvious to any intelligent child. I reverse this procedure. I begin with the sex and work backwards so that when I examine the end product I have a clear conception of what the artist was trying to say and why he said it in that particular manner.'

This brings us to the episode of the tattoos.

Bertie's body was covered from head to foot with a pattern of tattoos of quite exceptional obscenity. I cannot recall them in detail because the only occasion when he revealed them to me, on a sultry afternoon in a bedroom of the Villa Malcontenta, a fleeting glance was more than enough. His chest portrayed a couple of negresses in a position which no ladies should assume, either on one's chest or anywhere else. The most shocking mural—if it can be so described—was printed into his back. When he turned round one saw a weird hunting scene, of excessive indecency, in which a troop of nymphs and satyrs were chasing a sort of fox, whose tail was vanishing up his behind.

What does one do when one's host takes his trousers off, in such circumstances? What does one say? Something like this. 'Too amusing, dear Bertie. It must have been very painful. And yes ... I notice the fox's tail. And do put your trousers on again because there is a draught.'

That was roughly the dialogue. The point of the story is that somebody should write it, because it might offer an exquisite opportunity for an expert in black comedy. Somebody like Tennessee Williams. Catherine must have known about the tattoos but I do not think that they would have bothered her. Behind his strangely illuminated façade there was a brilliant brain and a very kindly heart.

The women in my life! Fifty years of women, of all shapes and sizes and degrees of intelligence. Where does one begin and where does one end? How are they to be catalogued in less than fifty volumes?

I cannot answer that question. I can only flick over the pages of memory, more or less at random, beginning with those ladies who are happily still with us.

The most brilliant woman whose friendship I have ever been privileged to enjoy is undoubtedly Rebecca West. Creatively and critically she stands alone. Compared with her, the ladies of Bloomsbury were pale moths, fluttering about as though life were a candle which they dared not approach too closely, lest they scorched their wings. Hugh Walpole once held her up to me as an example. Although he was a second-rater he was no fool, and his advice to young authors was usually sound. 'When you are writing,' he said, 'you must never write for the great, you must never speak to the crowd; you must think only of one person, and you must write only for him or for her.' I did not ask Hugh for whom *he* wrote, because he was at that time deeply involved, emotionally, with a middle-aged policeman. But I asked him if he had any suggestions as to whom I might choose as a ghostly audience for my future works. He immediately suggested Rebecca. He had happened to see a short 'documentary' in which I had interviewed her for a concern called the London Topical Film Company, and he had formed the conclusion that we had 'struck sparks', whatever that may mean. She certainly struck sparks with me and sometimes, particularly in the early days, they scorched. She was among the many distinguished writers who reviewed my early novel *Patchwork*. Some of them treated it kindly. Not so Rebecca. The final sentence of her notice read: 'We are more than ever regretful, after studying this book, that corporal punishment has ceased to be fashionable at Oxford. It would probably have been Mr Nichols's salvation.'

After this salutary crack of the whip, I read everything of Rebecca's that I could lay hands on, and she gradually became a sort of invisible censor; when my pen was running away with me I would catch a vision of her face and see the mockery in her very beautiful eyes, and throw the manuscript into the wastepaper basket. There is an analogy here with Evelyn Waugh and the Catholic Church. Somebody once asked him how he could reconcile his outrageous behaviour with his Christian faith. 'I don't reconcile it,' he replied. 'My behaviour is outrageous. But without the Church it would have been worse.' Looking back on a life-time's work I realise how much of it is second-rate. Without Rebecca it would have been worse.

To attempt to assess this extraordinary woman in a few paragraphs would be not only impossible but impertinent. The only excuse I can claim for writing anything at all is the fortuitous authority of age; we are roughly of the same generation and our paths have often crossed. I can remember her beauty in the twenties. And even as I am writing there is the sound of scrumpled manuscript rustling into the wastepaper basket because Rebecca would certainly not approve of the manner in which I have attempted to convey this beauty. When she was lying on the rocks, soaking up the sun in the South of France, all the other bodies in the neighbourhood seemed to be painted out. Sometimes, recalling her, I have tried to put a name to the artist who might have immortalised her in those halcyon days, when the Mediterranean was a deeper, cleaner blue and the rocks a deeper richer red, when the fire in one's blood captured the fire of the sun. Cézanne might have tried but he would have made her all body and no brain. John at his best, in his Suggia period, might have brought her to life. One would have thought that she would have been pestered by artists all her life, because she is eminently paintable. She could have posed for Goya. But the only portrait of her that I have ever seen, by Nevinson, does her less than justice. It is an intellectual exercise, a cunning contrivance of planes and angles; the woman does not emerge from the pattern.

One cannot discuss Rebecca the woman and Rebecca the intellectual without referring to H. G. Wells. I have some knowledge of this stormy relationship but the matter is best left to posterity, when it will emerge as one of the most absorbing love stories of the century. All I would suggest, at the moment, is that Wells was a very lucky man and Rebecca was not so lucky a woman. One must remember that the whole romance was played out many years ago, long before the days of the so-called permissive society, and though Rebecca was a natural rebel, by nature avant garde, she was also, through her breeding and background, what might be described as a delicately nurtured female. There was a constant conflict between life and letters and love, involving many painful compromises and tedious deceptions. It would have been easy for her to drift onto the rocks. One cannot help remembering Wilde, who tried to evade the responsibility for his disasters by inventing an epigram to explain his folly. 'I put my genius into my life,' he said. 'I put only my talent into my works.' Rebecca put her genius not only into her life but into her works. But before they are worthily assessed some years will have passed, and a good deal of increasingly polluted water will have drifted under the bridges.

A last trivial memorandum which I shall not throw into the waste-basket. A few months ago, when I was in an extremity of pain and more than half in love with easeful death, Rebecca came down to see me, and after an hour she had persuaded me that perhaps it might be worthwhile going on for a little longer. Suicide —particularly if one sometimes writes detective stories—is an absorbing theme for contemplation. Shall it be pills? There are plenty in the cupboard upstairs. Shall it be with the aid of a revolver? But that would make a mess, and one does not like loud noises, and anyway one has not got a revolver, and would not know how to fire it, even if one had. Something to do with the car. Crashing it over a cliff? Or just sitting in it, and switching it on, and suffocating? I can see the garage from my study window, the doors are open, and welcoming.

Yes—suicide is an excellent subject for an author's consideration, when the plot of his life seems to be inextricably tangled, when he can think of no other way to end the story. Rebecca made me realise that perhaps there are other ways. Not through anything she said or did. But because of what she was.

When she left I found a little parcel on the hall table. It was a sort of 'get-well' present which, typically, she had forgotten to mention. Opening it I discovered three bottles of scent, though on this occasion the word 'perfume' might be permissible, because they came from Paris and were imprisoned in phials of the greatest elegance. Rebecca must have guessed that I had an unmasculine addiction to such essences, like Baudelaire, who once confessed that the fragrance of fleur-de-lys caused his nostrils to *onduler*. I took the bottles upstairs and savoured them, one by one. Slowly the precious liquids are running out, but I shall keep the bottles even when they are empty, because the perfume will linger on.

More than fifty years ago, after the aforesaid interview with the London Topical Film Company, I walked home with a song in my heart. The evening was drawing in, and the lights were coming on in Bond Street. The windows seemed to have a special sparkle and all the charming follies of this enchanted thoroughfare were made more alluring by the memory of the woman who had just come into my life. Pausing outside a scent shop I noticed a display of bottles of a scent which had just come on the market. It had been created, I believe, by Guerlain, and the gossip writers had announced that it was much in vogue with the Bright Young People. Well, I was a bright young person, and I had just made contact with one even brighter young person, so I went in and bought a bottle, though it cost a guinea, which in these days would be at least twenty pounds.

I can remember the scent to this day, with a Baudelaire clarity, an undulation of the nostrils. Even if I could not remember the scent I should remember the title. '*Suivez moi, jeune homme.*' It might have been Rebecca speaking.

CHAPTER XII

🌹🌹🌹🌹🌹🌹

CRY HAVOC

This ramshackle work has long ceased to have any shape. The beginning has got mixed up with the end and the middle is meandering all over the place. This would not matter so much if any sort of clear self-portrait were emerging. But it is not—at least, none that I care to recognise. The features so far portrayed on the canvas have formed themselves into an unattractive pattern in which arrogant lines of conceit conflict with drooping curves of self-pity.

Worst of all, there is no hint in the design of any strength of character, no continuing rhythm to indicate that the sitter was inspired by any higher purpose than the need for survival, in as comfortable circumstances as he could contrive. Were there no ideals at all? Was I really so spineless?

I think that I can answer that question in the negative. And I hope that the answer may not only bring the self-portrait more sharply to life but may also shed some light on the history of the period we are discussing.

If there is a single word which illuminates, more vividly than any other, the chasm dividing the thinking of the post-war generations of 1918 and 1944, it is the word 'pacifism'. My own Oxford Dictionary is dated 1962 and still carries the conventional definition —'the doctrine that it is desirable and possible to settle internation disputes by peaceful means', but the Oxford Dictionary does not always march with the times. This may be fortunate for the philologist but misleading for the historian. A truly contemporary definition would read 'Pacifism. (Obsolete). A mental aberration afflicting the intelligentsia of the younger generation in the decades immediately preceding the Second World War. Now confined to minor religious groups such as the Quakers, *q.v.*'

But even this would not be enough. Pacifism was a great deal more than an 'aberration', even more than a philosophy. It was a religion and a way of life, cutting through every barrier of class and political tradition, setting husband against wife and father against son.

I have been doing some elementary auto-analysis, trying to discover why I had this intense loathing of the physical horrors of war, which was the passion animating one of the few books of mine* which had a definite impact on the thinking of my generation. The obvious Freudian explanation would be that it stemmed from the hatred of my father. He, when he was sober, was an obscene parody of Colonel Blimp. Reclining in his armchair, throughout the four years of the first great carnage, he gained a vicarious sadistic satisfaction through the blood-sacrifices of the world's youth. One of his bitterest disappointments was that none of his own sons was ever slaughtered.

But the Freudian theory, like many of the themes which came from the sombre jungle of the Freudian brain, would have been superficial. I may have been my father's son but I was more than that. I had a mind of my own, and though it may sometimes have been spurred by hatred there were other times when it was inspired, perhaps creatively, by love.

Another obvious explanation, of a different nature, though we are still in Freudian territory, would be that I was scared, concerned for the safety of my own skin. I believe that this did in fact apply to some of the most outstanding pacifists of the period such as Kingsley Martin, the editor of *The New Statesman*, with whom I was constantly in contact. Lord Boothby, who is a shrewd judge of everybody's character but his own, once said to me: 'There's only

* *Cry Havoc*

one trouble about Kingsley. He's yellow. Oh yes he is, as yellow as a banana, and with about as much spine. And I'm sorry to see you in such company.'

However, I was not scared on my own account. I had no reason to be. I had been graded as unfit for military service in my teens, and it was unlikely that I should be called to battle in my thirties, even if I had been physically stronger which, to put it mildly, I was not. And yet this obsession remained, dictating my conduct and haunting my dreams.

The least honourable explanation of my obsession would be a claim that I was more 'sensitive' than my fellows, more keenly aware of the agonies that were approaching. This would be an intolerable excuse. I was no more 'sensitive' than many of my contemporaries, though perhaps I had a sharper perception of what history had in store.

One of those contemporaries was Noël Coward, who could scarcely be accused of insensitivity. This reminds me of a story. At the height of the furore which had been stirred up by *Cry Havoc* the League of Nations called a mass meeting at the Albert Hall, with the object of convincing the nation that the League held the key to peace and that only if we would be faithful to its lofty principles, all would be well. The chairman was an amiable idealist called Lord Robert Cecil, who wrote to ask me if I would wind up the debate. I replied in the negative. I was fed up with the League. As a reporter I had attended its sessions in Geneva and been sickened by what I had seen and heard—the political parasites of Europe mouthing meaningless generalities while the world was hurtling to destruction—parasites who were overpaid, overfed, deaf, dumb, and blind, except when they looked under their desks to relieve the boredom of the proceedings by the naughty pictures in *La Vie Parisienne*.

So I wrote back and said no, dear Lord Robert, I did not think that I would have anything useful to contribute. Then I tore up the letter and accepted. Perhaps after all there was something that I could say.

The Albert Hall meeting has earned a place as a footnote to

history which can still be studied; the proceedings were filmed, and are sometimes revived in reviews of the period. The arena was packed from floor to ceiling by a very youthful audience—the potential cannon-fodder of the war that was waiting in the wings. They had come for inspiration; they did not get it. All they got was a parade of platitudes, a misty compound of meaningless internationalism. The audience coughed and shuffled, the film crews began to pack up their kit.

I was the last speaker. I was supposed to sum up the proceedings with a few more platitudes. But I was very angry indeed and when I got to the microphone I knew how to pitch my voice so that the opening words, 'My lords, your excellencies, ladies and gentleman,' had the impact of an insult. And I knew how to stop the coughing and the shuffling with a single phrase. *This meeting has been too damned polite.* The coughing stopped, the film crews hastily switched on their lights again.

Then I let them have it. As I was speaking impromptu I cannot—fortunately for the reader—quote myself at length and I should be the last to claim that this outburst had the oratorical authority of a Chatham or a Burke. All I can remember is the final passage which began with the same bitter invocation to 'My lords, your excellencies, ladies and gentlemen'—in the accents of hatred.

'What we are seeking, no, what we are demanding, is peace. And by peace we mean peace at the price of honour. Peace at the price of Empire. Peace at the price of security. Peace at any price. Peace at any price at all.'

A few days after the Albert Hall episode the newsreels took up the story in cinemas all over the country, and I went along to Piccadilly to see myself on the screen. There was a long queue on the pavement and when I joined it I found myself standing behind Noël. There was some polite conversation in which Noël made all the best remarks. When we were nearing the box-office I asked Noël why he had come.

'To look at your performance.'

'Thank you. I hope you like it.'

'I shan't like it at all.' A very beady look. 'I have come to hiss.'

And hiss he did, in the middle of the front row.

But it was only a fleeting consolation that he hissed alone, and that his hisses were drowned in applause.

Not so long afterwards, Noël produced a play called *Cavalcade*, which held up the traffic in Drury Lane at about the same time that *Cry Havoc* was being chaffered in the secondhand bookstalls.

We both believed in what we had to say. But Noël always had a genius for backing the right horse.

Cry Havoc was yet another example of my perennial conflict between the sacred and the profane. The passion that animated it can without affectation be called spiritual. In my personal life, and in the life of my 'home', when I was able to visit it, I was longing for a time of quietness, for an end to discord, for a stop to cruelty, and this longing was reflected in my attitude to international affairs. But if I was to do anything about it, if I was to translate these emotions into practical politics, I had to go out into the world and fight, and sometimes I had to go into dark and dangerous places.

The most extraordinary aspect of it all and from the contemporary angle the most inexplicable, was the conviction that one could 'do anything about it'. What young man today, armed only with a pen, could be so deluded? Where have all the crusaders gone? To claim the accolade of 'crusader' may seem an empty boast, but it was not, for many of us were prepared to lay down our lives in the cause of peace. How otherwise is the historian to interpret such bizarre phenomena as the 'Peace Army', which thousands of young men including myself, pledged themselves to join, with the object of marching out to the battlefields in the event of war and standing passively between the opposing armies, holding white flags, under the delusion that they might thereby compel the opposing armies to hold their fire? The idea, of course, was ridiculous, and came to nothing, but the fact that it was ridiculous does not imply that it was contemptible. Crusaders must be prepared to look ridiculous, and usually do. A classic example of this was given by A. J. Cook, the miners' leader, during the depths of the pre-war depression. He was addressing a hostile meeting, trying to compel the audience to share his own indignation with the harsh realities of work at the coal-face, which in those days were grim indeed. He was getting no response. Suddenly he stopped speaking, and fell on his knees, and began to crawl round the stage, again and yet again. The audience was shamed into silence. People who witnessed this demonstration, which might have been embarrassing, have told me that it was more effective than the most lurid mob oratory.

Here I must tell a story which sharply illustrates the vital import-ance of the role which luck plays in one's life. When I read contem-porary autobiographies I often have the impression that the writers are seeing their lives in a faulty perspective; they lack the gift of stepping aside and studying themselves objectively, as though they were sitting in the stalls and watching a stranger tread the stage. The successes think they did it all themselves, the failures conclude that it is all their own fault. Both are wrong.

Quote. 'Cry Havoc *was one of the few books of mine which had a definite impact on the thinking of my generation.*' This is not the sort of sentence to make the reader jump out of bed to see if the postman has delivered the latest instalment, but if you are still with me, you may care to know that it was only by chance that the book came to be written at all.

Chance, on this occasion, presented itself in the shape of a powerful and poisonous critic called James Agate. To the American reader the name Agate will mean nothing. Very few critics, *per se*, achieve an international reputation. (How many British readers have ever heard of Alexander Woollcott or Heywood Broun whose most casual utterances, in the Broadway of fifty years ago, could light up the stars or send them crashing to oblivion?)

One would have thought that Agate would have been forgotten even in his own country, but he is still very much alive. His diaries are being published and republished and the latest issue (1976 edition) has been favourably reviewed.* He has been built up into a legend of almost Johnsonian proportions, though he would have

* *The Selective Ego: An Anthology of the Diaries of James Agate.*

preferred to be compared with Hazlitt. He was a stocky, horsey man, who attended first nights wearing a cape and carrying a long black cane. Year after year in the columns of *The Sunday Times* he danced like a butterfly and stung like a bee, though perhaps a hornet would be a more appropriate insect. Since he did me great damage and since I have always regarded the *de mortuis* philosophy as not only muddle-headed but dishonest, I may add that his private life was quite exceptionally scabrous and would have supplied Freud with some sensational footnotes. So much for Mr Agate, for the moment, but there is worse to come.

The reason for my abiding hatred of Agate after forty years is because he killed a play of mine stone dead. This is not merely the moan of an aged and disgruntled dramatist, it is an essential feature in this self-portrait which I am trying to paint. It was early in 1931 that my pacific passions began to come to the boil; I had to get them down on paper; but in what shape? The very idea of writing a 'documentary', such as *Cry Havoc* eventually turned out to be, filled me with alarm and despondency. It would involve an immense amount of research, at which I had never been very good and a great deal of journalistic drudgery, of which I was sick and tired. I was longing to get out of the journalistic rut, to create a work of art. I cherished the illusion that a work of art might have as much impact on history as any essay in propaganda, however sensational.

So I sat down and wrote a play called *Avalanche*.* I set the story in a Swiss chalet, the home of 'a famous dramatist' who was, in fact, based on Noël Coward. There were eight characters apart from 'Noël', including an international financier, an American poet, a society woman, an idealistic girl, and a young man-about-town. I locked these people up in a snow storm, cut them off from all contact with the world, got them to grips with one another, and then—over the radio, their only source of information—announced the outbreak of a European war. The announcement was of course

---

* *Failures:* Three plays by Beverley Nichols, with a Preface by The Author. Jonathan Cape Ltd, 1933.

a fake, contrived by the central character whose object was to study the reactions of his guests. The hoax succeeded beyond his wildest dreams, and beyond my own, because as I worked on them the characters leapt vividly to life, and what had begun as a slick theatrical device ended as a very powerful play. It was finished in ten days and a few weeks later I was taking curtain calls in Edinburgh, with a cheering audience, a brilliant cast, and all the financial backing that any aspiring dramatist could desire.

Now we return to the villain of the piece, Mr James Agate. On the day after the production of *Avalanche* he rang me up from London. A little bird, he said, had whispered to him that a play of mine had been produced in Edinburgh. He would very much like to come North and see it. Could I arrange for a room at an hotel? A quiet room in a discreet hotel? I got the message, and booked him a room in an hotel where the hall-porter asked no questions if distinguished dramatic critics arrived in the middle of the night with scruffy young persons picked up in Princes Street. I did not feel too proud of myself. But Agate was a power, *The Sunday Times* was a voice to be reckoned with, and anyway, the play was the thing.

I did not see Agate when he arrived in Edinburgh, but something evidently went badly wrong with his visit. It could not have been the play, which was receiving standing ovations. Perhaps he had had an unfortunate encounter with one of the scruffy young persons in Princes Street. Whatever the reason he left his hotel before breakfast. On the following week he devoted the whole of his column in *The Sunday Times* to an attack on *Avalanche* so venomous that the backers took flight, the cast was dismissed, and the play was killed, as far as the English-speaking world was concerned, though it was later produced in Vienna where it was hailed as a masterpiece. And the most damning feature of his review was his accusation that I had treated the theme of war with flippancy, mocking the horrors and making light of the lunacies. This was very hard to bear. However I did nothing about it. What could I do?

This story at last is reaching its climax. Shortly after returning to London I walked into the Garrick Club, picked up a copy of

Country Life and began to turn the pages. Suddenly I came upon a long article about *Avalanche* by George Warrington, a writer who was unknown to me. Mr Warrington, it seemed, had also been at the Edinburgh first-night, and his opinion of the play was very different from Mr Agate's. Indeed, he took Agate to task for the violence of his stricture. *Avalanche*, said Mr Warrington, had given him a lot to think about.

I finished this article with a sigh. If only George Warrington had been the critic of *The Sunday Times*! However the damage was done and it was too late to repair it. All the same, I thought that it would be courteous to thank Mr Warrington so I rang up *Country Life* and asked where he could be found.

There was some humming and hawing. Mr Warrington was not in the habit of giving interviews. I told *Country Life* that I did not want to 'interview' Mr Warrington, I only wished to thank him. More humming and hawing. Then *Country Life* came clean. There was no such person, they informed me, as Mr Warrington. 'George Warrington' was the mask concealing a far more distinguished journalist. His name? James Agate.

When I put down the receiver I was trembling with anger. I rang up *The Sunday Times* and made an immediate appointment with the editor. When I told him the story he sat up very sharply indeed. This, he said, was most unfortunate. For me, I suggested, it was more than unfortunate. Of course, of course, agreed the editor, but I must understand his own embarrassment. Agate had an exclusive contract with *The Sunday Times*. He had broken it. Moreover he had already been paid a year's advance of salary and had probably spent it. Most embarrassing. What did I feel should be done about it?

There was quite a lot that I might have done. I might indeed have ruined Agate's career. No critic could have survived the exposure of such blatant duplicity. But I am not a vindictive man and though revenge might have been sweet, it would not have brought *Avalanche* back to life. So I contented myself with writing him a little note. In it I made no reference to his review, but I hinted that I knew rather more about his private life than he would wish to be made public and that if he ever gave me any further trouble I would put the information in the hands of the police. I should of course have done no such thing, but I wanted to make him squirm, and squirm he did, for the next two years. When *Cry Havoc* was published I sent him a personally inscribed copy, asking him to review it and suggesting, in faintly menacing erms, that the review had better be good. He got the message. This is what he wrote, with the same crooked pen that had accused me of mocking the horrors of war:

I regard this book as of immense importance because it is the work not of a politician or a pedant, but of a playwright whose seriousness is a matter not of profession but of passion. It is a book wholly without hysteria and its author has used his wit and his keen sense of drama to enforce cogency and no more, etc. etc.

Yes, all this is 'shop', but in the story of any writer's life, 'shop' must play a leading part. And if it is rather squalid shop we must remember that Fleet Street has always been rather a squalid thoroughfare, although its gutters, in the time of which I am writing, did not stink so foully as they do today.

On with the crusade, back to the grindstone. If God was not going to allow me to change the world through the medium of the theatre, I should have to use the medium of the press. It would not be nearly so enjoyable, nor half as profitable, but I was not in this business for pleasure or for profit; I was in it for peace, and I still thought, stumbling and starry-eyed, that something could be done.

In this endeavour I was greatly helped by a lady called Dorothy Woodman. She was an intimate friend of Kingsley Martin, the editor of *The New Statesman*, and she spent her time in an office collecting facts about the armament industry which were explosive enough to blow up the world. The only trouble about Dorothy was that she lacked journalistic flair. She had a genius for turning a sensation into a sedative. If she had suddenly been given the exclusive information that New York had been entirely destroyed by an earthquake she would have told you about it in the same tone of voice that would have been used to tell you that she had discovered an outbreak of greenfly in Hampstead Garden Suburb. All the same, she was a highly intelligent woman, and a very brave one, for the forces against which she was pitting herself were among the most powerful in the world, and the most ruthless.

On the glass door of Dorothy's dusty office in Victoria Street were printed the words 'Union of Democratic Control'. This sounded impressive but it meant nothing at all until I came along, one afternoon in the Spring of 1932. I had been lunching with Noël Coward at the Ivy and though we were poles apart in our political convictions Noël was a kindly man and he was always ready to help a friend, even if he felt the friend was making a fool of himself. We talked a great deal about war and peace, very loudly and both at once. I wish I had a tape of the conversation which would have been an illuminating record of the clash of two young schools of thought. I can only remember Noël's summing up. Chinese eyes, a glass of *crême de menthe frappée* in the left hand, and a great deal of finger-wagging with the right. And his words: 'If you insist on carrying the white flag at least you should learn to carry it properly.' What was that supposed to mean? 'It is supposed to mean that you pacifists need a producer. All the world's a stage and you ought to think in terms of the theatre. What are you all doing, all over the world? Mumbling your lines and missing your cues. If you made *me* your producer there wouldn't be any bloody war.'

'Why not take us on?'

'Darling Beverley, it's not my sort of play.'

Armed with these instructions from the Master I took a taxi to Victoria Street and found Dorothy Woodman sitting in her dusty office in a dusty brown dress surrounded by quantities of dusty pamphlets. The first one she handed me bore the title 'The Secret International' and it was so discreetly presented that it might have been a travel brochure. By the time I had finished it my blood was boiling, so I excused myself and asked if I might take it home for further study, and perhaps we could lunch tomorrow. Of course, said Miss Woodman, not realising what she was letting herself in for. I was about to suggest the Ivy, but no—not in that dress; and

Noël might be there and he would not be impressed by my first recruit. So we fixed on Brown's Hotel.

When I got home I read the pamphlet again, came back to the boil, and sat down at my desk. First, I changed the title. Then I wrote:

THE BLOODY INTERNATIONAL
(DEATH LTD)

Then I wrote two more titles:

TO MAKE YOUR FLESH CREEP

And then . . .

THE MICROBES OF MARS

After which, I began to ring people up. H. G. Wells. Lord Beaverbrook. Aldous Huxley. The French Ambassador. Bernard Shaw. The Archbishop of Canterbury. (*Sic*) Some of these eminent persons I knew, some I did not; all of them—or their secretaries—seemed faintly puzzled by the urgency of my demand to see them. It was as though I were announcing a declaration of war. Well, I was, and that was how it all began.

The only person who did not seem puzzled was Shaw. A few weeks later, when I was beginning to feel intimidated by the magnitude of the task I had undertaken, he sent me a letter that was like a shot in the arm. A study of Dorothy's pamphlet had convinced me that the international armaments industry, behind the scenes, was playing a far greater part in the fomentation of war than was generally understood, particularly by the world's pacifists. Our eyes were on the wrong people. We were hissing Hitler and booing Mussolini and bewailing the ineptitude of our own leaders, and we were quite right to do so. But the dictators were only puppets and so were the men who tried to stand up to them. The real target must be the armament industry, in Europe and America, and somehow or other I had to get inside it and expose it for the horror which in those days it was. (And to some extent, though the scene has drastically changed, still is.) I drew up a rough plan of campaign and forwarded it to Dorothy who forwarded it to Shaw. He wrote:

Dear Beverley Nichols,
Dorothy Woodman tells me that you are doing an important piece of work and doing it very well. You will need all the encouragement you can get. Here is mine.

It will come as no surprise to you to learn that I have already said all that you seem to be trying to say, but it cannot be said too often. And though nobody listened to me they might conceivably listen to you.

I have marked a passage which seems particularly apposite. If you wish to quote it, please do so.

Yours sincerely,
Bernard Shaw.

With the letter he enclosed a typed extract from *Major Barbara*, and the passage he had marked was a speech by the character of the armament maker, to whom he had given the name of Undershaft.

The Government of your country? I am the Government of your country. Do you suppose that you and half a dozen amateurs like you, sitting in a row in that foolish gabble shop, govern Undershaft? No, my friend, you will do what pays us. You will make war when it suits you and keep peace when it doesn't. . . . When I want anything to keep my dividends up, you will discover that my want is a national need. When other people want something to keep my dividends down, you will call out the police and the military. And in return you shall have the support of my newspapers, and the delight of imagining that you are great statesmen.

With Shaw's permission I was eventually to use this quotation to conclude the fourth chapter of *Cry Havoc*, which was called 'Mystery at Le Creusot'. The title of this chapter is in itself a proof that I had taken Undershafts literally and was frenziedly trying to back them up with the force of facts. Le Creusot was the headquarters of the vast Schneider armament industry. The manner in which I wormed my way into this closely guarded citadel still makes dramatic reading but the drama had no last act; the citadel kept its secrets. My assault on the British armament firm of Vickers was equally unproductive and to me personally, very embarrassing. I passed through the gates of Vickers under false pretences, playing on my friendship with the managing director, who was unaware that I was arranging to stab him in the back. This was one of several occasions when I had to choose between playing the role of a gentleman and the role of a pacifist. The two roles were incompatible. I put aside all thoughts of behaving like a gentleman. In such a cause it was easier to play the cad. I accepted Vickers' hospitality, was received as an honoured guest, and got on with the stabbing.

By the time that the 'crusade' was nearing its end, when the storm clouds were sweeping more swiftly over Europe, I had completely lost any semblance of a sense of humour. Clinging desperately to the hope that a miracle was still possible I approached Ribbentrop, the German ambassador, and arranged with the Anglo-German Fellowship to entertain a group of Hitler Jugend at—of all places—the Garrick Club. I also rang up Ivor Novello, who was starring in *Henry the Fifth*, and got him to give me a box for a matinée. Ribbentrop was delighted; he was in bad odour with the British press and any gesture of co-operation was to be welcomed. So was Ivor, because the play was not doing very well, and this would be good publicity. So was I, because I cherished the illusion that this might be the occasion for building a frail bridge between one or two nations—the youth of Germany meeting in friendship with the youth of England, inspired by the spirit of Shakespeare. The idea was quite insane and the whole thing turned into a farce. The Hitler Jugend arrived at the Garrick and gave the Hitler salute, to the considerable astonishment of my fellow-members, some of whom seemed to think that war must already have broken out. I did not accompany the party to the theatre because I was beginning a nervous breakdown on a grand scale. Just before they took me off to the nursing home, which was a sort of expensive private lunatic asylum, Ivor rang up to tell me what a great success it had been. The Hitler Jugend had behaved impeccably. They were 'lambs' and extremely photogenic. And business was picking up.

CHAPTER XIII

MARKING TIME

I am one of those readers who needs guidelines and signposts, which is one of the reasons why I cannot get on with the novels of Proust. I never can be sure who is doing what or where or when or —most important of all—why. The art of autobiography, surely, should offer an author no excuses for such obscurity. But if one has lived to a considerable age, and met a vast number of entertaining people, one gets mixed up. If one has not kept diaries one cannot produce a tidy account of 'what one was doing or where or when'. The only thing one can be reasonably sure about is why one was doing it. I think that I can claim with assurance that my patterns of behaviour have been dictated by certain deeply held convictions that have guided me from my earliest youth. On the credit side, my conviction that . . .

1. *Cruelty, in some form or another, is the only sin.* Quite literally the *only* sin. There are endless degrees of misconduct and irregular behaviour, legal or illegal, but if no element of cruelty is involved, they cannot be classified as 'sin'.

2. I also believe that no man's opinions can be of much value unless he constantly submits them to the scrutiny of a higher Power who, for the sake of convenience, may be called God. Even if he decided that God does not exist, he must at least try, at some time in his life, to answer this ultimate question. Perhaps my own answers would have been clearer if I had been able to express them through music. Which brings me to my third conviction . . . 'on the credit side' . . .

3. *Music is man's nearest approach to God.*

George Orwell once wrote an extremely perceptive article about me to the effect that though much of what I have been saying over the years was worth saying my style of saying it was often more likely to antagonise than to convince.* He also said: 'You write too much. You should put down your pen for at least a year.' In this he was certainly correct. In the past sixty years I have written at least ten million words. All of them have been written by hand and if the script were put into a computer it would probably stretch from Land's End to John o'Groat's and would demand hundreds of gallons of ink.

Of those words approximately fifty per cent were written for love (or in anger), twenty per cent were written for laughter and the rest for money. Is there much difference? I think not.

As a boy at Marlborough I once went for a walk over the Wiltshire Downs with William Temple, the only Archbishop of Canterbury of the present century whose opinions still command respect outside their religious context. He used to come down every term and one of his duties was to go for a walk with a boy who had distinguished himself in the classroom or on the playing fields. I was chosen because of some essay I had written. As soon as we got into our stride the Archbishop began to talk about my future. What was I going to do? I could not very well tell him that I wanted to play Chopin so I told him that I thought I would be a writer. Whereupon he replied, firmly and unequivocally, 'In which case, Nichols, you must never forget that Shakespeare wrote for money.' It was years before I fully understood what he meant.

The heart of the matter is that there are a great many pleasanter ways of passing the time than sitting at a desk putting words on paper. Lying in the sun, picking flowers, talking idly in a café, making love, watching the clouds go by. Only in the case of a very rare spirit is the urge to create so overwhelming that he is compelled to put everything else aside. Authorship is a highly pro-

* *The Observer:* October 29th, 1944.

fessional affair—as professional as medicine or the law. Doctors and lawyers, however dedicated, do not work for love; an extra spur is needed; and in the great majority of cases the spur is economic. Shakespeare is not the only genius who wrote for money; Mozart is another. His miraculous output was only possible because he was as methodical as a chartered accountant, and sometimes, particularly in those pieces which were produced for court consumption, his music sounds as if it had been written by one.

Surveying my journalistic output over half a century I am astonished that I so seldom got into trouble. I was not a timorous journalist and I did not mince my words. I was the first journalist to print two words which are now in common currency, 'pregnant' and 'syphilis'. In my early days, no woman was ever 'pregnant', even if she was swollen out like a captive balloon; she was 'in a certain condition'. Nor had any man contracted syphilis, even if his nose was dropping off; he was suffering from 'a certain disease'. This was sickening hypocrisy, and it was also highly dangerous. There were two editorial confrontations in which I threatened to resign if the words were struck out of my copy. In each case I won.

There were only two occasions when I was nearly sued for libel. The first was in my capacity as dramatic critic for the *Sunday Dispatch*. I was beginning a bout of 'flu and before setting out for the theatre I fortified myself with several large whiskies and soda. The piece under review was Carol Kapek's *The Insect Play* which had arrived with a great flourish of trumpets. It was a symbolic drama in which all the players were cast in the roles of insects, of various shapes, sizes, and significance, who spouted at interminable length about nothing in particular. It was pretentious nonsense but that was no excuse for getting the insects mixed up in my notice. Staggering back to the office I wrote that the beetle had given a powerful performance but that the bumble-bee had fluffed its lines and that the ant had been inaudible. On the following Monday there was a great buzzing and hissing in the office. The bumble-bee, apparently, had not given a powerful performance at all, it had only made rude noises in the wings, whereas the ant had brought the house down. I had to write an abject apology to all concerned.

The other incident was more serious. I had written a book called *A Village in a Valley* which was the third volume in the trilogy of country books which had begun with *Down the Garden Path*. In order to convey the rural atmosphere of our village I bought a copy of the local newspaper. In those days newspapers of the English counties gave a unique picture of country life. Every flower-show was reported and every concert in the village halls and all the funerals, which were usually described as 'sorrowful assemblies'. There were discussions of sermons and news of crops, and dances in stately homes; even the advertisements were delightful with their country flavour; in them you could hear the whistle of the ploughboy and the homely noises of the farm-yard.

Reading this newspaper I suddenly came across a paragraph about a local lady that was almost too good to be true. Here are three sentences:

'One can truthfully say that Mrs Graham,* wife of Town Councillor E. W. Graham, is a "live-wire" in many ways, whether it be politics, social service, golf, hockey, or even the mundane things of ordinary life.'

As if this were not enough, the next paragraph began:

'Of Scotch extraction she revels in the fact that she played for Wales at hockey.'

There was more about her sporting activities, and finally . . .

'In the County Library, she has proved herself a tower of strength.'

Prose such as this was too precious to be wasted on a little country paper. A Scotch-extracted 'live-wire', with so many interests, revelling in her hockey, and proving a 'tower of strength', deserved a wider public. I gave her one. I changed her name, and also the name of the newspaper, and made various speculations as to what she looked like and the sort of activities in which she might have been involved. The whole thing was written in a spirit of the lightest comedy.

The scene now switches to New York, where I was beginning a coast-to-coast lecture tour. *A Village in a Valley* had been published

* This name is fictitious.

in England, Mrs 'Graham' had got hold of a copy, and she was not at all amused. Indeed she was in a flaming rage.

The Personal Column of *The Times* for Thursday, January 3rd, 1935, begins with the following item:

Apology. Mr Beverley Nichols, the author, and Jonathan Cape Ltd, the publishers, of *A Village in a Valley* wish to apologise for the insertion in this book of a derisive and libellous passage reflecting upon Mrs — (here followed the name of the lady and a description of her activities). To a lady enjoying the prominent and distinguished position which Mrs — does in local public life the derogatory and offensive comments which the passage contains, and which are without the slightest foundation, must have been extremely hurtful and aggravating. There is absolutely no justification for the aspersion cast upon Mrs —, and we trust that this Apology in conjunction with our offer to pay £100 to a local charity will be accepted by her as the expression of our sincere regret at the pain and annoyance which she has been caused.

'Mrs Graham' was the most expensive lady who ever came into my life, though in fact she did not come into my life at all. She existed only in my imagination.

As a result of this bizarre experience I took out an insurance policy with Lloyds to protect me in case I inadvertently libelled anybody again. It costs a hundred pounds a year, and as it has been in operation for forty years, and as I have not yet had occasion to use it, Lloyds have done pretty well out of it.

So have I, for at least it has given me peace of mind.

There is not much that anybody can teach me about popular journalism; I have been crime reporter, magazine editor, war correspondent, gossip writer, dramatic critic, music critic, political commentator, financial expert, horticultural mentor, and even sartorial adviser.

Perhaps the most striking proof of virtuosity was provided by a series under a feminine signature, on the trials and tribulations of having a baby. A great many female journalists were having babies all over the place but none of them seemed able to describe their experiences in convincing prose. They made them sound as boring as if they were writing a recipe for chicken casserole. They did not seem to understand the agonies and the ecstasies of it all. I was poignantly aware of these things, so I sat down and had a baby in six vivid instalments. The series was a great success, and was widely quoted in maternity magazines.

One of the lessons of this long and arduous conduct of the journalist's craft is that what one has to say is often less important than the platform from which one says it.

Somerset Maugham was bitterly aware of this. It was not till he was well advanced into middle-age that the critics began to take him seriously. Why? Because his earlier stories were published in popular American magazines. They were the best stories he ever wrote and if they had come out in *The New Statesman* there would have been plenty of earnest young critics to acclaim them. As it was, for many years he was dismissed as a lightweight. Once, at the Villa Mauresque, he gave a literary cocktail party in honour of a group of international journalists. As they drifted about the terrace, weaving their way around him, paying him homage, sipping their dry Martinis—(which on these occasions were apt to be watered)—the air resounded with a persistent hiss, a single adulatory phrase . . . *'Cher Maître.'* Over and over again. *'Cher Maître.'* Dear Master. The phrase with which one would have greeted Balzac.

When they had gone Willie sat down, sipped a dry Martini (unwatered) and mimicked them. *'Cher Maître!'* And then . . . 'They never called me that when I was being published in *Cosmopolitan.'*

Another phrase of Willie's which I remember. It concerned Max Beerbohm, for whom he had no great fondness.

'If M . . . m . . . ax had been here, they would have called him *"Cher Maître"* too. But *not* if his little pieces had appeared in *Tit-Bits.'*

'M . . . m . . . ax,' he continued, 'knew nothing about t-t-tits. And his b-b-bits were not as good as all that. But he never made the mistake of speaking from the wrong p-platform. Never forget that, Beverley. Never get onto the wrong p-platform.'

Shortly later I was to leap onto the wrong platform, feet foremost, and stay on it for fourteen frustrating years.

* * *

But first there was an interlude of a few weeks in which I did what I wanted.

Melba died, and in doing so made it possible for me to write a novel about her. This sounds callous but we had been estranged for years, and I could not pretend to be heartbroken. She had severed relations at a stroke, without a word of explanation; at one moment we were devoted friends, at the next she was an implacable enemy. It is a very strange story. At the time when I was moving into my first London house in Westminster she was also moving into her own very grand house in Mansfield Street, and since she had far too much furniture, and I had almost none, she gave me everything for which she could not find room. I would not have asked even for the loan of a teapot, but she decided that she wanted to furnish my little house, and furnish it she did, in a manner which I could not possibly have afforded—exquisite pieces of Louis Seize, Queen Anne chairs for the dining-room, and even a couple of Guardi gouaches to hang over the mantelpiece. She was a constant visitor and always a welcome one except that every time she arrived all the furniture had to be moved into different positions and all the pictures rehung.

This went on for a long time until one day a furniture van arrived at the front door, from which stepped two large footmen with a note addressed to my factotum, Mr Gaskin. It was curt and very much to the point. It requested Mr Gaskin to give the footmen every assistance in removing the furniture which Dame Nellie Melba had lent to Mr Beverley Nichols as she needed it herself. There followed a long and detailed list of everything that she had given me, down to the last coffee-spoon. This enraged Mr Gaskin as it meant stripping almost the entire house, and he had grown very fond of it. It also astonished myself, possibly because I was in bed with 'flu and not thinking very clearly.

I rang up Mansfield Street and asked to speak to Melba. There must be some mistake. I was told that 'Her Ladyship was in Paris.' (She always used the title of 'Ladyship' because she was a 'Dame', and all dames can legally call themselves 'ladies' though few of them claim the right to do so. If anybody had ever called Sybil

Thorndike 'm'lady' she would have had a fit.) When would Her Ladyship be back? Nobody knew, and who was it speaking please? Mr Beverley Nichols? Down went the receiver, and stayed there.

The footmen were admitted, and clattered up and down the stairs, bearing everything away. The only thing they did not remove was the bed, which she had also given me—a very beautiful bed decorated with a golden Regency swan. I refused to get out of it; after all I had 'flu. I sent it back the following week, and I sincerely hope that it broke its neck in transit.

Reflecting on the Melba saga, which greatly influenced my life, profoundly affecting my whole relationship with women in the years that lay ahead, I have come to believe that its abrupt and mysterious conclusion was the result of my love—the word may now be used without embarrassing either of us—for another woman, who has not yet appeared in these pages. Her name was Betty Hicks. She was the daughter of Seymour Hicks, who was one of the greatest actors of the era, a master of comedy and tragedy alike, though his genius was not fully recognised till shortly before his death.

I first met Betty on the voyage to Australia, when I was sailing out to take up my appointment in the services of the Queen of Song. Seymour and his enchanting wife Ellaline Terris were on the same boat, and we all became a family party. Betty was then a beautiful young lady of eighteen, with a magnolia skin, who might have posed for Rossetti. It is impossible to analyse the elements of the attractions which draw young men to young women, but I think that—*au fond*—what brought us together was the saving grace of laughter. We could, and did, and still do laugh at the same things, even when there was no obvious reason for doing so. We would lean over the ship's railings, lulled by the soft rhythm of the waves, watching the crimson sunsets which grew ever more spectacular as we headed south, and we would begin to smile and then to laugh, simply at the beauty of it all, because beauty often carries laughter in its wake.

Melba was waiting for me at the dock when the ship arrived at Melbourne, and as soon as her beady eye lit on Betty, who was walking by my side, I realised that we were in for trouble. Who was that girl? The daughter of Seymour Hicks? Of course. What a great artist he was! And his wife, Ellaline Terris—so attractive! We must ask them both to dinner. And Betty too, I suggested. Was that the girl's name? Oh yes, she must be included. I must send the invitations at once. And what a pity it was that Betty bore so little resemblance to her mother.

They came to dinner about a week later, and it was a disaster. There were a number of the Australian aristocracy, in dinner jackets. Seymour, out of courtesy to his hostess, wore a white tie. I can still remember his bewitching smile as he bent over Melba's hand and murmured . . . 'I seem to be somewhat overdressed.' Ellaline, as always, sailed through it all, looking delicious, quite unaware of any social tensions. Darling Ellaline had the priceless gift of being able to ignore the tensions of life, whether they were social, financial, or emotional—and as Seymour's wife she had more than her share of these. But she was able to smile them all away. Perhaps this was why she lived to be over a hundred, and died with so serene a smile.

But for poor Betty the evening was a great ordeal. Melba terrified her. She made her feel gauche and ill at ease. When she left she was near to tears. As Melba began, so she continued. My attempts to meet her were cunningly frustrated, and on the solitary occasion when I accepted an invitation to stay the night with the Hicks family there was such a pyrotechnic display of temperament on my return that the experiment was never repeated.

If I were to tell the whole story of Melba, Betty, and myself in the years that lay ahead, it would involve me in so many convolutions, queries, and speculations that I should end up by writing a quite different sort of book, and it is impossible to speculate on the sort of book it would be. If it had been a romance I think it would have been a happy one. It began with laughter, and thanks to Betty, her bravery and her understanding, the laughter has lingered on, even through the times that called for tears.

Here comes one of those periods which, in every man's life, he wishes that he could live again. In order to write the novel about

Melba, to which I gave the title of *Evensong*, I had to escape at all costs—escape from the social idiocies and the Evelyn Waugh parties and all the journalistic hackery and lock myself up in a quiet room. So I got into the car and motored down to Roquebrune, which perches on a cliff between Monte Carlo and Menton.

At Roquebrune there was a little hotel on the cliff called the Maison Imbert, and I decided to take the entire hotel. This was not as opulent as it sounds, because it was a tiny place, with only five bedrooms, sparsely furnished. But there was a large terrace overlooking a pebbly beach, and I wanted to lie alone on the terrace, thinking my beautiful thoughts about Melba, and turning them into a story. I worked very quickly; 2,500 words a day. Piles of manuscript mounted up on the sun-drenched desk. Then, out of the blue—and the whole of life was drenched in blue, Mediterranean blue—old Madame Imbert came tottering down the stone steps, knocked at the door, and handed me a telegram. It was from my agent, informing me that a paper called *The Sunday Chronicle* wanted me to write a weekly page at a fee of £1000 a year. My reply was short and sweet. OVER MY DEAD BODY. Two days later there was another telegram. *The Chronicle* had upped its offer to £1500 a year. This gave me to think for a moment, but only for a moment. I cabled back my regrets. I had *Evensong* to write. A week passed. Then came the final offer. £2000 a year. Generous expenses. Complete freedom to write what I wanted, when, and where I chose, with no editorial interference, and I need not begin until *Evensong* was finished.

Whereupon I cabled—'Accept.'

Of all the many mistakes in my life, this was the one that I most bitterly regret. It was a despicable decision. And yet, searching around for excuses, I can understand why I made it. £2000 a year in those days was equivalent to at least £10,000 a year today. And I could write what I wanted to. I should look forward to that. There were a great many things that needed to be said in the modern world and *The Chronicle* would give me a platform from which to say them.

But it was the wrong platform.

CHAPTER XIV

❀❀❀❀❀

THE HACK

We have now reached the year 1932, when I sprang onto the platform of *The Sunday Chronicle*, with full star-billing from the powerful propaganda machinery of the Kemsley Press. Once again I turn to *Who's Who* to check a few dates. To my surprise I find that *The Chronicle* is not even mentioned. A number of other achievements are recorded for this year—the publication of *Evensong* as a novel and its production as a play, the production of another play called *When the Crash Comes* which was inspired and indeed suggested by Orwell. It was very much Orwell's cup of tea, for it dealt with the tribulations of an English upper-class family after a Communist take-over. I began it the day after he had told me that I ought to stop writing for a year, and finished it ten days later. Some of it is exciting but the last act is a sentimental mess.

Still in 1932, I am reminded that I published a collection of dialogues called *For Adults Only*. There were innocuous little conversations, of a satirical nature, between a little girl and her mother. They would have passed unnoticed if a copy had not fallen into the hands of Tallulah Bankhead, who learned some of them by heart and recited them at parties, with obscene interpolation. Last but by no means least, in 1932 I published *Down the Garden Path*.

This should have been enough for a single year.

But *Who's Who* does not even mention *The Sunday Chronicle*. Why did I cut out all reference to it in my little dossier of achievement? *The Chronicle* was a highly respectable paper, edited by a journalistic genius called Jimmy Drawbell, who chose Monica Dickens as my feminine counterpart, and a host of other distinguished contributors, such as A. J. Cronin. There was nothing to be ashamed of, appearing in such company, particularly as our joint efforts set the circulation soaring.

So why did I discreetly push it into the background? Here again the answer must lie in some form of character deficiency. *The Chronicle* was an old-established working-class newspaper, of radical political persuasions, with its grass-roots in Manchester. I had not a working-class background nor a working-class mentality. It would have been ridiculous to try to write with a Manchester accent. And yet, this was what I was supposed to do, while at the same time I was expected to play the role of the smart young man-about-town. One week I had to be seen in white tie and tails, escorting beautiful young females to glamorous first-nights, and the next week I had to put on an old suit in order to be hail-fellow-well-met with a crowd of workers at a trade-union 'social evening'. I was expected to lie on the rocks at Cap d'Antibes, exchanging confidences with millionaires, and then to rush back to the London docks, in order to spend the day with a shipload of bargees, shipping crates across the Thames. And always I had to be photographed, in a variety of costumes, looking decorative and, of course, smiling. In those years there was no difficulty in looking decorative, but the smiles were often hard to contrive.

My most anguished ordeals were concerned with social dilemmas. I had no right to regard myself as a member of 'society', either by birth, or money, or inclination. But I was presentable, I knew the drill, I had a 'talent to amuse', I was attracted by elegance, and as such I often found myself, very happily, in the company of people who were greatly my social superiors. And I was expected to write about them.

But how could one write about them? One would never have been asked to their houses again. It would have been different if I had been Valentine Castlerosse, who for many years was my chief competitor in Fleet Street as a 'columnist'. Apart from the fact that Castlerosse was a Viscount, to whom most social gaffes are forgiven, he was also a vulgarian, who was incapable of realising when he had committed a gaffe at all. I detested Castlerosse. He was gross and lecherous and fundamentally dishonest. One of the abiding mysteries of Fleet Street is the affection that Lord Beaverbrook had for him. Beaverbrook had a natural chivalry towards women and an almost ferocious affection for the British Empire. He was scrupulously honest in his personal and political dealings. And yet, he stuck to Castlerosse through thick and thin, paying his debts, giving him a free hand in his most powerful paper to propound a philosophy which, one would have thought, was the antithesis of everything that Beaverbrook held dear.

My first meeting with Valentine Castlerosse was unpropitious. I happened to be a member of the St James's Club which was one of the most 'exclusive' clubs in Europe. When I first walked into the elegant hall Castlerosse asked me to join him in a game of back-gammon, and as I liked the game and played it rather well, I sat down and he started to rattle the dice. I was under the impression that we were playing for sixpence a point, and when the score reached 256 I offered him a double, which he refused, with a snort of indignation. He staggered out of his chair, in a drunken rage, muttering something about 'chalking it up'. I was surprised because 256 sixpences is less than £8, and though this was quite a large enough sum for me, Castlerosse had the reputation of being a reckless gambler. From a distance I saw him glaring at me. He was talking to the Duke of Westminster and I heard him say 'Who let *that* one in here?' A few moments later Westminster was chuckling over my shoulder. 'You don't seem to be very popular with Valentine. How much did he lose?'

'Nearly £8.'

'But the score says 256.'

'Well . . . that means £7-16.'

'I see.' He gave me a friendly smile. 'I suppose he didn't inform you that in this club we usually play for £1 a point?'

This was typical of the late Viscount Castlerosse. He had seen me wandering in, rather lost, looking around for somebody to speak to, and he had decided that I was a lamb ripe for the fleecing.

His little ruse misfired, and he lost £256 which, needless to say, he never paid.

In the Northern outskirts of London there is a drab, featureless suburb called Colindale, which contains one of the most remarkable research institutes in the world, the British Newspaper Library, which was originally a section of the British Museum. It contains the largest collection of newspapers ever gathered together under one roof from the first historical edition of *The Times* to the latest contemporary edition of *The Evening News*. I have recently been a frequent visitor, travelling on the District Railway disguised—not very heavily—as an 'Elderly Person'.

My reason for these visits has been to study *The Sunday Chronicle* from 1932 till some time after 1947, or whenever it was that I stopped writing for the wretched thing. It is a daunting task and I have small hope of completing it. But to any historian of imagination, who had the courage to extend his researches to such an unacademic source, the diary of Page Two by Beverley Nichols might provide some valuable material for the story of our times.

The first weekly instalment of the diary appeared, after a loud preliminary flourish of Fleet Street trumpets, on September 25th, 1932, and was to continue almost uninterrupted, through peace and war, for nearly fifteen years.

It began, quite literally, with a bang. I quote:

The Great North Road sparkled into the distance. There was no traffic in sight, barring the lorry a little way in front of me. I sounded the horn and put my foot on the accelerator.

And then, according to the police reporter's notebook, I said to my companion: 'My God, we're for it!' I don't remember saying that.

All I remember is a black shape that suddenly loomed across the road as the lorry swerved, an appalling crash as we hit it, a sound of tearing boards and splintering glass, and a roar from the engine as though it were going to explode.

I pulled out the switch. The roar stopped. There was a strange silence. A piece of metal fell to the road, tinkling inanely. The sun shone through the broken glass. The road still gleamed ahead. I was still on this earth.

This happened a few days ago. And my first thought as I got out a little shakily on to the hard road was: 'This will be a grand beginning for my new diary.'

This is good journalism, but it tells a sad story. If a man's first instinct, after coming within a few inches of death, is to reach for a reporter's notebook in order to translate the episode into a newspaper paragraph, it is a proof that he is already hooked as a journalist and is abandoning his career as a writer. With shaky fingers I scribbled a detailed account of the accident, laying particular emphasis on the difficulty of giving evidence in a state of shock. I described the colour of the flowers by the road side, the behaviour of the sightseers who had appeared from nowhere, and then, turning from my own little car to the giant lorry that had been responsible for it all I suddenly hit upon a theme. My own car was a smart little Renault, which I had bought for the sole reason that it was such a pretty shade of pale blue. Through the shattered windows I could see the stout figure of my passenger, who was adjusting his monocle with a look of pained surprise. Then across the road, I noted the two lorry drivers. They were also in a state of shock, but the police were being much rougher with them than they had been with me. Maybe rightly, because they really had been very naughty boys. But the police had called me 'sir', and they had bowed to my passenger as though he were a peer of the realm. Whereas, they were treating the lorry drivers as though they were the scum of the earth.

So there was the theme, handed to me on a plate, through a chance turn of the wheel of fate. Class distinction. The injustice of the social system. I was not thinking very clearly, because I was beginning to feel faint. But I was a good enough journalist to fumble for a pen and scrawl these words in my notebook, and the fact that they are quite ludicrous will not prevent me from reprinting them . . .

How damnably unjust all this is! The lore of accent, the deceit of dress, the illusion of dirt or cleanliness . . . these mean nothing. I see only eyes that are bright or dull, lips that have a lilt or a sag, hear only a voice that has music or a voice that is flat. I am utterly 'equalitarian'.

After which I passed out. Not a moment too soon, the reader will agree.

I could not possibly write such rubbish today. In a modern version of the same situation it would be the lorry drivers who would be the dominatory figures, receiving the courtesies of the police. My accent would tell against me, and my passenger's monocle would be damning evidence. Apart from all this, I have never been and never could be 'equalitarian'. Such a philosophy is morally indefensible, aesthetically meaningless, and socially disastrous, as we have learned to our cost.

And yet, in this very first article, I nailed my colours, as it were, to the mast of the 'workers'. What was I doing, writing this stuff? The answer, of course, is prostituting myself. I was not enjoying it; and it was to lead to a lot of trouble.

CHAPTER XV

❀❀❀❀❀

FULL STEAM AHEAD

Meanwhile in the next few weeks everything and everybody was grist to my mill. Page Two was a smash hit and *The Sunday Chronicle* put on 100,000 circulation. But as I sit in the Newspaper Library, reading these faded headlines, I shudder.

Here are some typical examples:

ELINOR GLYN DOES NOT LIE ON TIGER SKINS

GENE TUNNEY IS A MASS OF NERVES

THE ATTORNEY GENERAL CONFESSES TO ME

WHY DID THE LORD CHAMBERLAIN TELL ME TO WATCH MY STEP?

I AM BANNED BY RUSSIA

ORANGES AND INFINITY

H. G. WELLS ADMITS THAT HE HAS AROUSED A HORNETS' NEST

IS LADY ASTOR A LIAR?

THE MAN WHO LOVES LUMBAGO

FEAR DRIVES A NOVELIST FROM HER BATH

I DANCED WITH A QUEEN

WITH OSBERT SITWELL IN TRAFALGAR SQUARE

I AM PSYCHO-ANALYSED IN BUDAPEST

WHY OLIVER BALDWIN WILL NEVER HAVE A SON

P. G. WODEHOUSE IS SO FOND OF SNAKES

CHILDREN OF THE RITZ

THE MAN WHO BOTTLED ECTOPLASM

THE CRUEL PRESENT THAT I WOULD GIVE MY WIFE

I AM SNUBBED BY BLOOMSBURY

*   *   *

Et cetera, et cetera. All this in the space of a few weeks. And there are thirteen years to come.

I sit in the Newspaper Library, rubbing my eyes. Is it conceivable that I—or indeed any human being of normal stamina—could possibly keep this sort of thing up, week after week, year after year, without losing his sanity, and giving up all hope of doing any serious work? The answer is 'yes'. I did not lose my sanity and I did quite a lot of serious work, which has lasted rather longer than some of the productions of the Bloomsbury clique, which were currently hailed as masterpieces.

Today, the bloom seems to be fading from Bloomsbury, and none too soon, though Virginia Woolf will linger on as a tragic ghost, long after her works have been put on their proper shelf, which was not so high as she imagines.

Here I must tell a Bloomsbury story, which would have been unprintable forty years ago. In the twenties—the days of the curly hair and the schoolboy complexion—I attended a party given by George Rylands at King's College, Cambridge. Mr Rylands should need no introduction; he was, and is, a brilliant scholar; he has been—and is—a creative figure in the history of the English theatre. He was an exceptionally decorative young man, a physical and intellectual asset to his college, and I was so flattered to be invited to one of his parties that I lost my head and got drunk.

In a state of stupor I was carried into Mr Ryland's bedroom, and promptly fell asleep. The party continued next door, but I slept on, until I was contorted by a nightmare. I dreamt that I had fallen into an ants' nest, and that the ants were crawling all over my face. As indeed they were. The ants were provided by Mr Lytton Strachey's beard. He had noticed my exit from the party, and had evidently been allured by the hair and the complexion, and had decided that this was the time to pounce. And pounce he did, precipitating himself upon me, murmuring phrases of adoration. I have never been attracted by beards, even if they are attached to the chins of eminent authors, and Mr Lytton Strachey swiftly found himself flat on the floor. After this episode there was, as they say, a coolness between us. He joined the gang of the detractors, inventing little

194

snippets of malice. One of these is mentioned in Michael Holroyd's monumental work about him. I was staying in Rome with Lord Berners, accompanied by an amusing young American; Lytton Strachey came to lunch; and went away hissing, because neither I nor my friend showed him much attention. He was a great hisser, but after all I had given him something to hiss about. He became a regular reader of *The Chronicle*, and used to cut out Page Two and recite some of the more lurid passages at Bloomsbury parties.

What Strachey did not realise was that under even the most ridiculous captions there was a story which might have been enlarged into a comedy of manners or a tragedy of our times. Consider Elinor Glyn and her tiger skins. I think that I was the first man to draw a picture of Elinor Glyn as she really was—an ageing woman desperately trying to preserve an image of eroticism and at the same time behaving as what she would have called an 'English gentlewoman'. It was when she was acting in this latter capacity that I first saw her at a Hollywood party. William Randolph Hearst had engaged her, at a large salary, to act as a sort of chaperone to his mistress, Marion Davies. It was an impossible assignment, because Marion Davies was an incurable alcoholic, who resented Elinor Glyn and lost no opportunity of humiliating her. At this particular party she waltzed round Elinor Glyn, hiccuping a parody of the famous jingle . . .

> Would you care to sin
> With Elinor Glyn
> On a tiger skin
> Or would you prefer to err
> On another sort of fur?

Then . . . after a swig out of the bottle . . . she pointed to poor Elinor. 'Come along gentlemen! Or would you like to sink? On a bed of mink?'

The author of *Three Weeks* rose above this scabrous performance. She had to; she needed the money.

I could not of course print such a story then, but I could, and did, pay tribute to Elinor Glyn as a gallant and extremely courageous human being. Admittedly there were occasions when she seemed to invite ridicule. I once went to interview her in New York when she was living at the top of the Ritz Tower, and the whole setting was so modern and she was still looking so beautiful—though the legendary auburn hair now came out of a bottle—that I thought it was time to update her, so I boldly mentioned the word 'sex' which, oddly enough, she seldom discussed in the abstract. The effect was electric. She threw back her head and proclaimed ... 'Sex has never touched the hem of my garment!' The phrase was immortal, and as I walked home I tried to put it in its historical context. It did not belong to the twenties or the thirties, nor even to the Edwardians; it was firmly late Victorian. I did not print her words but I wrote a 'profile' which showed her in a new light. She sent me, as a reward, a bouquet of tiger lilies.

Flick over another page. *The Man Who Loves Lumbago*. What on earth can that mean? I read on, and discover myself dining with Arnold Bennett at the Savoy.

We had been joined by a publisher who had given us some absorbing details about the publishing profession. When he had gone Arnold said . . . 'That's always the way. Get a man on his profession and he's invariably exciting. Now over there . . .' and he waved his cigar in the direction of an old gentleman sitting at a nearby table, 'is a man who is amazingly interesting if you get him on his profession, but he'll send you to sleep if he talks about anything else.'

'And what is his profession?'

'Being ill. He's got lumbago now, and he's loving it. If anyone were to cure him of it he'd die of a broken heart.'

To continue: *Why Did The Lord Chamberlain Tell Me To Watch My Step?* And why a few weeks later am I asking, *Is Lady Astor A Liar?* Oddly enough, these two questions were interrelated.

I had always been interested in Christian Science. Was Mary Baker Eddy an inspired prophet or was she a phoney? Today, I feel that she was something of both, but when I was writing Page Two I was prepared to be 'swept in'.

Two people helped me to make up my mind. One of them was

Mrs Winston Churchill, as she then was. Once at a dinner party she held me spellbound with an account of a book she had been reading about Mrs Eddy. It was a vitriolic piece of debunking by an American author called Arthur Dakin, and it was she who suggested that I should write a play about her. She had just seen *Evensong* and she said, 'You've written a play about one prima donna . . . here's your chance to write another. Mary Baker Eddy was first and foremost a prima donna.' Then she added, with a twinkle . . . 'But please don't tell Lady Astor that I said so.' (Lady Astor was a passionate adherent.)

I got hold of the book and realised that here was a tremendous theme for a great star. The final curtain would be sensational, showing Mrs Eddy—who had always denied the 'reality' of disease—as a sick old lady, near to death, with rouged cheeks and a faltering voice, giving her last gallant interview to the American press. I began to make notes.

Then, by chance, I ran into Victor Cazalet, and told him what I proposed to do. Victor was a young member of Parliament, one of the rising hopes of the Tory party, who was to meet his death in the aeroplane accident which was carrying him on a secret mission. The Cazalets were immensely rich, with a vast house in Grosvenor Square and an equally imposing mansion in Kent. Although they were not averse to entertaining royalty they were genuine, warm-hearted people and they were all sincere Christian Scientists. 'Before you write your play,' said Victor, 'come with me to one of our services.' He took me to the Ninth Church of Christian Science in Marsham Street. I was greatly impressed. I quote again from Page Two:

A woman in black got up in the front row. I whispered to Victor Cazalet. 'Isn't that Lady Astor?' He nodded.

Lady Astor told the most astonishing story of one of her boys who had congestion of the lungs when he was at school. They wired for her to come to him, and she wired back that she was coming at once, and that on no account were they to send for a doctor until she had seen him.

When she arrived the authorities said to her: 'We haven't sent for a doctor, but the boy's in a desperate way.'

Lady Astor was not frightened. Even when she went up to the boy, and saw his state ('there was terror in his eyes') she was not frightened. She had this all-conquering faith in her religion.

She took him away, at once. They said it was madness for him to travel at all. Within an incredibly short time, she had cured her son completely. How? I imagine by telling him that there was nothing wrong with him.

Well? What are we to say about it? Are we to call Lady Astor a liar, too? I do not suppose she would mind if we did—she has taken many hard knocks in her time, and she has always come up smiling.

When I took the copy to Jimmy Drawbell he grinned. 'This is grand stuff. Mrs Churchill, Lady Astor, the Cazalets. There'll be no trouble with the illustrations.'

'I thought you didn't want me to write about God.'

'I didn't. But *your* God seems to move in very superior circles.'

After this I felt ready to write the play. But before putting pen to paper I thought I had better go and discuss the matter with Lord Cromer, the Lord Chamberlain, who would have to censor the play before it was licenced for production.

With the greatest courtesy he turned me down.

'But I haven't even written the thing yet.'

'You don't have to. From what you have told me you couldn't have chosen a subject which would be more difficult for any Lord Chamberlain to licence. One of the objects of my office is to prevent the appearance on the stage of anything that is likely to cause real pain and stress in the minds of any considerable body of people. I think your play would do that, don't you?'

I walked away feeling sad and frustrated, and if, at that moment, anybody had asked me to sign a petition for the total abolition of all dramatic censorship, I should have signed it. Today, I am not so sure. I have seen so much filth bubbling over the world's stages that I am beginning to wonder if it is not time that somebody were authorised to put a lid on the sewers that run through all men's minds.

A few days after the publication of the paragraph about Lady Astor I was summoned to lunch at Cliveden. So much has been written about Nancy Astor and the 'Cliveden Set' that I will not write much more. In Christopher Sykes' outstanding biography* she emerges as a woman of infinite charm and generosity, with boundless courage and a keen appreciation of the political problems of the day. She was certainly generous—and she does not seem to have known the meaning of fear. But Sykes was bewitched by her, as were so many other men; his picture is inspired by the same adoration as emerges in Sargent's masterly portrait. He seems to have fallen on his knees while he painted it, which may account for the curious foreshortening of the figure. He made her tall; she was in fact diminutive. He also presents her in a most elegant dress, which suggests that he must have designed the costume himself, for she had no dress sense whatever. She gave the impression that she had bought her clothes, in a great hurry, at a supermarket.

Cliveden struck me as a house of the dead. The immediate effect was of a luxury hotel. It reeked of money but it had no feeling of welcome. And though every room brimmed with flowers they were arranged with less taste than the bouquets in the foyer of the Savoy.

Nor was there any warmth in the greetings of our hostess. There were about twenty of us and as she strode into the room she waved her hand towards the drinks tray. This was an item that I had not expected. It was loaded with every conceivable variety of alcoholic refreshment, from vodka to Pimm's Number One.

'If you want to poison yourself,' she announced in strident tones, 'you know where it is.'

Then, without a pause, she made straight for me. 'Why do you write for that rag?'

'Didn't you like what I said?'

'What you said was excellent. But *The Chronicle* isn't a gentleman's paper.'

There were a lot of replies to that comment, but I let it go.

Although I was among the least important of her guests she put me on her right. That is one of the points in Nancy Astor's favour; she was never a stickler for the rules of social *placement*. But if I were

---

* *Nancy* by Christopher Sykes: Collins, 1972.

writing the article today there would have to be drastic revisions. In *The Chronicle* I had suggested that she was not a liar. She was in fact a ruthless liar, particularly where her religion was concerned. The most striking proof of this was provided by her daughter, Phyllis, who was involved in a serious accident when hunting with the Pytchley. Nancy arrived on the scene with a Christian Science practitioner, convinced that the whole affair was an 'error of mortal mind', and could safely be left to the spiritual guidance of Mary Baker Eddy. While her daughter lay in agony she argued and prevaricated, and it was only after twelve vital hours had been wasted that she finally agreed that she should have proper medical attention. Three eminent specialists were summoned and arrived just in time to avert disaster. And yet, when discussing the incident, Nancy later denied that any 'orthodox' doctors had been consulted at all. No radiologists, no orthopaedic surgeon? Certainly not. Nobody.

During lunch, I was subjected to an endless torrent of Christian Science propaganda. This was brought to an abrupt conclusion by her son Bobbie who leant across the table and said in a loud voice, apropos of nothing, and addressing the table at large ... 'Darling, isn't it rather cold for the time of year?'

'So what?'

'If you're so anxious to convince Beverley that all our physical sensations are illusions there's one very simple way of doing it ...'

'Such as?'

'Turn off the central heating.'

She retorted, 'Bobbie, you're drunk.' After which, conversation became general, and soon I made my escape.

Bobbie was one of the crosses in Nancy's life, and her relationship with him shows her at her best. Although he was an attractive and amusing man his life-style inevitably led to troubles which need not be recalled; the scandals of yesterday are merely the indiscretions of today. In the present climate of opinion, charm and money are adequate excuses for any irregularity of behaviour. Bobbie had more than his share of charm but he also had more than his share of irregularity. Many women in Nancy's position would have kept him in the background; instead she pushed him forward, and he was constantly in attendance. Her only reproaches, which were delivered in public, concerned his drinking habits.

Nancy was reluctant to release a possible convert and after the Cliveden luncheon I was invited to St James's Square. But I made no effort to cultivate the friendship, if such it can be called. I was impatient with the incessant propaganda, and the sheer silliness of the opinions which she expressed so raucously. And yet, nobody writing a serious study of Christian Science can ignore the career of Nancy Astor. She sums up, in a single dynamic figure, the whole philosophy in all its bewildering contradictions—its weakness and its strength, its madness and its sanity, its denial of the world's reality coupled with its bland acceptance of the world's most glittering prizes.

I am beginning to feel slightly dizzy. Even the short list of headlines from Page Two, in the brief space of a few weeks, makes me wonder how I managed to get it all in. For example: *I Am Psycho-Analysed In Budapest*. Was I? And why? And how? The last time I tried to get to Budapest, a few years ago, the ambassador warned me off, with the suggestion that I might end up behind the Iron Curtain. Yet, in those days, one could waltz off to this enchanting capital, and live like a prince on a few pounds a week, with no questions asked.

I went to Budapest to stay with two attractive young American women who were living together under the firm impression that they were lesbians, when they were in fact nothing of the sort. All that was the matter with them was that they both had too much money, and had both married cads. They had retreated to Budapest to be psycho-analysed, at enormous expense. But they were getting a little bored with it, and decided that I might cheer them up.

This was obviously grist to the Page Two mill, so I went to Budapest, and—judging from the flagons of Tokay that were consumed every night—we all cheered each other up. I immediately fell in love with the city. The women were the most elegant in Europe, and though the blue Danube proved to be a vivid shade of grey, there must have been some elixir in the water, because after bathing in it one could dance all night.

After a few days my two friends decided that I too must be

psycho-analysed. They were really trying very hard to be lesbians—so much so that they had even adopted boys' names; one was 'Robbie' and the other was 'Ned'. But they were getting bored with lying on their backs three times a week at fifty dollars an hour trying to think up complexes, and they decided that I must share the burden, and go along to consult Professor Plonk. (Not his real name, but something very like it.)

So I went along. I could not publish a verbatim account of the ensuing analysis, which started in the gutter and stayed there. It was sex, sex all the way, some of it so ludicrous that I had difficulty in preventing myself from laughing. The Professor discovered instincts and impulses in me which I had never dreamed of. The climax came when the hour was up.

'It's all quite simple,' said the Professor. 'You may relax. You are quite normal.'

'It didn't sound very normal to me.'

'Oh, but yes. Quite typical. You see,'—and here he wagged his finger in my face—*'you are in love with your father.'*

This was really too much. 'It may interest you to know that I have tried to murder him.'

He nodded. 'Quite so. Just as I thought.' He opened the door and called to his secretary. 'Will you please tell the Countess that I am ready for her?' Whereupon he waved me out.

The readers of Page Two got a very modified account of this episode.

But it had some effect. It made 'Robbie' and 'Ned' laugh, and it persuaded them to give up their visits to the Professor. A year later they married men who were both convinced that they were homosexuals. This did not prevent them from producing large families who were strictly reared in the conventions of the American way of life.

For a time I obeyed Drawbell's injunction to keep God off Page Two, if only to appease the art department, who were constantly demanding names—names of people who were in the news, preferably women. Whether they were in the news for any good reason was apparently a matter of minor importance. Shortly after the Budapest episode I found myself in Norway, staying with the Baron Wedel-Jahrlsberg who was Norwegian ambassador to Paris. He lived in a palace which was somewhat larger than the royal palace, and in his will he left it to the Crown Prince, so that it is now the official residence of the royal family. This was undoubtedly 'le high life' and I greatly enjoyed it, particularly the food, because the Baron had the best chef in Europe. The best item on the menus was the fruit, because the month was September when in Scandinavia the fruit surpasses any fruit in the world. The gooseberries were the size of tangerines, with the most exquisite fragrance.

When I got back to Drawbell he demanded, 'Any news from Norway?'

I told him about the gooseberries.

'That's a hell of an illustration! Gooseberries! Didn't you meet anybody? Didn't you go anywhere?'

I mentioned that we had dined with the royal family.

'Why didn't you say so before? Did you talk to them?'

'Well, I danced with the Queen.'

He stared at me in despair. 'When will you ever learn any sense of news values? You dance with a queen and all you can talk of is gooseberries!' He lifted the telephone. 'Get me all the pictures we have of the Queen of Norway.'

We sat in silence, glowering at each other. It was not for me to warn Jimmy that the Queen, though great fun, was not what one calls photogenic. She was very tiny and she reminded me of an agitated shrimp. Nor had the dance been a romantic interlude; after a few turns round the floor she had broken off with a charming laugh. 'Mr Beverley Nichols, you talk very much better than you dance. We will sit the next one out.'

When the pictures came down from the art department Jimmy stared at them with increasing distaste. 'We can't possibly use any of these. But we have to keep that caption ... *I Danced With A Queen.*' Pause. Then, with marked irony ... 'Are there any *other* queens you've danced with?'

'Of course.'

'Such as?'

'I once trod on Queen Mary at a charity ball.'

'I'm asking for pictures.'

'Well—Queen Marie of Rumania.'

On to the telephone again. 'All the pictures we have of Queen Marie of Rumania.'

Page Two, that week, was dominated by a large picture of Marie of Rumania, who was hardly mentioned in the copy. Nor was the Queen of Norway. The gooseberries were not mentioned at all. I still think that the Manchester housewife might have been more interested in the gooseberries. But this was 1932, when Fleet Street was a hive of snobbery. It still is, but the social standards have been downgraded to fit the requirements of the Welfare State.

We are still only half way through the list. The mention of Gene Tunney reminds me that all this gadding about included numerous visits to America, because the interview was set on the terrace of one of the great hotels in Miami. He was carrying a Russian novel under his arm and anybody less like the conventional picture of a boxer I have never seen. The conversation was almost exclusively about 'nerves', which was fortunate, because if he had talked about his exploits in the ring I should have been at a loss. He said: 'People laugh at me because I always read Bernard Shaw before a fight. But a Shaw preface with its cool logic is a grand preparation for any struggle—mental or physical.' The Tunney interview was published on the same page as the 'confession' of the Attorney General, who was a charming man called Sir William Jowitt. When one compares him with the present holder of that distinguished office one is inclined to sigh for the past.

I Am Banned By Russia, strangely enough, ended up as pure comedy. I was quite sincere in my wish to go to Russia; I still had a few lingering illusions about the brotherhood of man, and—here God pops up again—I was foolish enough to think that I might find somebody in Russia who would give me a factual comment on the Marxian thesis that 'religion is the opium of the people'. (As it happens this well-known shocker, in its context, was not so far from the truth.)

But, as I was saying, it ended up as pure comedy. After weeks of shuttling about between the Consulate and the Embassy, in which nobody seemed to know his way about, even to the lavatory, I was back in the Consulate in a room plastered with photographs of naked young men, gazing in apparent ecstasy, at rows of very large chimneys. I found myself facing the head of the Russian propaganda machine. He was dressed in deep black and was sunk in gloom. He stared at me with obvious distaste and then said:

'Why do you want to go to R-r-russia?'

I could have told him the truth, if he had been a human being. I could have told him that in spite of my Page Two dossier, which was spread before him, I was still a pacifist, and that I still remembered my Tennyson, with his pathetic vision of the Parliament of Man, the Federation of World. But you cannot communicate with robots, particularly when you have been kept waiting so long that you want to go to the lavatory. So I kept it short. When he asked me if I had written any books, I scribbled a few titles and pushed them across the desk.

'Any more?'

By now I was nearly bursting.

'Several more.'

'You will give me please the titles?'

I snatched back the paper and added: *Three Weeks, The Eternal City, Wuthering Heights.* I never got my visa.

We will skip the titles referring to H. G. Wells and Osbert Sitwell; we will also skip *Oranges And Infinity* and *The Man Who Bottled Ectoplasm* because they are both connected with my preoccupation with the Almighty, and caused the usual complaints in the art department. But I should like to mention the Wodehouse piece, if only to recall the funniest remark he ever made. We had gone to the Zoo together to see the snakes, for whom he seemed to cherish a curious affection, and we found ourselves standing outside the monkey house. We were surrounded by a group of schoolgirls, who were in the charge of a very prim-faced mistress. Suddenly from the background emerged an enormous mandrill, which stalked up to the bars of the cage, turned its back, and presented its spectacular behind to the prim-faced lady. Even for a mandrill it was an exceptional behind, scarlet and purple and orange, and it embarrassed the lady, who began to direct the attention of her charges towards the Smaller Cat House. But not before Wodehouse, in ringing tones, had observed ... 'That monkey seems to be wearing its club colours in the wrong place.'

Only one caption remains ... *Children Of The Ritz*. This was the title of a number from Noël Coward's revue *Words and Music*. It is interesting as one of the few examples of the fact that Noël, although he always refused to be drawn into any sort of theological discussion, had a very strong moral sense. I feel partly responsible for this number, because I gave Noël the title for it. We were lunching at the Ritz together and Barbara Hutton was sitting at the next table. Her finger nails were tipped with mother-of-pearl, and she was waving them about in front of a dish of quails. I drew Noël's attention to this phenomenon.

'Good God,' he exclaimed. 'And yet she still has the face of a child.'

'Cue for song,' I murmured. 'Children of the Ritz.' The second verse of Noël's number begins ...

Children of the Ritz
Sleek and civilised
Frightfully surprised
We know just how we want our quails done
And then we go and have our nails done.

It sounds, and is very trivial, but under Noël's direction it emerged as a brilliant piece of theatre and a pointed commentary on the contemporary scene.

That will be enough of Page Two, even though we have covered only a few months of it, and it was to carry on for thirteen years. Earlier in this chapter I wondered how any man could lead such a life and keep his sanity, and I claimed that I *had* kept it, at least for a while. Perhaps it is time to explain how I managed to do so.

CHAPTER XVI

🌹🌹🌹🌹🌹🌹

THE GARDENER

If I am remembered at all, in the years to come, I would wish it to be as a gardener; and if there is indeed such a person as the Recording Angel I believe that he might give me credit not only for the gardens that I have created but the gardens that I have helped to bring into being.

The man who plants trees is performing an act of pure virtue. He is creating choirs for the songs of innumerable birds and orchestras through which the winds may play an infinity of music. He is giving shelter to a multitude of humble creatures and providing canvas on which Nature may paint her fairest pictures. He is enriching the earth and bringing the hills nearer to the heavens; without arrogance he might claim that he is playing the part of God. Indeed he might claim that he is playing it rather better.

My first garden, as we have seen, was born in the elevator of a luxurious Chicago hotel during the last hectic hours of the First World War. It was here that chance threw me into the arms of a stout middle-aged woman called Emily Borie Ryerson who immediately became a friend for life. Emily had a brother called John Borie, who owned an enchanting Tudor cottage in the sleepy village of Glatton in the county of Huntingdonshire and when, a few years later, he died, I bought it from Emily for a ridiculously low price.* Borie was a passionate Anglophile and he was buried

* As I wished to keep some privacy I altered the name of Glatton to 'Allways'. Not long after the publication of *Down the Garden Path* the postal authorities were obliged to accept this as an authentic address, although it was never on the map.

in the local churchyard. He lay under a slab of grey marble, on which Emily had chosen the words by which she wished him to be remembered. 'Here lies John Borie . . . An American who loved England.'

'Allways' was the only place on this earth where I have known true happiness, and this must obviously have been reflected in the book where I recorded it.

But what is happiness? The question has a thousand answers, some of them unexpected. To the man who has known intense physical agony, when the tortures are so intense that no drugs will assuage them, happiness is quite simply the absence of pain, to which the logical solution is death. I have known the craving for this sort of happiness all too well. This is of course an extreme example; even so, I believe that all happiness is in some way or other the fulfilment of a longing to escape, and that this escape can best be achieved in a garden.

Here I must remind the reader that in spite of the superficial glitter of the years I have been recalling my public life had a very dark background, the pattern of which was designed and dominated by John Nichols Esquire, my father. He was always there, waiting in the wings. As far as John Nichols Esquire was concerned, he did not exist, on any of the innumerable printed pages that I was churning out for public consumption. But he existed all too vividly in reality.

A quick flash shot, to illustrate this damnable dilemma. I am going to a first-night, in white tie and tails. I call at our 'home' to give my mother a bunch of flowers. There is a body at the bottom of the stairs, with blood over its unshaven chin. Thank God, the doctor is there, and a male nurse. I cannot stay, because the curtain will be up in half an hour. I leave the flowers, I give her a kiss, I get back into the taxi. Twenty minutes later I am in the foyer, being photographed with Marlene Dietrich. It makes a nice picture, which will brighten up next Sunday's article.

What has this got to do with gardening? Everything. 'Allways' was my refuge, my escape from hell. And the garden itself was primarily created as a place in which to hide. It was this need for a hiding-place which dictated the entire design and even the nature of the flowers and shrubs that I planted.

Thus, when I arrived my first action was to ignore the formal little plot which John Borie had planted, to walk out into the surrounding fields with a bundle of bamboo sticks, and to start digging holes. As each hole was finished I rammed in a bamboo stick to mark the site of a tree which would form part of the green rampart which was to shield my private world, to keep out the ghosts. I had seven acres of barren clay to deal with, so I used a great many bamboo sticks, and wrote out hundreds of labels and involved myself in a very considerable expenditure. Being a complete amateur, knowing nothing of the subtle relationship between soils and plants, the mysteries of the wind and the rain and the sunlight and the shadow, I made innumerable mistakes. But I was a quick learner and I had the gift of 'green fingers', which is not an old wives' tale but a scientific fact. Most of all, I had this passionate need for a hiding-place.

Those long, lonely interludes in my seven barren acres, tramping up and down through the frozen grass, plunging the spade, almost at random, into the sullen and reluctant soil, were the happiest that life has ever given me. For I was not only building a fortress against fear; I was creating—so I imagined—an enchanted forest. A plunge of a spade, a thrust of a bamboo stick, a tying-on of a label with numbed fingers, and suddenly, as though in a dream, the tree stood before me, laden with blossom, and from a far distance came the scents of summer.

That was the first stage.

Again, what has this to do with the creation of a 'garden?' Again I repeat 'everything'. Still ignoring the garden proper, which was pretty enough in itself in a picture-postcard fashion, I continued to set it aside, making straight for the open fields, which were now sprouting with a forest of bamboo sticks. It was not till I had prepared my protective rampart that I could indulge myself in the delight of artistic creation. The nature of this delight was purely musical. I saw those seven acres as an opportunity for musical composition, as though it were a blank page of manuscript on which no notes had yet been written. There are endless analogies between the creation of a garden and a piece of music, and if I were a millionaire and at least forty years younger I can imagine no more delectable occupation than the creation of gardens inspired by the music of the great composers. There would be a Mozart garden, preferably in the outskirts of Salzburg, planned as formally as a classical sonata in three movements. There would be a Beethoven garden, high up in the Harz Mountains, with giant oaks and in the far distance the faint roar of a great river. Every composer has a garden which echoes his genius and some of the gardens would need little artifice for Nature has already designed them. In every English woodland you can hear the music of Delius; all you would need to do is to contrive avenues through the trees, through which the music might sing more sweetly.

The third reason for beginning the garden with a wood, spending all those days tramping up and down the barren acres, was because it was only in the shelter of a wood that I could indulge my passion for winter flowers. This was really how it all began.

It was all quite unexpected. Here I was, in my first garden, aflame with excitement, surrounded by catalogues of seeds and trees and shrubs, offering all the rainbow allurements of Spring and Summer and Autumn. And I swept them all aside and stepped, in imagination, into the heart of Winter. I spurned the gold of April, the crimson of the June roses, the scarlet flush of the October maples, and headed straight for December. Why? At first I did not understand; neither to myself nor to anybody else could I explain this irresistible inclination. It was not until I put it down in writing that the mystery began to solve itself.

Here is a passage from *Down the Garden Path* which goes to the heart of the matter:

This passion for winter flowers has its roots deep, deep within me. I have a horror of endings, of farewells, of every sort of death. The inevitable curve of Nature, which rises so gallantly and falls so ignominiously, is to me a loathsome shape. I want the curve to rise perpetually. I want the rocket, which is life, to soar to measureless heights. I shudder at its fall, and gain no consolation that in falling it breaks into trembling stars of acid green and liquid gold. I can hear only the thump of the stick in some sordid back yard. The silly thump of a silly stick. The end of life. What does it matter that a moment ago the tint of night was spangled with green and gold? It is gone now. The colour is but gas, a feeble poison, dissipated. Only the stick remains.

I believe that my love for winter flowers has its secret in this neurosis. I want my garden to *go on*. I cannot bear to think of it as a place that may be tenanted only in the easy months. I will not have it draped with Nature's dust-sheets.

That was written nearly fifty years ago, but it is so penetrating a fragment of auto-analysis that I shall let it stand, though if I were to attempt to write it again today the prose would no doubt be severely pruned. The supply of purple ink available to elderly authors must be strictly rationed for it is pumped from their own hearts.

It was not long before 'Allways' began to echo to the laughter of my friends—most of them young men who, like myself, still had their way to make in the world. None of us had much money and few, as yet, were celebrities, but we were all convinced that riches and fame were just around the corner. There must have been some magic about the place because as soon as my guests had groped their way through the hall, bumping their heads against the low beams, and stepped into the peace and perfume of the garden, they seemed to relax and show themselves in their true colours. One of my first visitors was John Gielgud. He arrived on an evening of acute international tension, when the skies of Europe were dark with the thunder-clouds of war, and we were sitting round in a state of unaccustomed gloom, wondering what was going to happen to us all, whether we should be able to finish our books or our poems or our paintings or our music, or whether we were all going to be swept up in the approaching holocaust. 'If you're all so worried about what's going to happen,' said John, 'why don't you turn on the radio?' 'There isn't one,' I said. 'That,' replied John, 'is excellent news, because I shall be able to listen to myself talking. . . .' And talk he did, brilliantly, till the small hours of the morning—not about Hitler or Mussolini or any of the other ogres who were haunting us, but about the theatre, which was all he knew about or thought important in this distracted world.

On the following morning I rose early, to get the papers from the village post office. But I found that John had forestalled me. He was sitting in the music room, surrounded by scattered copies of the Sunday papers, whose headlines were double-decked with disaster. Ultimatums, troop movements, diplomatic scurryings, mobilisations. His face was dark.

'What in heaven's name has happened?' I demanded.

His face grew darker. But he had not noticed the headlines. He was scanning the theatrical pages.

'The worst,' he proclaimed in sepulchral tones. 'Gladys has got the most appalling notices. And so has the play.' He strode to the window and stared out. 'I don't know what the world is coming to.'

Among the most constant visitors was Rex Whistler, whose exquisite drawings were to give to my little book, and to its two successors, a very special *cachet*. When he first saw the garden he shook his head. 'This is not at all my cup of tea.'

I felt desolated. 'But why? Don't you think it's one of the prettiest cottages you ever saw?'

'That's the trouble,' he sighed. 'It's the Tudor cottage to end all Tudor cottages. Roses, sweet-briars, even honeysuckle round the porch. Not me at all. I'm only good at stately homes. With long avenues and lakes in the distance and balustrades and cherubs holding heraldic arms over the roof.'

'You won't find anything like that here.'

He picked up a watering-can. 'What could I do with a thing like that?'

I had a moment's inspiration. 'You could give it to a cherub. And by his side you could draw another cherub with a spade.'

His eye lit up. 'So I could.' Out came his pencil and within five minutes he had completed a drawing of a cherub with a spade and another cherub with a watering-can. It was printed, without any alteration, as the introduction to Chapter One. It was one of the happiest examples of collaboration that there can ever have been between an author and an artist.

'Allways' was a place where people seemed to shed their inhibitions and to reveal their true personalities as soon as they stepped into the garden. As a result there were constant surprises. One of these was provided by Hugh Walpole, who was among my first visitors. He was then at the height of his influence in the literary world, not only because of his own novels, but because of his tireless intrigues in every aspect of the literary roundabout, which were eventually rewarded with a knighthood. He never lost an opportunity to cultivate the friendship of those who might forward his progress, to join the right club, to be photographed at the right first-nights; and he was very active in his attendance at the memorial services of eminent literary persons, especially if he had contrived to be the author chosen to deliver the memorial address, which he did with great skill, drawing tears from the eyes of the distinguished audience and thereby attracting to his own person some of the glory of the dear departed.

So when Hugh came, I was prepared to entertain a hardened cynic. Instead I found an endearing sentimentalist. He had been driven down in a large Daimler, chauffeured by an immense middle-aged ex-policeman whom he introduced as 'Harold'. I had arranged with my housekeeper that he should sleep in one of the two 'spare' bedrooms, and that he should have his dinner in the kitchen. But Hugh had not been in the cottage for five minutes before he drew me into a quiet corner of the garden, to make an alternative suggestion.

'So kind of you,' he murmured, 'to give Harold such a comfortable room. But would you mind if he moved in with me? And if we could all dine together?'

'But of course, Hugh.'

'And perhaps, after dinner, we could play Hearts?'

'Play what?'

'It's a card game. Very simple. Harold loves it. I will teach it to you.'

So we all dined together, on the terrace, to the scent of wall-flowers. I cannot say that the conversation went with a swing, but the game of Hearts was a great success and went on till the small hours. When the two of them stumbled up the little staircase, I knew that the evening had been a success. For one of them, at least, it had been an evening of romance.

'Allways', indeed, seemed designed for romance, and there were several occasions when young couples, as though bewitched, fell in love as soon as they stepped into the garden. When this happened I let them use the cottage for their honeymoon. One of these couples was the Duke and Duchess of Leinster. I met Rafaelle Leinster soon after her arrival in London from America. The quality that most attracted me to her was her innocence, her touching conviction that life was a fairy tale. When she met Leinster, the premier Duke of Ireland, and when he fell in love with her, it all seemed part of the fairy tale. He had an abundance of charm, but unfortunately he had very little else, for he had squandered his inheritance and mortgaged his estates. This did not deter Rafaelle in the least. To suggest that the Dukedom had nothing to do with it would be untrue, but she did not marry him because she wanted to be a duchess, she married him because she was in love and because . . . well, duchesses fit into fairy tales. So she transformed him into a fairy figure, and when I suggested that 'Allways' might be a fitting setting for their honeymoon, she was enraptured, and immediately transformed the cottage, in her imagination, into a fairy palace.

The fairy tale did not last for long. The plot went awry and the music turned to discord. The marriage was dissolved. But the little girl from Brooklyn took it on the chin; the fairy-tale duchess behaved as a duchess in her own right, she held her head high, and there is still laughter in her eyes.

As for Leinster, he drifted slowly downhill. Once, in New York, I saw his arrival chronicled in the *Herald Tribune*, and rang him up to see if I could help in any way because I knew that he was down on his luck. To my surprise, he asked me to a dinner party at the

Ritz. 'A birthday party,' he explained, 'but I shall be providing the presents, so don't worry.' It was the oddest birthday I have ever attended, consisting of about a hundred guests, and I soon realised that it was in fact a publicity stunt for a firm of watch-makers. At the end of dinner we were all given very expensive gold wrist-watches by the man who was paying the bill. It was supposed to be a perpetual motion watch that never had to be wound up. It was set for midnight, when the party broke up. When I returned to my hotel I noticed that the hands still marked the hour of midnight, and there they stayed however violently one shook it. I eventually gave it to the bell-boy.

I last saw him in the South of France. He had remarried and was running a sort of boarding-house de luxe. Once again, he asked me to dinner and once again the experience was embarrassing, because the 'guests', to say the least of it, were rather second-rate.

When I left he glanced at my wrist, which was unadorned. 'You're not wearing my watch,' he said, reproachfully. 'Don't tell me that it stopped? It was supposed to go on for ever.'

'No. It didn't stop.'

'Then why?'

'It never stopped,' I said, 'because it never started.'

It was not till I was falling asleep at my hotel that I realised how aptly this comment reflected those far off days of his honeymoon, when he was leading Rafaelle down the garden path at 'Allways', playing the role of prince in the fairy story which she had created. The fairy story was finished all too soon. But it did not stop; it never really started.

CHAPTER XVII

🌹🌹🌹🌹🌹🌹

THE MACHINE
BREAKS DOWN

In spite of the impact which *Down the Garden Path* made on my life
and on my fortunes, its very success carried the seeds of destruction.
Who's Who reminds me that it was published in 1932; the sequel—
A Thatched Roof—in 1933; the final volume—*A Village in a Valley*—
in 1934. All of them were immediate bestsellers; as a result my
secret hiding-place began to be invaded by the outside world and
long before the little wood had grown high enough to serve as the
protective barrier which I craved, people were beginning to peer
through the hedge. There were even occasional charabanc parties,
loaded with females who looked suspiciously like Manchester
housewives, eager to discover if I bore any resemblance to the
handsome young gentleman who was regularly presented to them,
week after week, on Page Two. This was flattering in its way. I
remembered how Lord Tennyson had complained to Meredith that
he was constantly irritated by the hordes of admirers who came to
catch a glimpse of him over the garden wall. To which Meredith
replied, 'You'd be much more irritated if nobody came at all.'

All the same, I was disturbed by these intrusions. I was trying to
make something beautiful and I needed total privacy, if only for a
few days at a time. Creating a garden is like making music: the least
distraction is apt to destroy the melodic line. I have written so
much about the making and marring of gardens that I will resist
the temptation to ramble on at length; but it is perhaps interesting
to note that as soon as I had dealt with the all-important problem
of the protective wood, I knew, when I came to make the garden

proper, precisely what I wanted. And what I wanted was water. So the first task was to dig a pond.

This, as I now realise, was yet another variation on the theme which has so often been explored on these pages—the eternal confrontation of the sacred with the profane. Later I was to write ... 'A garden without water, even if it is only a pocket-handkerchief of a lily pond, is a garden without a soul. For, like a mirror in a room, water gives to the garden a fourth dimension, capturing a glimpse of the heavens and bringing them down to earth.' I have felt this more and more strongly with every garden I have ever made for myself, and have tried to impress the lesson on the owners of the gardens that I have made for other people, but few of them get the message. They remain blind to the magic of the mirror.

But it was all too much. The making of one pond led to the making of another, and as the wood grew I bought more land to make sure that my refuge was protected. The expenses mounted at an alarming rate, the whole place swarmed with workmen, while the courtyard overflowed with bundles of bushes and stacks of trees waiting to be put into the ground. And I could seldom be at hand to supervise the planting. Almost before I arrived I had to rush away again.

Nor could I relax when I had returned to London. I used to lie awake at night, and instead of sleeping I wandered distraught down the paths of the garden where I was longing to live and eventually to die—the garden which I was being forced to neglect through the folly of my own way of life. There were a hundred and one tasks that needed to be done, week after week throughout the seasons, if this precious plot were to be saved from reverting to the jungle. There were trees to be staked, and there was nobody there to stake them, for my gardener and his wife had suddenly departed after a domestic storm, leaving 'Allways', for all practical purposes, untenanted. There were brambles to be cut back, orchards to be scythed, roses to be pruned, creepers to be tied back to the walls from which the winter winds had wrenched them. I longed to get out of bed there and then, and motor through the darkness up the Great North Road, and make breakfast in the empty kitchen while the dawn was breaking, and hurry out to the tool-shed to throw myself into this rescue work. That would have been true happiness, and that might perhaps have proved—at least to my own satisfaction—that there was one role in life which I could play with total integrity—the role of Adam.

But it was not to be, because always, tomorrow, I was lunching with a film star at the Savoy or speaking at a literary luncheon on the trends of the modern novel, of which I knew little and cared less.

I knew that the end was near when I went to the cottage for the last time and said goodbye to my dog. His name was Whoops, and he had been given to me by Lady Cunard when he was a puppy. He was a most endearing mongrel, the result of the unexpected union between her poodle and the black chow who used to sit on the steps of the Chinese embassy opposite her house in Grosvenor Square. I loved him very much, and he loved me, but he was pining because of my constant absences. My companion on this melancholy occasion was a very old friend, Geoffrey Harmsworth, who later proved to be one of the most brilliant members of the empire founded by his uncle, Lord Northcliffe. Geoffrey realised that there was something wrong with Whoops; he also realised that there was something wrong, very wrong, with me. He had a large house in the country, he adored dogs, and he had fallen in love with Whoops at first sight. 'Would you like me to take him when you are away?' Yes, I said, I would. 'When?' As calmly as possible I said, 'As soon as you can.'

'You mean tomorrow?'

'No. Tonight. No, now. For God's sake, now.'

We stared at each other in silence. There was a great deal that might have been said, but we did not say it. Then I looked down at Whoops. He was gazing up at me with an expression of puzzlement in his big brown eyes. From time to time he glanced at the open window, and his tail began to wag, for he was waiting to be taken for his walk. Then his tail stopped wagging, and he lay down quietly, with his head on his paws, and a long deep sigh. He knew, I think, that this was the end.

Geoffrey took him away that night. As I watched his car turning the corner of the lane, a chapter of my life was closing. But not for Whoops, who was to live happily for another fifteen years.

I did not sleep that night for the greatest ordeal still lay ahead. I had to say goodbye to the garden.

It was a translucent morning in early May. As I stepped through the door I heard the chimes from the clock in the old church. They struck six times, sweet and tremulous, on the note of A flat. With a twinge of bitterness I realised that I still had perfect pitch—and a lot of good it had done me! I walked down the path and entered the wood. By now there were several hundred trees, and I knew every one of them, every twist and turn of every branch; I could have walked through them blindfold. They stood there in the morning silence, and I had the uncanny feeling that they were watching me, that they knew what was happening, that they were aware that I was deserting them. I made the tour slowly, in a sort of dream, touching every one of them, gripping my fingers round the trunks, and even lifting some of the leaves to my lips. If there was a tree that I thought I had missed, I went back to it, and touched it again. I stumbled through the harsh branches of the conifers—the main bulwark of my barrier against the world—I lifted my arms to the wild white cherries and my eyes to the laburnums, whose blossoms were luminous in the early light. From time to time I paused, as I caught sight of weeds and brambles—rogue convolvulus climbing up the stakes—a sinister patch of ground elder. They were perhaps the most agonising moments of all, for I swear that the wood was watching me; the trees knew that they were in danger, and that they were being deserted.

Then I went back into the cottage. I stood in the doorway, looking round me. I wanted to fix every detail of the old place in my mind—every curve in the dark beams, every fold in the faded curtains, every shadow on the faded carpet, as the sunlight filtered through the honeysuckle. But there was no need to stand and stare, the whole scene was printed irrevocably on my memory; it was in my heart, and always will be.

219

From the garden room to the music room, where all the books had been written—on an old desk, by the light of a window that looked out onto the secret garden. On the desk lay some pages of manuscript, the opening chapter of a novel whose name I have forgotten. I pushed the pages aside. The novel would never be written. From the desk I walked to the piano, and rested my fingers on the keys. My mind was tormented with music, my whole body was aching with music, but it would not be released and it would never be written down. Once again there was a shadow over the keyboard, the black shadow of my father. I closed the lid.

I am trying to describe a nervous breakdown, and not doing it very well. Because a nervous breakdown, surely, should present a picture of total disintegration, in which the mind loses all control, and concedes complete surrender. I did not lose complete control. For at this point, the old pro took command. Thirty-five years of self-imposed discipline, thirty-five years of controlled ambition . . . these leave their mark, and impose their own standards. After closing the lid of the piano, I went back to the desk, looked out to the secret garden, and spoke to myself. This is what I said, and I spoke aloud:

'You are about to commit a form of suicide and you must do it efficiently. There must be no bungling, no hesitations, no regrets, no looking back. You must do it cleanly and quickly, at a single stroke.' What does this imply? I paused for a moment, thinking with the relentless clarity of the insane.

Then I wrote four letters. One to my lawyers, one to the bank, one to my publishers, and one to a firm of house-agents. They were to the effect that 'Allways' and its contents were for sale, with immediate possession. With the letter to the house-agents I enclosed a photograph of the cottage and the outline of a publicity brochure, suggesting that 'Allways' was the scene 'made famous by the books of Mr Beverley Nichols'. The old pro was still in control.

I went outside, picked a spray of honeysuckle, and walked down the lane to the post-office. After posting the letters I crossed the road and entered the churchyard. I placed the honeysuckle on John

Borie's grave and read the inscription 'An American who Loved England'. A lot of things had happened since that armistice night in Chicago nearly eighteen years ago. The church clock chimed . . . eight strokes, on the familiar note of A flat. Within the past two hours my life had entirely changed.

I returned to the cottage, and opened the door, making for the crooked staircase. There were things I needed to take away . . . shoes, dinner-jackets, razors, even bottles of scent from the ancient town of Floris. Then I stopped. If I went up I should be opening another floodgate of memories. Memories of laughter, of sadness, of romance. I should go to the window and look out onto the garden and the distant fields and say to myself, as I had so many times before . . . 'This is where I want to die.'

So I stopped at the bottom of the stairs and turned back. I was desperately reminding myself of the suicide motif, and the need to carry it through. 'No bungling, no hesitations, no regrets.' My eye caught a gleam of sunlight reflected from a decanter on the drinks table—a charming piece of Victorian papier-mâché which had been placed there as a welcome for weekend guests. It was an early eighteenth-century decanter of Waterford glass, and it was filled with a rather special vintage of Madeira. Why not take it, and put it in the boot of the car? Then I said, still speaking to myself aloud: 'No. If I take this I shall start taking other things—I shall go round the house collecting this and that. I shall fill my arms with memories, there will be no end to it. And the whole object of this operation is that the memories must be exorcised, cleanly and quickly. I must draw down a curtain over part of my brain and keep it drawn. This may be madness; if so, I am mad. But I am still in control.'

I went outside and stepped into the lane. I did not even bother to lock the door. Then I got into the car and drove to Oxford. I was only a few hours from collapse.

The trip to Oxford was the last frenzied teeth-clenching struggle of the old pro to keep a grip on himself. It deserves a moment's explanation.

I had to go to Oxford because I had been billed as principal speaker at the annual meeting of the Oxford Group. There had been a great deal of publicity about the occasion and I could not let them down.

My brief enchantment with the Oxford Group is one of the spiritual contortions with which I have not bored the reader. It was an awful warning against the dangers of rushing into print without adequate reflection. I had nearly completed *The Fool Hath Said*, which was an apology for the Christian faith and—for me, at any rate—quite a scholarly piece of work. It had involved a great deal of research, and when it was eventually published the theologians were favourably impressed. However, at the last moment, I was swept into the Oxford Group and dashed off a chapter about the movement which was incorporated as the book was going to print. I was soon to regret this. As I came to learn more about the Group my enthusiasm changed to distaste. Dr Buchman revealed himself as a brash American salesman who was selling Christianity as though it were a new form of cosmetic, expensively packaged. He was doing very well out of it and so were his followers, gallivanting about the world and proclaiming the Word from a background of luxurious hotels. Perhaps the most revealing remark about his spiritual inclinations was delivered during a press conference at Brown's Hotel when he was being asked an awkward question about the Group's finances. He replied with a counter-question ... 'Isn't God a millionaire?' This was the final disillusionment; something had to be done about it; and I was on the way to Oxford to do it.

But what could I do? I had to make an important speech, in a blaze of publicity, and I had not the faintest idea what to say. Looking back on it all I think that this was the final straw that broke the old pro's back. The four principles of the Group, which at that time were echoing round the world, particularly among the richer nations, were Absolute Honesty, Absolute Purity, Absolute Unselfishness, and Absolute Love. If I were absolutely honest on this occasion I should have to say things which were insulting about Doctor Buchman and this would have disagreeable repercussions. As for the purity and the unselfishness and the love—the words meant nothing. I could only think of 'Allways', and the empty cottage, and the deserted wood, which were slowly fading further into the distance as the car sped on.

I reached Oxford and found my way to the college of Oriel, where the Group had arranged a large and expensive luncheon party. There were the usual flash-light photographs and introductions and back-slappings. In the distance I saw a *Sunday Chronicle* reporter who drew me aside for an 'exclusive'. I must have looked rather odd because he peered at me anxiously and kept on asking me to smile. 'Come on, Beverley—a nice smile. Come on. A million readers are watching.' I managed some sort of grimace, and retreated to the bar.

Of the luncheon I remember nothing, except that I drank a lot. So did the jet-black African archbishop who had been seated next to me. Our conversation cannot have been very illuminating, and was not, I suspect, exclusively confined to Absolute Honesty, Absolute Purity, etc. Then there was the familiar banging on the tables, the ringing announcement of the toast-master—'My lords, ladies, and gentlemen . . . pray silence for—Mr Beverley Nichols.'

I walked up the steps to the platform. Quite steadily, because I could still put on an act, and I was sober enough to control my body, even though I had destroyed my soul. I stared out at a crowded hall of complacent faces—healthy, hearty, well-nourished young men, who were giving a splendid exhibition of the collective honesty, purity, etc. that, as they firmly believed, would change the world.

Then the faces faded, and once again I saw only 'Allways', and the forsaken wood, and the abandoned cottage. I tried to speak but I could say nothing. I could only weep.

Have you ever wept in public—standing alone on a platform, under the bewildered scrutiny of a crowded audience? It is not an experience to be recommended. Men do not weep gracefully; their shoulders hunch, their features contort, they gulp and look ridiculous. I provided the audience with this remarkable exhibition for . . . how long? A minute? Half a minute? To me it seemed an eternity.

While I wept, there was total silence. Not a single member of the absolutely honest, pure, unselfish, and loving assembly of Oxford Groupers rose from his seat to help me. To this day, I wonder why? Surely one of them must have realised that they were in the presence of a man in great distress? That some sort of tragedy, however minor, was being enacted before their bright and loving eyes? But no. In silence I was allowed to stagger from the platform and collapse outside the door from where I could hear the next speaker ringing out the familiar platitudes. I had let the side down and if there were any good Samaritans in the audience they did not show themselves.

The next nine hours are a blank. Somehow or other, I must have driven back to London, because the car was discovered in a side street about a mile from home. At midnight Gaskin, my factotum, arrived and found me standing in a hall blurting out a single sentence . . . 'I can't stop crying. I can't stop crying.' Later there were doctors and injections and eventually I woke up in a sort of luxurious loony bin on the borders of Hampstead Heath. Everything was very quiet and very sinister and the nurse looked at me with an expression clearly indicating that one of us was mad, and it certainly was not herself.

None of these distresses were reported in Page Two. How could they be? The art department would not have known how to illustrate them. As I gradually returned to some sort of normality it was suggested that a collection of celebrities should be assembled at the loony bin and be photographed round my bed, raising glasses of champagne to my swift recovery. I refused to co-operate; it would have been too like a macabre parody of an early novel by Evelyn Waugh. I also refused to have anything to do with the sale of 'Allways' or even to glance at an inventory of the contents. This, to say the least of it, was an act of folly and lost me a great deal of money. Some of the objects I had collected, guided only by my own taste, proved to be more valuable than I had suspected. The dining-room table alone was later sold at Sotheby's for five thousand pounds, which was more than twice what I had received for the entire property, lock, stock, and barrel. I did not care. Over and over again I kept on saying to myself, 'I have committed suicide and that is the end of it.' Sometimes I said it aloud, thereby summoning the attention of the nurse who had a room next door, and had evidently been warned that I might do something foolish when she was looking the other way. 'Come, come, Mr Beverley, we mustn't carry on like this, must we?' Bang bang on the pillows. 'We must sit up and look out of the window and enjoy the sunshine and the beautiful garden.'

I will end this sombre patch of my life with a letter from Rex Whistler, one of the few that I kept from the bundles that were being daily delivered.

> My dear Beverley,
> I am so sorry to hear that you are in the Slough of Despond and that you have said goodboy to 'Allways', where I spent such happy times making innumerable sketches (for which I was grossly underpaid!). There must have been some very deep-rooted reason for this decision and I shan't be so impertinent as to enquire what it was.
> But I refuse to believe that you have really said goodbye. Your books on 'Allways' were the record of a love affair, which is why they have inspired so many people, including myself.
> Of all the drawings I made for you my favourite is the little one at the end of the last chapter of *A Thatched Roof*. It is only a scribble, done very quickly, to meet the publication date-line. But I think it expressed what you were trying to say. At any rate, you told me so at the time, and we celebrated it with a glass of very special Madeira, which you poured out of a decanter of very special Waterford glass, that stood on a very special papier-mâché table in the hall.
> I think that you should look at it again, and read what you wrote those two long summers ago.
> > My blessings,
> > As ever,
> > Rex.

I have just read again the passage to which Rex was referring. I had forgotten it, and if I were to try to write it today, no doubt it would be written differently. But I could not write it today, for it is, as it were, a 'preview' of my own death, and one of the mysteries of life—from the writer's point of view—is that the closer he approaches to death the more distant does death become. As one grows older, death retreats, gliding silently away, assuming various, changing shadowy shapes of promise or threat or foreboding. But always at a distance. In youth, death is ever close at hand.

Here is the passage of which Rex was speaking . . .

I know that whenever I die, in the last moment my spirit will fly to that white room over the quiet fields. I may die in poverty or in exile, but no man will be able to bar me from this place which I have loved and will be mine for always. It may be in some shabby hotel bedroom, in some southern country—with a concierge knocking at the door, and peering in through the thickening dust, to see if the old Englishmen who lives there alone, is still alive. Or in a café, when suddenly I see the mirrors darken before me, and the noise of the orchestra is blown darkly away by the last gusts, as the wind blows away the howling of a dog on winter nights. Or at sea, when the waves leap up for the last time, and remain stiff and frozen, while the immense sky closes in, with no star to give me light.

But wherever the hand of Death may seize me, near or far, rich or poor, alone or in a gay company, I shall escape him. I shall escape him utterly. Over sea and forest and city, in that strange, tortured moment of consummation which all must know, I shall fly, and I shall get there before Death. Yes . . . I shall be in the white room over the quiet fields, even if it is only for the last second, for the last 'look round'.

CHAPTER XVIII

❀❀❀❀❀

INTERLUDE
IN AN INFERNO

When a man is making a record of his life he should remember not only what he did but why he did it. After a lapse of several decades many of one's actions seem incomprehensible. So it was, when I emerged from the Hampstead loony bin. I had been ordered complete rest and, if possible, mountain air; I must avoid crowds and tension and any sort of involvement in public affairs. Whereupon I promptly set off for Berlin, which in the summer of 1936 was the most hectic capital in Europe. For this was the year of the Olympic Games—Hitler's final and most spectacular effort to dazzle the world with a display of Nazi might and Nazi efficiency.

As a companion I had a friend called Peter Claas, a young German from a distinguished family in Wiesbaden. He had sacrificed the chance of a brilliant career in his own country because he was horrified by the excesses of the Nazi régime. When he arrived in England he was glad of the few pounds I was able to put in his pocket for giving me German lessons. When I suggested that he might care to come to Berlin, driving the car which I was not yet strong enough to manage myself, he agreed with alacrity. This was very gallant of him because he might easily have ended up in a concentration camp.

But why Berlin? Why did I make for this demented city? I hated the place. I had only been there once before, at the beginning of the thirties, when inflation was raging like a forest fire. My main reason for hating it was because everybody in the city, by which I mean every pair of arms and legs, was for sale. If a man had a fancy for

227

small girls or small boys he had only to lift his finger and they would be fluttering around him, like hungry sparrows, waiting for crumbs of bread. He could be old and ugly and cruel but if he had the bread in his pocket, in the shape of dollars or francs, the sparrows would fly to him and do his bidding, however degrading it might be. I imagine that in the entire history of civilisation there has never been such a sexual extravaganza as was presented by Berlin at the beginning of the last decade before the war, and I have a feeling that this chaffering in young bodies was in no small degree responsible for the war itself. 'The Sexual Origins of the Great War' might prove a fruitful theme for the historian, explaining some of the excesses of the German troops when war began. Some of the brutality, I believe, had its origin in memories of the male brothels which sprang up in all the great German cities, with the tacit approval of Goebbels, who realised that they were not only a tourist attraction but also a convenient setting for espionage. The youth of Germany was getting its revenge.

I have never been an ardent habitué of brothels, but in Berlin, on this occasion, it would have been impossible to avoid them even if one had tried to do so. One very special brothel will always remain in my memory. I was wandering with Peter down a side street. We were both tired, and both in need of a drink and when we saw a discreet-looking bar, dimly lit, we decided to go inside. At least, in this sort of place, we should not be pestered.

We went inside and sat down in a quiet corner. A waiter approached, and surveyed us with a rather unfriendly expression. Peter ordered two Schnapps. There was a pause. An even more unfriendly expression. Then, a click of the heels. '*Ein Moment, meine Herren.*' With which he departed.

As we waited for our drinks, I looked around and it occurred to me that we had wandered into a very curious establishment. The average age of the customers was well over sixty, with a fair sprinkling of septuagenarians. Moreover, they all had beards—some of them snow-white; and without exception they were staring at us with undisguised hostility.

I began to feel embarrassed. '*Was ist los?*' I demanded of Peter.

(He was trying, without much success, to persuade me to speak German.)

He shrugged his shoulders. Then, suddenly he began to laugh. At which moment the waiter returned, without the drinks. There was a rapid interchange in German, which seemed to increase the hostility of the watching clientele. One white-bearded ancient, who must have been nearly eighty, rose to his feet, and shook his fist.

Peter, still shaking with laughter, led me outside and explained the situation. By chance we had wandered into one of Berlin's most exclusive brothels, which was reserved for the use of elderly gentlemen who happened to find their pleasure only in the arms of other elderly gentlemen, and could only express their endearments if their beards were closely entangled. And when we had entered, young and sprightly and clean-shaven, they must have felt a sense of outrage, as though we had come to violate their sad and secret world.

All this is in anticipation, because the flight to Germany did not begin in Berlin. It began in Hamburg, with Peter at the wheel of the car, and me sitting by his side, seeing the landscape through a mist of tears. Although we had escaped from England, I could not escape from 'Allways'. I was still in spirit a prisoner of the garden, still wandering through the deserted wood. This was morbid and ridiculous; for all I knew, the cottage no longer belonged to me; some stranger would be sleeping in my bed, picking my flowers. I had to take a tight hold on myself; I wanted to stop the car at the nearest post-office and send a sheaf of telegrams cancelling the whole transaction. It was not to be. I had to keep reminding myself that I had committed a sort of suicide, and when one has done that, one is like a ghost, incapable of logical thought, let alone of logical action.

Besides, there was another reason why I could not turn back. I had an appointment in Berlin which must be kept at all costs, even if it were the last I was ever to make. It might be called an appointment with Peace. However dazed and bewildered I was after this breakdown, however muddled my standards and muddled my principles, there was one cause I would never desert—the cause of pacificism. And I was impelled by a final desperate illusion that Berlin, at this moment of history, was the last city left where a single individual might actually *do* something for peace. Like the suffragette who jumped to her death in front of the horse at the Derby in the cause of women's suffrage.

As it happened, life was to give me the chance of making an even more sensational gesture, to which we will revert.

We started off in Hamburg in very grand style, staying at the Vierjahreszeiten Hotel.

'But, Beverley, this is the most expensive hotel in Germany.'

'Never mind. We can afford it.'

'But, Beverley, this is the hotel where *Lolotte* stays. She was here only last week.'

It must be explained that 'Lolotte' was the pseudonym by which we referred to Hitler. We often discussed the Führer in our conversation but it was wiser not to mention his name in public.

'So much the better. We will take the royal suite.'

And we did. Peter—assuming a thick English accent—approached the desk and informed the management that I was a *berühmte Schriftsteller* (distinguished novelist) who had a high admiration for the Führer and would be honoured if he could sleep, even for a single night, in the same bed which His Excellency had occupied. It worked like a charm. Within a few minutes we were installed in Hitler's suite, and a large bunch of roses had appeared on the centre table, followed by a bottle of champagne with the compliments of the management.

That night we went to a music-hall. The house was packed from floor to ceiling, the show was going like a bomb. Turn after turn was applauded with a hoarse Teutonic roar—every singer, every comedian, every acrobat was received with rapture. And every one of them was a Jew. They were not merely tinged with Jewishness— they were flagrantly, outlandishly Semitic. Of the many minor mysteries of the period this was one of the weirdest. The Jewish concentration camps were already beginning to fill up, the Jewish fortunes were already plundered, and at the entrance to all the villages giant signs were springing up bearing the chilling slogan *Juden Sind Hier Nicht Erwünscht*. And yet, in this great German city of Hamburg, it was to the Jews that the Germans were turning for the saving grace of laughter. I do not pretend to understand it, I only record it.

On the following day we set out for Berlin. We arrived in a city that was in an advanced state of hysterics, beflagged and beribboned, the streets choked with ramparts of the military marching—so it seemed—in a choreography of intimidation; over the ceaseless clamour of the city echoed the strident voice of Goebbels, broadcasting through giant loudspeakers which spouted at every street corner.

I have set out the facts of the astonishing climax to the Berlin episode—which also marked the climax of my own struggles in the cause of pacifism—in a volume of short stories called *Men Do Not Weep*.* The story is too long and complicated to recount in detail. The final scene tells all that matters. It is laid in the Führer's box at the spectacular opening of the Olympic Games. The whole world has flocked to Berlin, the great ones of the earth have converged on the Stadium, and the Holy of Holies is Hitler's box. It is packed with glittering uniforms, royalties, heads of state, ambassadors, field marshals. In the front row the Nazi hierarchy are taking their places, Goering, Goebbels, Himmler, the entire infernal crew. Hitler's seat is still unoccupied, but in the distance one can hear the roar of the multitudes and the shrill flourish of trumpets as his cavalcade approaches.

And immediately behind the Führer's empty seat stands a solitary figure, in a shabby dark blue suit, very pale, very rigid, waiting. Myself. Wondering what to do. I am so near to Hitler's seat that I could have leant forward and touched it. And if there had been a grenade in my pocket—as there might have been—I could have blown the whole hideous collection to kingdom come.

* *Men Do Not Weep:* Jonathan Cape Ltd, 1941.

How did this situation arise? The answer to this question is told in the story. Very briefly it was due to an extraordinary error on the part of the British contingent who had made a mistake with the tickets and presented me with the places which had been reserved for the Spanish ambassador's party.

The bitter irony of it all was that there was no hand grenade in my pocket, as, I repeat, there might have been. For one of the *dramatis personae* in this whole sensational script was a young communist with whom I had struck up a friendship—a fanatical blond giant called Hans Bruckner, who could easily have provided me with one. Owing to the muddle at the embassy he also had a ticket for the Führer's box, but he was arrested at the entrance and executed on the following morning.

A question remains to be answered. If this book can claim any validity as a self-portrait, if it is authentic autobiography, would I have sat down, taken my place, and pulled the pin of the grenade that might have been in my pocket? Had I done so, I should have changed the whole history of the world. They were all immediately in front of me—Hitler, Goering, Himmler, Ribbentrop, Goebbels, Hess, the whole poisonous gang. A flick of the finger and they would have been blasted from the face of the earth. Would I have used that grenade? I would like to think that the answer would be 'yes', but I doubt it. The act would have involved my own suicide and I had not got that sort of courage. A great deal of pious nonsense is talked about suicide, particularly by the Roman Catholic Church, which has decided—for reasons which defy all rational or spiritual examination—that suicide must be damned as a mortal sin when, in fact, it may often be numbered among the highest virtues.

Anyway, my courage was never put to the test. My pockets were empty. I stood there, a shrunken figure in a shabby suit, while the athletes of the world sped by in the arena, and the leaders of the Third Reich sat a few yards away, shouting their acclaim, because Germany was sweeping all before them. In the middle of a particularly thunderous outburst of applause I slunk away.

*   *   *

On leaving Berlin, I bade an affectionate farewell to Peter and set off to drive to Vienna alone. It was time to learn to stand again on my own feet, and to grapple with the various problems of language and transport which beset the traveller in unfamiliar countries. In the thirties if you had a British passport and an adequate supply of sterling there were no problems at all. The present generation can have no conception of the ease and delight of European travel before the war. The hideous device of the 'package tour' had not yet been invented, the great hotels had not yet been commandeered by swarms of uncouth holidaymakers, the stately squares were not jammed with charabancs, the winding streets did not echo to the shuffle of plebeian queues, gazing like sheep at ancient monuments which they neither understood nor cared about. And the landscape —the magical panorama of mountains and lakes and forests—was not yet desecrated by giant concrete matchboxes erected for the convenience of the *canaille*. It was still possible, in short, to travel like a gentleman.

I had special reasons for wishing to visit Vienna. One of them was because it was a city of music, and after the brazen uproar of Berlin I was longing for a musical interlude. In Vienna music is in the very air one breathes, it even seems to echo from the taxi-horns. My most vivid realisation of this came on my first visit to the Prater, where I decided to join in the fun and sprang onto a merry-go-round. As I jogged up and down on the brightly-painted wooden horse I suddenly realised that the little mechanical band was puffing out selections from *The Magic Flute*. In what other capital would such a fiesta be celebrated to the music of Mozart?

My other reason for visiting Vienna was to see the German version of *Avalanche*, my own play, which as we noted in a previous chapter, was killed by James Agate, the king of critical crooks. It was drawing the town, and the star part was being played by Basserman, who might be described as Germany's John Gielgud. If I had been sensible, I should have watched the performance from a box. But that would have meant dressing up, and I thought it would be more fun to go along anonymously and sit in the back row of the stalls. It was a curious experience, sitting in the crowded theatre, listening to my puppets making the speeches that I had put into their mouths. My German was not fluent enough to catch the nuances of everything that was being said, but after a few minutes it was evident that the play was gripping the audience. On the following morning I went round to the theatre and was received *en prince*. More important, the management gave me quite a large bundle of schillings which were due in royalties.

After which I got lost.

There is something uniquely exhilarating in being quite alone in a strange city where one knows nobody and where nobody knows or cares who one is or where one has come from. Anonymity becomes a sort of magical cloak; it is a form of rebirth. One can assume a new personality, adopt poses that one has never adopted before. For a space I enjoyed the delights of this anonymity to the full. I had made sure that it was total. Nobody at home had the faintest idea where I was. For all anybody knew—relations, secretaries, agents, friends—I might be dead, or murdered, or mad. As it happened, I was staying at Sacher's, which was one of the most glamorous hotels in Europe. Sacher's was pure Strauss and the creaking corridors echoed to the sound of deceased Austrian arch-dukes, as they made their way to the private suites where they entertained the ladies of the ballet. Sacher's was, *par excellence*, the place where the Austrian aristocracy drank champagne out of ladies' shoes. This had always seemed to me an unattractive and faintly unhygienic introduction to romance and I wanted to discover if it was true. (The memory of Page Two was beginning to haunt me again and I could not help thinking that *I Drink Champagne From A Lady's Shoe* would make a good paragraph and would present no difficulties for the art department.)

Sacher's was haunted, but some of the *ancien régime* still lingered on. Among these was a seedy old gentleman who was a distant cousin of the Emperor Francis Joseph. He was obviously down on his luck, and he used to wander into the lounge to study the visitors' book, in the hope of finding some acquaintance of the old days who might give him a drink. In a rash moment I had entered myself in the book as Sir Beverley Nichols; the adoption of a title seemed to enhance my anonymity. It proved a bait to the old gentleman, and one evening he made an excuse for sinking into the chair next to me. I asked him if he would join me in a drink, and ordered a bottle of champagne, choosing a Louis Roederer 1911. A sparkle came into his eyes when he saw the label, and after the first glass he began to unwind and talked about the past, in fluent, flawless English. This seemed the moment to inquire about the shoes. Did the Austrian aristocracy really indulge in this curious habit?

'Of course,' he replied. 'It was almost *de rigueur*. The ladies would have felt insulted if we had not suggested it.' Then he gave a charming smile. 'But they were very small shoes. And we did not fill them with a vintage of *this* quality.'

I took him out to dinner that night. The bill was staggering, but with the exquisite diplomacy of the old régime he conveyed the impression that he was paying it.

On the following morning I packed up, left Sacher's, and went to stay at the König von Ungarn. When I settled the account I handed the concierge an envelope to give to the old man. With it I enclosed a note for a thousand schillings and a slip of paper ... 'With the compliments and thanks of Sir Beverley Nichols.'

This fleeting encounter in Sacher's was to prove the first step on the voyage home. For it was a bitter reminder that I was a journalist, and I was longing to kill the journalist in me. Here I was in Vienna, with a successful play running, but I had done nothing about it. Here I was, paying the bills with royalties, from books which had been acclaimed in Germany, and I was still doing nothing about it. And here I was, masquerading as a titled Englishman in one of the most romantic rendezvous in Europe, and I stumble on a story, and I do nothing about *that*. The fatal spell of Page Two encompasses me. I can see the title all too clearly. *Beverley Nichols Drinks Champagne Out Of A Lady's Shoe*. If I had been Somerset Maugham, I should have written the story and made a fortune out of it. As it was, I threw it away on a couple of paragraphs for the Manchester housewife.

It was because of Maugham that I told the taxi to drive me from Sacher's to the König von Ungarn. This hotel had been Maugham's favourite haunt when he stayed in Vienna. My bag was carried by a very decorative page-boy who looked as if he had been engaged for the exclusive service of the Master. When he had departed I sat down on the bed to think, but after a while I came to the conclusion that I had nothing to think about—or rather, a great deal too much. The air was full of music and the streets were alive with stories, but the music evaded me and the stories were not taking shape.

Worst of all, the cloak of anonymity was beginning to become a bore. Admittedly, it allowed me to indulge in outrageous behaviour which would have been unthinkable in London, where I might have been recognised, but I am not by nature all that outrageous, and my occasional surrenders to *nostalgie de la boue* have been few and far between. I found myself afflicted by the melancholy sense of isolation which comes to all who travel alone in great cities, sitting at cafés drinking Tokay in solitude, edging up to marble-topped tables in order to strike up a conversation with persons in a similar situation. One of these encounters was unexpectedly rewarding. I caught the eye of two American matrons of piercing respectability and introduced myself as a guide. By now I had acquired a flawless Anglo-American-German accent and they engaged me to conduct them round the Kunsthistoriches museum. They were deeply impressed by my knowledge of the masterpieces in this unique treasure-house and when we parted they slipped me a thousand-schilling note, and a visiting card, which bore an address in Cincinnati. Years later I was to lecture there, and I have often wondered if they were in the audience.

But I could not go on being a nobody, a non-person. A few days later, after a final surrender to *nostalgie de la boue*, I paid the bill and set out for home.

CHAPTER XIX

❀❀❀❀❀❀

BACK TO
THE GRINDSTONE

Number 1 Ellerdale Close, Hampstead, North London, was a very desirable little residence. Although it was only twenty minutes from Piccadilly Circus it stood among giant trees and was a mere five minutes' walk from Hampstead Heath. It lay at the top of a quiet hill and had a modest elegance, for it had been designed by one of the most distinguished architects of the day, by name Clough Williams-Ellis.

I had bought it for £2800 on a '999-year lease', which is one of the legal eccentricities of British property conventions. Today it would probably fetch £80,000. When I signed the lease there was a moment of misgiving. I was still at an age when one has intimations of immortality. Other people would die, but one would go on for ever. Would it not have been wiser to invest in a freehold? 999 years was only a flick of the fingers of Time, a reminder that all good things, and all bad things, must come to an end. It seemed hardly worth while planting the hyacinths in the front garden.

As it happened, a great many good things and a great many bad things were to come to an end in less than 999 days.

The door was opened by Mr Gaskin, my factotum, who seemed not at all surprised to see me, although I had been vague about the precise date of my return.

The house was spick and span, there were freshly cut roses on the piano, and before I had even suggested it he had produced an ice-cold sidecar cocktail on a brightly polished silver tray. (Equal quantities of brandy, Cointreau, and lemon juice.) Had there been any crises? No more than usual, sir. Were there many letters? Yes, there were a great many, but my secretary had been doing her best to cope. And the cats—were they well? Had they been missing me? Yes, they were very well. As for missing me—he raised his eyebrows—'Well sir, you know what cats are.'

I did indeed. When I walked out onto the terrace, the cats (two jet-black half-caste Siamese) stared at me with marked disapproval. Then they yawned, stretched, and jumped onto the wall, safe from any attempt to stroke them. This was as it should be. One of the many enchanting characteristics of cats is that when one has been away for long periods one's return is greeted, not with ecstasy, but with reproach. There are no leapings onto laps, no ecstatic purrings —there are only chilling reminders that they feel neglected, that some explanation is due. As I walk upstairs to my bedroom I realise that it will be several days before they condescend to sleep with me again.

I remove my travel-stained garments and throw them on the floor. Gaskin will deal with them. I take a bath, powerfully perfumed with rose-geranium bath essence from the ancient house of Floris. Get out of the bath, dry myself, and walk over to the full-length triple mirror to survey myself from all angles. It had been installed as soon as I took possession of the house, not for any reasons of conceit, but because it seemed a sensible precaution. Over the years I had suffered a number of operations with which the reader has not been bored, and I wanted to keep a check on the scars. I seem in pretty good shape.

The physical survey completed, I went to the dressing-room to choose a suit for the evening. Here comes a twinge of acute nostalgia. The suits were hung in a fitting which I had designed at the same time as the triple mirror. It was fronted with plate-glass and it slid back at the flick of a finger.

The suits came from the firm of Kilgour French and Stanbury Ltd who were the best tailors in the world. On my first visit to this gilded establishment Rudolf Valentino was being fitted in the next compartment and behaving in a very prima-donna manner. Something was amiss with the padding of the shoulders and he was not satisfied with the action of the crutch. This was a revealing confession. I later had occasion to discuss the sexual prowess of the world's most legendary lover with two of the ladies with whom he had dallied, and neither of them, it seemed, had been satisfied with the 'action of the crutch'. One of the ladies was Nazimova. She told me that he was the most boring man she had ever gone to bed with. 'What's more,' she observed, with marked resentment, 'he snored.'

I am now washed, dressed, and in my right mind. I go to the window and look out. The prospect is pleasing. Nothing but gardens in full flower, and great trees, chestnut and apple and lime, and little houses—mostly late Georgian—keeping themselves to themselves. At the top of the hill I can see the graceful façade of Church Row which is pure Queen Anne, and beyond that, the tower of the old church, surrounded by a churchyard which recalled the setting for Gray's elegy.

The telephone rang. It was Gloria Swanson calling from Hollywood. She would be passing through London in a few days and would I be free to dine? I certainly should, on condition that nobody made any suggestion that I should act in anything, even with her—or even, if it came to that, as an extra. No such suggestion, she assured me with some amusement, would be made. She was well aware that I could not act. (She must have heard about the hilarious fiasco of my first Hollywood film test.) She did not want me to act, but to write. What about? 'Me,' she replied sweetly.

After dealing with Gloria—who should certainly have been included in the chapter on the 'Women in my Life'—I went to the bookshelf and took down a copy of *The Star Spangled Manner*, to refresh my memory on something that I had written about her in New York, a few years before. I quote her opening remarks.

My life is like a street and I never know when I shall cross that street. All I know is that when I have crossed it, I am a different person. And when that moment comes, the crowds drift away, and there is nothing but myself in the middle of the road, and a lamp-post, shining against a sky that is dark and without a star.

239

And again . . .

When I grow old, I want to have an old brain as well as an old body. I shall pray for wrinkles in my spirit to match the wrinkles on my face. I shall pray for the fire to die down in my mind just as it dies down in my body.

But the incomparable Gloria, I fancy, will never grow old. At various times in recent years—one of them was when death was knocking rather too loudly and insistently at my door—Gloria has appeared, as it were from outer space, and invariably she has given me spiritual consolation.

The telephone rang again. This time it was another woman who should have been included among the 'Women in my Life'. Lady Juliet Duff. I mention her in order to remind myself of the exceptional historical span of my mixed-up social life. For Juliet's mother was the famous Lady de Grey, who takes us way, way back through the Edwardians to the Victorians. She was already a mature woman when she commanded the musical establishment to engage Melba to sing at Covent Garden. My favourite story about Lady de Grey is laid in Paris. She had her moments of abandon, and once, when she was staying with the British Ambassador, she had a fancy to visit a certain notorious red-light district. Would it be possible? Of course, said His Excellency, and proceeded to make a few telephone calls. When the Ambassadorial party eventually arrived the most disreputable section of the brothel area had been railed off and she was able to make her inspection without embarrassment. Apparently she had an instructive experience, but it cannot have been popular with the ladies of easy virtue who could not understand why business was so slack.

Lady de Grey's daughter Juliet had inherited her mother's patrician assumption that all doors would automatically be opened for her, and they usually were. But on one occasion something went wrong. By chance we found ourselves on the same boat crossing from Calais to Dover and she invited me to her cabin for a game of backgammon. As we drew near to Dover I suggested that we ought to get up and take our places in the queue. Eyebrows were raised.

She had never stood in a queue, and she had no intention of doing so. 'They' would come and tell us when it was time to go and we should of course be the first to leave the ship. But 'they' did not come; instead of being the first we were the last. The ship was so overcrowded that we were jostled and hustled and eventually missed the train, so that there was no car to meet us in London and we had to take a taxi. Juliet entered into it as though she were stepping into a tumbril.

As I recall that evening, driving down to the Savoy, the tides of nostalgia sweep over me in a flood. London looks so beautiful, Regent's Park is like a Canaletto; the Georgian architectural heritage is still largely intact, there are no traffic jams, and there is no speed-limit. I am at the Savoy in twenty minutes and when I get there Juliet is already established at the best table, which in those days was the first on the left as you entered the room. She is lighting a cigarette from a Fabergé case, and as I glance round the room I notice that the clientele is composed of a breed of persons who are now largely extinct, known as 'ladies and gentlemen'. There are no pop singers, no Arabs, and no presidents of jet-black republics being rude to waiters with diplomatic immunity. And when, long after midnight, I pay the bill, there is plenty of change out of a fiver.

It was with some misgiving that I reported to the office of *The Sunday Chronicle* on the following morning. I had only been away for a few weeks but it seemed like years. What had been happening? Had I been sacked? Not at all. Thanks to the journalistic ingenuity of Jimmy Drawbell Page Two had continued almost uninterrupted, though it had been largely a scissors and paste job, created from the débris of previous articles which had been kept in reserve. However there had been no complaints.

This was the year when my journalistic stock seemed to be running high. In a national opinion poll I was elected one of the six most popular young men in Britain. What this proved is anybody's guess, but it is a minor pointer to the climate of the times because I was still associated with extreme pacificism. Oddly enough, the number one favourite was Jim Mollison, who was anything but a pacifist. Although his name is largely forgotten today, he was one of the greatest airmen whom Britain ever produced. Noël Coward came second—and nobody could describe him as a pacifist either. Was he not the author of *Cavalcade*, which was one of the most effective pieces of Imperialist propaganda ever written? I tied for third place with Ivor Novello, who had no political opinions whatsoever, and lived exclusively in Ruritania. I forget the names of the other two successful candidates. We were certainly a mixed bunch.

So the year sped by, and I will not attempt to get it into focus. Obviously I was mentally and spiritually in an appalling mess. I was going everywhere and getting nowhere. I was meeting everybody and meeting nobody—nobody who had any vital impact. Such friendships as I formed were superficial. The women in my life were women of no importance. Quite a number of them were in love with me. This statement is not so outrageous as it sounds. Every reasonably personable bachelor who attains some celebrity inevitably attracts the affection and sometimes the adoration of women of all ages, shapes, and sizes. If he is rich enough to engage the services of an efficient army of secretaries and bodyguards—or if he is lucky enough to be equipped with a chromium-plated heart —this problem need cause him no anxiety. But I had not a chromium-plated heart.

Life was very successful from a material point of view. I had made a 'name', but I began to sell it in ways which I secretly despised. London was suddenly placarded with posters informing the world that 'If Beverley Nichols offered you a cigarette it would be a de Reszke.' The slogan gives me an excuse for telling a story about Noël Coward. One night we were the reluctant guests at a cocktail party given by a celebrated columnist called Godfrey Winn, whom I had every reason to detest. He was a humourless egomaniac, who wrote excruciating prose, hated cats, and was tone-deaf. But because he was also a 'columnist', the more malicious gossip writers of Fleet Street sometimes mentioned us in the same context.

Noël came up to me at the cocktail party which was not going with a swing, because Godfrey was not a generous host. The drinks were few and far between, and the cigarette boxes were all empty.

Noël. 'Beverley, darling, I adored your trumpet-blast about de Reszke cigarettes.'

Beverley. No reply. No invention of dialogue.

Noël, groping in an empty box, draining a last drop of watered martini, and preparing to make his exit . . . 'I have only one thing to suggest, as a postscript.'

Beverley. 'Yes?'

Noël, with his eye on Godfrey, speaking with that incomparable clarity, which resounded round the room . . . 'If Godfrey Winn were to offer you a cigarette, it would be a bloody miracle.' Exit.

With such trivia, time flew by. I even toyed with the idea of standing for parliament, egged on by old Mrs Ronnie Greville, who offered to provide substantial funds if I would stand as an independent conservative against Duff Cooper in a by-election, thereby splitting the Tory vote. But here, for once, I had the courage to say no. Apart from the fact that I admired Duff Cooper, and had a distant adoration for Lady Diana, I was not an independent conservative nor, indeed, an independent anything. Again, a few visits to the House of Commons were enough to convince me that whatever career God had planned for me it would not be a political one. A drearier collection of nonentities, featureless, inarticulate, and uncouth, it had never been my misfortune to listen to. I could not conceive the idea of spending my life in the company of such creatures. Maggie Greville was not at all pleased that I had flouted her wishes; she told me that I was losing the chance of a life-time, and there were dark hints that I must not expect any benefits from her decease. There was a temporary coolness between us, but it did not last for long and I was soon back in favour.

Of course, the trouble with me in this blank period was that I had nobody, and nothing, to love . . . and that meant 'Allways'. Beneath the title of *Down the Garden Path* I had written 'A garden is the only mistress who never fades, who never fails.' I had deserted my only mistress. Often, coming home late at night I would go upstairs and open the window and lean out and survey my patch of garden and heave a sigh, for all I had was a tiny triangle. The most uncompromisingly triangular triangle that had ever been traced since the days of Isosceles, and what could one do with *that*?

If you lean out of a window late at night, in all weathers, with turmoil in your heart and desolation in your soul, and if you have, in however minor a degree, the temperament of the artist, something happens. Almost certainly, you will catch a cold. But that will not be the end of it. You may also catch a gleam of magic.

This was, I believe, what happened in my case. Little by little, as I leant out of the window, the triangle seemed to change its shape, to soften its outlines, to be modulated in my mind, in the same way that a bleak and uncompromising melodic line can be modulated by the arts of harmony and the skills of counterpoint.

This proved to be one of the most fascinating challenges I have ever accepted. At first, it was entirely a question of geometry. I spent long hours totally absorbed with sheets of squared paper, measuring heights and levels, wheeling barrowloads of bricks, erecting temporary walls, knocking them down, rebuilding them, lowering them, heightening them, curving them ... contriving cunning devices of *trompe l'œuil*. Finally, I designed an exquisite little Regency conservatory, with a domed roof of silvered glass, floating like a bubble in the distance. The miracle of 'Allways' was repeating itself in miniature. When it was finished I had created a refuge, a hiding-place, in which I could shelter from the world's alarms.

Needless to say, while I was making this garden I was writing a book about it. I called it *Green Grows the City*. It had, and still has, a considerable influence on the craft of landscape gardening. It also had a considerable influence on myself, because it was not only an act of defiance but an act of faith. Here I was, in the centre of a city which would soon be the target for prolonged and violent assault, and how did I face up to the situation? By creating a frail bubble of silver glass, which could be destroyed by a whiff of grapeshot. I had a curious conviction that whatever disasters might strike the city, my little bubble would emerge unscathed.

And so it proved to be. Meanwhile, the grindstone went on grinding. Page Two went from strength to strength and once again my salary was raised. There were no longer any problems with the art department because my weekly copy shimmered with celebrities. Nor was there any need to feel diffident about mentioning the various people who crossed my path. They were positively clamouring to get onto the page.

A crowded life, a star-studded life, and—when all is said and done—an excruciating bore.

Then, of a sudden, life took a dramatic change. In some ways for the better, in some ways for the worse. But a change that was long overdue.

꧁ ꧂ ꧁ ꧂ ꧁ ꧂

CHAPTER XX

A TALENT TO AMUSE

Paris, spring 1937. To quote a lyric of the times . . . 'April in Paris, the chestnuts in blossom, the holiday tables under the trees.'

I had never been happier, more fully stretched. Out of the blue a benevolent American impresario had appeared and I had played him some songs after dinner and made him laugh, and within a couple of days I had a contract to write a revue. Not just to contribute a few lines and sketches, but to create the entire thing from start to finish, from the opening chorus to the final curtain.

The word 'revue', in these days, has fallen into disrepute. In the twenties and the thirties revues could be regarded as works of art in their own right, thanks largely to the genius of Cochran working in perfect harmony with Coward . . . though there were many other collaborations that were almost as fruitful, such as those between Charlot and Gertrude Lawrence.

Every amateur who can tinkle a tune and scribble a lyric thinks he can write a revue. No idea could be more mistaken; it is a very difficult, delicate, and intricate medium of entertainment. I discovered this when I wrote Cochran's 1930 revue. The material I gave him was second-rate but his magic gave it the sparkle of success and it ran for a year.

Now I was on my own, with no Cochran to guide me. I should have been scared, but I wasn't.

I took a suite of rooms on the first floor of a very grand hotel near the Étoile. Catherine d'Erlanger had suggested it. Her

daughter Baba had married a charmer with the romantic name of
Prince Jean de Faucigny-Lucinge who apparently had something
to do with the hotel, and she had arranged for them to give me a
ten per cent deduction. 'You see, *mon enfant*, the things I do for you.
It will be *pour rien*!' It was in fact astonishingly expensive. She had
also arranged for them to fill the salon every day with baskets of
fleurs-de-lys. The piano I chose for myself, and on the night that it
arrived I sat down to play.

And then something rather extraordinary happened.

Set the scene, with the sparkle of Paris flickering through the
leaves of the chestnut trees, the white candles of their flowers
glimmering through the gathering dusk. Fill the room with the
lingering scent of lilies. Place a glass of champagne on the table by
the piano, rest your hands on the keyboard, and listen. Listen to
what? You have no idea, but it will come. Although the salon is
almost silent there are muted hints and echoes from the distant
traffic in the Bois—the eternal music of Paris dancing her way into
the night.

Sit still and listen. It will come.

And it came. But it was not the music which I had wanted, nor
the music for which I had been waiting. It came in the form of a
prayer—and I knew that it had to be the prayer of a girl whose
lover was setting out for the wars. The words and the music came
so swiftly that I might have been taking them down from dictation.

Noël Coward once admitted that even the most popular lyrics
sound trivial and ridiculous in cold print. This did not deter him
from publishing his own, at considerable profit, and it will not deter
me from publishing mine.

> I will pray
> Every hour of the night and the day,
> And I know that each whispering word
> Will be heard
> And will guide you . . .
> I will pray
> And my prayer will be happy and gay

It will ring like a song
All night long
Echoing beside you . . .
Through the thick of the fight
Like a lamp in the night
It will lead you,
Through the fire and the fear
You will know I am near
And I need you . . .
I will pray
Every hour of the night and the day,
And I know that each whispering word
Will be heard.

So that was that. As I wrote the last bars I knew exactly how the
song must be sung, and where and why. The occasion would be the
Waterloo Ball, there would be the muffle of drums in the background, and the whole stage would be bathed in red . . . the curtains,
the costumes of the dancers, all would be red . . . the blood red of
war.

I finish the champagne, and stay by the piano, thinking. This
has been a good night's work. The Waterloo Ball will be a marvel-
lous finale for Part I. It will look exquisite, with all the girls
swirling round the stage in every shade of crimson and scarlet and
blood red. Tomorrow I will go down to the Place Vendôme and
see Schiaparelli and try to persuade her to design the dresses. It will
sound lovely too, for the tune is simple and direct, a slow waltz
which will lend itself to many variations of tempo and of key as the
story progresses—and already, in my mind, a story is taking shape.
But for the moment I am too tired to write it down.

I get up and walk to the windows, pausing to sniff a bowl of
Catherine's fleurs-de-lys. The national flower of France. I throw
open the windows. In the early hours of this spring morning Paris
is hushed, but one sound comes very clearly into the room—the
tramp of soldiers' boots, a regiment of *poilus* marching down the
Champs-Elysées. I am brought sharply back to the present. I had

been living in 1815, to the music of a waltz. I had come back to the present, and though the rhythm had switched to a march, the theme was unaltered.

The revue, which I decided to call *Floodlight*, was finished in rather less than eight weeks. Considering that it contains twenty-two 'numbers', four star parts, three ballets, and a first-act finale which was a miniature operetta in its own right, I could scarcely be accused of wasting time. I flew the whole mass of manuscript over to London and arranged an audition. Everybody seemed delighted, particularly the backers. A brilliant cast was engaged, including John Mills—now Sir John—Hermione Baddeley, and Frances Day. By an extraordinary piece of good fortune Freddie Ashton—now recognised as one of the most inspired choreographers of the century—agreed to arrange some of the dances. I think he had fallen in love with a song I had writted called 'Dancing with the Daffodils' which was based on Wordsworth's poem.

One of the most charming theatres in London was booked—the Saville—and we went into immediate rehearsal. I could not believe that all this was happening—that so many charming and talented people had suddenly been assembled to sing my songs, dance to my music, act my sketches. I should have been on top of the world, but I was not. I was in an agony of apprehension, for a very simple reason. There was no master-mind to knock the whole thing into shape. No Cochran. Instead, the whole production—for reasons which could not possibly interest anybody but a very ancient and stage-struck fanatic—was in the hands of a charming but unpredictable young man called Denis Freeman. I pray that the soul of Denis Freeman is resting in peace. But I cannot help regretting that in spite of occasional flashes of genius he was, *au fond*, a crook, who fiddled the accounts, sniffed cocaine in the wings, was always late for rehearsals, and sometimes did not appear at all. I have nightmare memories of arriving at the theatre and finding groups of disconsolate chorus girls wandering about with nothing to do.

I will not dwell on the nightmare. When *Floodlight* at last appeared . . . and it was actually produced on time . . . it had what is known as a *succès d'estime*, which is the very last sort of success that any professional author wishes to be credited with. The notices were kind and the audiences seemed enthusiastic. For a brief period it looked as though we were set for success. Royalty appeared on several occasions—which is supposed to be good for business—and I had the agreeable experience of being summoned to the royal box to click my heels and answer ridiculous questions. One night Shaw arrived and beckoned to me in the foyer. 'Your Waterloo Ball conception was charming,' he observed. 'But you should have talked to me about it before you wrote it.' I asked him why. 'Because you were recording an historical event and you didn't check your facts.' I resisted the temptation to suggest that the same criticism might apply to *Saint Joan*.

Then suddenly everything began to go wrong. There were violent quarrels between the stars. One of the backers went bankrupt, creating a financial crisis. Worst of all, Denis Freeman, who should have been dealing with these matters, disappeared in a drunken haze. Very shortly afterwards the notices went up, and *Floodlight* flickered out.

The analysis of failure in the theatre is always interesting, if only to the author. In nine cases out of ten Shakespeare said all that was needed, in his terse comment that the 'play's the thing'. But there are exceptions. Brilliant plays can be ruined by insensitive directors, and Denis Freeman was to no small extent responsible for the collapse of *Floodlight*. But so was I. Even if it had been brilliantly directed it was probably doomed to failure, and it failed because I could not encapsulate myself in the theatre and forget the outside world. The most obvious example was at the end of the first half when I brought down the curtain on a prayer for peace at the Waterloo Ball. Nobody goes to the theatre to listen to prayers for peace, however melodious. But there were many other examples. There was a little song about a love-sick young man, with a good tune and an effective lyric but I made the fatal mistake of connecting it with the unemployment problem. How banal can one get? Listen to this:

My heart is out of work
It's on the dole
I stand in Cupid's queue
Without a goal
Until the moment you
Will condescend to save my soul

All this is excruciatingly trivial, but it has a place in this book, not only as an example of self-revelation in the past but because it gives me the opportunity to say something of importance in the present.

We must switch back three months. The only thing that really interested me about this unprofitable exercise, as I have already suggested, was the chance of hearing my music properly played by a decent orchestra, and at last it had come. The man whom I had chosen as orchestrator was a brilliant young musician called Benjamin Frankel, who was an exciting composer in his own right. I gave him a complete score, with a full piano version and a fairly comprehensive lay-out of the various instrumental parts. He expressed astonishment. 'This has never happened to me before,' he said. 'All I usually get from the so-called "composer" is a rough melodic line, and sometimes I don't get even as much as that. They simply come along and pick out a few bars on the piano with one finger and expect me to do the rest.'

He set to work and the result was enchanting, particularly in one of the ballets which I had composed as a parody in the style of Rossini. Came the day when the printers sent me the programme for correction.

FLOODLIGHT
Book, Lyrics and Music
by
Beverley Nichols

I stared at the programme. Something was wrong. Why was there no credit for Benny? Against the word 'Music' I scribbled an

251

asterisk. And after my own credits the asterisk added the information 'Orchestration by Benjamin Frankel'.

Never do a kind action. How long does one have to live learning these primitive precepts, which are the foundations of worldly success?

As the immediate result of my gesture with the asterisk I received a slap in the face from an important newspaper. The beady eyes of the dramatic critic had lighted upon the asterisk. He had been puzzled, he said, to see the name of Mr Beverley Nichols connected with the composition of music. Mr Nichols had surely gained enough notoriety in other spheres. 'Orchestration by Benjamin Frankel' obviously meant that it was Mr Frankel who had himself composed the music. Or words to that effect.

I was very angry. I wrote out an apology to myself and telegraphed it to the important newspaper, adding that I should be obliged if they would print it on the following morning and send me a cheque for a hundred pounds which would be presented to the People's Dispensary for Sick Animals. They printed the apology and sent the cheque by return of post.

What has all this to do with the present day and age? How can it interest the common reader? To answer these questions I must switch from autobiography to propaganda.

I have always resented the acclaim that is given to 'composers' who sail under false pretences. Even when those composers were capable of inventing an original tune I have felt this resentment—even with men like Noël Coward. One sits in a great theatre like Drury Lane; the lights are lowered, the overture strikes up, and the music begins—the sweep of strings, the murmur of the wood-wind, the golden sparkle of the harps, the cunning intervention of the percussion. And the audience sits back and marvels. 'Is it not amazing that Noël can contrive this magic . . . that he has such a mastery of counterpoint?' To which the answer is that Noël did *not* contrive the magic, and that his knowledge of counterpoint was nil.

It is all a vast confidence trick. The magic is wrought by the little men behind the scenes. The men and women who take the bare bones of the tune, and give it the authority and glamour of sophisticated instrumentation. Does that really matter? At least, it may be argued, Coward could create *tunes*. Is it of any consequence that if they had been given to the world through the medium of a mini-piano, they would never have been heard of again? Maybe not, though to me it would still be extremely irritating. I once had the melancholy experience in the twenties, in Paris, of hearing an early Cole Porter musical in which the tiny orchestra was unrehearsed and incompetent. The audience walked out. I had the even more melancholy experience, in Hollywood, of hearing Charlie Chaplin fumbling about on the piano making piffling little noises which were later transformed into quite impressive theme songs. By the little men behind the scenes.

This was forty years ago. Today the popular musical scene has changed, and greatly for the worse. The so-called 'composer' has faded further into the background, the little men have assumed more importance, and the machines have begun to assume the most vital role of all. We have now reached the stage where any illiterate errand boy with a primitive sense of rhythm can grunt into a complex of electronic devices, and in due course be hailed as a 'composer'. And if he has the right physique and an astute manager, and if he wears his trousers tight enough, and if his sex-life is sufficiently outrageous, he will shoot to the top of the pops and end up with a villa in the South of France. All in the name of 'music'. Of all the inventions of the last century, I believe the most likely to hasten the decline of western civilisation is the electric guitar, even more swiftly than the invention of the internal combustion engine.

I will end this jeremiad with a dirty story.

When I was writing Page Two the editor sent me to the provinces to write a piece about the latest pop group—not The Beatles—which was rousing the teenagers to new frenzies of hysteria. After twenty minutes of ear-splitting cacophony I could stand no more and sought out the manager in his office. He was in a state of nervous stress and I asked him what was wrong.

'It is a matter of dirt money,' he said.

And what was that?

He explained that it was the extra wages he had to pay his staff for cleaning up the unsavoury mess which was made on the carpets by the hordes of sexually demented young women who had been driven to orgasmic extremities by the screaming youths on the platform, strumming their instruments as though they were phallic symbols, as indeed they were.

Only an old man could write in this manner? Perhaps, but in these matters my feelings have not changed since boyhood. Over forty years ago, in one of the 'Allways' books,* I expressed them in a chapter called 'A Symphony of Silence', and as I turn back to its pages I am struck by the consistency of my early loves and my adolescent hatreds. The silence which I celebrate is not total, for there can be no such thing on this side of the grave; it is a sort of musical silence in which every sound is pianissimo. I begin the chapter by leaning over an old well in a cottage garden, recording the music of drops of water that slowly fall in a simple sequence of four notes . . . C, C♯, E and—after a pause—E♭. I stay by the well, and after a few moments the silence is broken again by a fairy-like percussion. A thrush is knocking a snail-shell on the old pavement that leads to the rose garden. I leave the well, and walk to the orchard and lie down under an ancient apple tree. There is scarcely a breath of wind, but the leaves are singing, very softly, and there are mysterious hints from the long grass, and through them I can detect other instruments in Nature's infinite orchestra—the swift whispers from the wings of a dragonfly, even the unique sound of a mole burrowing in the sweet-scented earth. I described it as 'the sort of sound that a goblin grave-digger would make.'

I ended the chapter in this book with a paragraph of unashamed sentimentality.

I am writing far from Allways, and the traffic roars by in the street outside, so fiercely that you would say that the street was full of wild animals, bellowing and screaming after their prey. But above the din I hear, clear

---

* *A Village in a Valley:* Jonathan Cape Ltd, 1934.

and sweet, the tiny sounds of Allways, which are so far clearer to me because I hear them with my heart, and not only with my ears . . . the soft patter of petals onto the parched earth when a rose in summer passes, the hard knock of a chestnut in the road when the November winds are full, the hiss of apple logs when the fitful rain spits down the chimney. These sounds I hear, high above the clamour of the city. Maybe I walk with dreams. But the dream is clearer than the reality.

So it was, nearly half a century ago. And so, thank God, it remains today.

CHAPTER XXI

✿✿✿✿✿

WHITE COCKROACHES

I have always believed that success may be snatched from the jaws of disaster and after the failure of *Floodlight* I sat down and wrote a novel about the whole experience. I called it *Revue*. Thanks to the brilliance of my French translator, René Brest, it was very well received in France, particularly on the radio, where it proved to be a welcome source of francs. The royalties continued to mount up throughout the war, and when peace came it was turned into a television spectacular by Radiodiffusion Française.

This was among the rare occasions when I felt that perhaps there was some point in being an author. To sit in a café, with a pocketful of foreign currency, conjured up through the workings of one's own imagination, to share—anonymously—the emotion of the audience as they followed the fortunes of the characters one had created, this was gratifying. I had never wanted to set pen to paper at all, as long as there was a keyboard available. I could have said in a few chords things that were more important than I had said in many chapters. But I had this fatal facility with words. I was a very mixed-up kid.

The 'fatal facility with words' reminds me that it is time to explain the title of this chapter, which is singularly unpleasant. So unpleasant, indeed, that it evoked a typical postcard from Bernard Shaw. Like all his postcards it was short and to the point. 'Your cockroaches make me shudder. Keep it up. G.B.S.'

But what *were* the white cockroaches, and where did I encounter them? In answering that question I shall be able to give some momentum to our story.

We are still in the middle thirties. To all outward appearances I was in the full flight of success, not only in England but in America, where I was beginning to demand high prices on the lecture platform. An American lecture tour would hardly suggest itself as a theme for romance but my own tours, which had to be streamlined and cunningly organised, were among the most vivid episodes in my life.

There was only one snag about them; one was never quite sure what to expect. I had three 'standard' lectures, which I adapted to the quality of the audience. They came into three classes—'literary', 'political', and 'general'. But sometimes I was really up against it, because my agents had been misinformed about the audience. I will recall only one occasion. Arriving at a middle-western town in a violent snow-storm, I was greeted by a reception committee of elderly gentlemen in deep black who were the leading figures in the local Presbyterian community. As soon as we got into the car they made it clear to me that I had been engaged to preach a sermon in the parish church. They would not expect me to lunch, they would take me straight to my hotel, where I would doubtless need to meditate before delivering the sermon at two p.m. Meditation, in these circumstances, was obviously demanded. It took the form of two dozen oysters and a bottle of Californian chablis. At precisely two p.m. I mounted the pulpit, cleared my throat, and delivered the sermon. It went like a bomb. In concise and vigorous prose, I delivered a sustained attack on the moral attitudes of St Paul who has always seemed to me the least attractive of the figures in the Christian story. I laid special emphasis on his complex about women's hair, and his fanatical insistence that it must be covered in places of worship.

Nobody walked out. When I stepped down from the pulpit the leading Presbyterian escorted me outside, where the blizzard was raging even more furiously. He couldn't have been more friendly and assured me that I have given his 'flock' something to think about. With which he handed me my cheque and I returned to

New York, travelling in an over-heated carriage, and thinking that this was a very agreeable way of earning a living, even though it might be an unorthodox method of spreading the gospel.

Spreading the gospel. At last we can approach the white cockroaches.

If any sort of living portrait has emerged from these confused confessions it must by now be clear that whatever my other failings and absurdities, there was one thing about me that was constant. I was, *au fond*, a missionary. Behind the bright façade lurked a very different sort of person, a man who really had a genuine desire to make the world a better place. Up till now, my missionary zeal had been confined to two themes, expressed in *Cry Havoc* and *The Fool Hath Said*. It was time that I widened my horizons. Oddly enough it was the late Duke of Windsor, of all people, who unwittingly provided the inspiration. When he was Prince of Wales he went down to the distressed areas and was so upset and befuddled by what he saw that he delivered himself of a short sentence of four words. He said . . . 'Something must be done.' Throughout his lamentable life they were the only four words he ever uttered that had the faintest relevance to the horrific situation of the British Empire, of which he was the titular head, but they echoed round the world. The reason why they had this remarkable impact was that he had thought them up all by himself. They had emerged quite spontaneously, from his tiny weasel brain. Having delivered them he went back to London and danced till dawn.

It was too much to stomach. I had to do something about it. What I did was to get into a train and hasten to Wales, the area over which the clouds of misery were most thickly concentrated. If 'something had to be done' I might conceivably be the man to do it.

Enter, at last, white cockroaches.

When I sped to Wales I was inspired by an almost masochistic determination to do things the hard way. I wanted to be hurt, to share in the squalor, and to learn the reality of hunger. Through the help of one of the miners' M.P.s I was put up by a family called

Williams, who lived in a small town of indescribable desolation called Ynyscynon. I was given a room the size of a large cupboard, the bed was propped up by packing-cases, and there was only one blanket. The Williams family was on the starvation line. I was glad that I had brought down a hamper of food which included a large ham and two bottles of whisky.

On the following day I put my masochism to the test and went down one of the coal-mines. Nowadays, everybody goes down coal-mines—princesses and pop stars and publicity-minded politicians.

When I went down my coal-mine, forty years ago, the experience was not quite so pleasant. To say that every mine in those days was a death-trap would be an exaggeration, but it would not be so far from the truth. To me, at any rate, it was a death-trap, because I have always suffered from acute claustrophobia.

As we walked I noticed how quiet it all was. The tunnel was hushed, as though the mine held some terrible secret. Our feet sank into the piled dust, as into a thick carpet. And there were strange winds that blew down the tunnels, bringing with them a smell that was entirely new, faint but persistent, a compound of coal-dust and sweat and ancient poison.

We trudged on, further and further into the depths. I had asked to see the ponies, and was comforted to find that they looked plump and well, and that they were not blind—as yet. All the same, I longed to take them back into the world outside, into the fresh air, where they could roll in the green grass.

And it was when I was coming out of the stables that I met the white cockroaches.

This is what I wrote that night, before going to bed ...

Cockroaches have never been my favourite form of domestic pet. There is something sinister about them, and he who crunches a cockroach has a terrible feeling of breaking bones, of murdering something foul but very much alive and sentient.

If ordinary black cockroaches are sinister, white cockroaches are far more so. They have the unhealthy pallor of fungi in dark woods, those fungi that you feel the sun has never touched, not because it cannot reach them, but because even the sunlight would be poisoned if it were to come into contact with that damp and evil flesh.

And here were the white cockroaches crawling round my ankles, getting very near to the gap between my socks and overalls. I bent down and brushed them off. As I did so, I felt more than slightly sick.

This, I maintain, was good reporting, and so apparently, did Shaw. The reason it was effective was because I had deliberately contrived a situation to which I knew, instinctively, that I should react with horror. There were many more horrors to come before at last, crawling on hands and knees, we reached the coal-face. Again I quote . . .

It is impossible to look for the first time, at this small black square, without a feeling of deep emotion. Here on this foundation, an Empire has been built. From here has come the power which has sent great ships over the seven seas, has levelled mountains, spanned rivers, created life in deserts. All from this small black square. And now it is near its end. A few more years and the last of it will be shovelled into the trams and will rattle its way to the pit-head. And then the tunnels will be deserted, and the lights will flicker out, and the pit will be closed, and the black rats and the white cockroaches will reign supreme.

This may not be immortal prose but it was apposite forty years ago, and even today it has its point.

Deliberately, in this Welsh adventure, I sought out ways of torturing myself. I wanted to see how much I could bear without breaking down. At the end of the desolate street where I was staying there was a house in which a man was dying. He was an ex-miner called John Morgan. The causes of death were cancer of the lungs and tuberculosis, both contracted in the mines. He was dying in a bed that lay under the window, which had no curtains, because they had long ago been pawned. Since the light from the street lamp shone directly onto the bed, he was dying in spot-lit publicity, and from time to time little groups of neighbours gathered outside to watch.

I cannot remember how I obtained entry to John Morgan's house. Probably by muttering the word 'Press' which was a sort of abracadabra, particularly to the very poor. I joined the little group that was keeping vigil. There were eight of them, his wife, his mother, his brother and his five children. The light was failing, and he was failing too. The pain was almost past bearing. 'Oh God! Oh God!' he cried. The whole room was permeated with pain. We stood and looked at each other. An old woman bent over him and wiped the sweat from his forehead. His face twisted to a grotesque and tortured smile.

I tiptoed away when the death-rattle was beginning. I had a compelling desire to weep, but suppressed it. Was I not writing a 'story', and was it not essential that the story should be authentic? So I walked into an alley, and sat down on a wall, and wrote a description of the death-rattle. And was I not fully qualified to write it? For the death-rattle is a form of music—the music that ends the dark discords of the lives of those whom God has forgotten. In terms of music, it should be scored for the percussion section. Muted drums, dying away, with sudden sinister crescendos, fading at last into a very empty silence.

So I sat on the wall, in the drizzling rain, and wrote it all down. Eventually it was to form a chapter in a book called *News of England*.* And nobody took the least notice of it. Nobody cared.

I am far too old to cherish resentments about my failures, but I am not too old to be puzzled by them. As far as I can remember *News of England* was the only book of mine which never went into a second edition.

Why? What was wrong with it?

The answer is quite simple. Nothing was wrong with it.

But I was the wrong person to write it, for two reasons. First, because it represented a total rejection of all that I had previously stood for; it celebrated the death of the pacifist and the final burial of the author of *Cry Havoc*. Secondly, because—in spite of the quality of the material, which was sombre and often brutal—some of it had been written, as it were, in white tie and tails. A single

* *News of England:* Jonathan Cape Ltd, 1938.

example will suffice. A few days after returning from Wales I attended one of the last of the great receptions at Londonderry House. This was perhaps an unwise thing to do, because the Londonderrys and their circle had mining interest, and my excursion—though I had not yet written about it myself, had caught the attention of several gossip writers. To make things worse, I stood at the top of the great staircase next to Lady Londonderry. When I took my leave I ran into Valentine Castlerosse, who had noticed my brief elevation to this position of grandeur, and had also heard about the Welsh adventure. He surveyed me with intense dislike. He said . . . 'Well Beverley, you have certainly mastered the art of getting the best out of both worlds.'

I seem to be going on at inordinate length about this long-forgotten work, but there is justification for doing so. For one thing, it should not be forgotten, because it is packed with hitherto neglected material. For another, because it throws a vivid light on my own motivations while I was writing it. These were primarily masochistic.

My own tendencies, from boyhood onwards, have always been masochistic. This does not mean that I enjoyed being beaten in dormitory, nor that I have ever had the least desire to recline on coaches in houses of ill-fame, being briskly caned on the behind. (As I have gone through life I have been surprised by the large number of quite respectable middle-aged gentlemen who have been allured by this curious method of passing a dull Sunday afternoon.) My own masochism has been expressed by a constant tendency to force myself into situations where I knew I should be hurt. Without agony there could be no ecstasy, and without pain there could be no creation.

In *News of England* we have already seen an expression of this tendency in the Welsh adventure. There were to be many more as the book progressed. Here is another example. I had never mastered my fear of flying, but I wanted to draw attention to the appalling state of Britain's air defences. In order to write with authority I had to conquer my anti-flying complex. This meant not only getting into aeroplanes and sitting back with a fiercely artificial smile while somebody else did the job; it meant climbing into the cockpit with the pilot and, after a few elementary instructions, taking over the controls. It needed a certain amount of string-pulling to contrive this situation, but eventually I found myself at Brooklands air-centre, on a wet windy day, struggling into a leather coat, goggles and helmet, and clambering into an ancient machine that looked as if it should have gently been towed by the nose into a neighbouring meadow and put out to grass.

This was unmitigated masochism—so much so that when I came to write about it I chose the medium of pure farce. If one was about to die, one might at least die with a smile on one's lips. When I first gripped the joy-stick I pushed it forward with such force that we went into a nose-dive, from which I was rescued by the pilot, who shot the machine up again, narrowly missing the steeple of a church. When we were high enough to manœuvre we plunged into deep cloud, and I heard the instructor shouting, 'Keep her straight!'

'How?'

'With the rudder.'

I pulled another lever. I seem to remember that when we came out of the cloud we were upside down, but I righted myself and for the next ten minutes I had the sheer joy of flying, and I had conquered my complex.

More masochism, and more farce. Surveying, as I was, the whole spectrum of British society, it was meritable that I should eventually come face to face with the Comrades. With the Russian menace. In 1938, for a great many otherwise sane people such as Bernard Shaw, Communism was a respectable and reasonable philosophy. (Some day some dramatist will write a tragi-comedy about Shaw's acceptance of Communism, and a very bitter work it will be, based on his Russian visit, where he laid aside his mantle as a passionate playwright, and struggled into the costume of a pathetic old pantaloon, spouting wicked nonsense and getting paid for it.)

I put a good deal of hard work into my researches on pre-war British Communism. This involved me in long arguments with some of the most pretentious bores whom God has ever created. I only persevered because of a deep conviction that the bores were dangerous. But how was one to get this across to the British public? There were a mass of alarming statistics, but would anybody ever read them? The answer was provided, unexpectedly, by P. G. Wodehouse. We were lunching together, and I put the problem to him. 'What would *you* do in my position?'

'You really care about this Communist business, don't you?'

'Of course I care.'

'And you want to know what I'd do about it? Very well.' He fumbled in his pocket and drew out a crumpled copy of *The Daily Worker*, the official organ of the Communist Party. 'Read this. I'd thought of giving it to Jeeves, but maybe you'd make better use of it.'

He had underlined some of the passages in an essay entitled 'For Purity of Marxist-Leninist Theory in Surgery'. He read it aloud with a dead-pan expression, and observed, 'If I were having my piles out and saw that article sticking out of the surgeon's pocket, I should leap off the operating table like a startled antelope'. That has the authentic Wodehouse touch. There was a great deal more in the same vein. One reflection I can quote with a clear conscience, because he gave me permission to scribble it on the menu. It was inspired by an exceptionally ridiculous article under the heading of 'For Party Spirit in Mathematics'.

Plum said, and this is a literal quote: 'Add a capitalist 2 to a communist 6. Divide the result by a Trotskyite 4. What is the answer? Whatever the result may be in Russian, I have a shrewd suspicion that in England it would be a lemon.'

I tore up all that I had written about the Communist menace and decided to attack with other weapons—the weapons of laughter. I tried to keep my sense of humour about it all, but on one occasion I failed. There was a meeting in a suburban town hall which was to be addressed by a young woman from an opulent background who had paid two brief visits to Russia, and had emerged so scrupulously brain-washed that her mental processes were atrophied. The title of her lecture was 'Russia Revisited' and after speaking at great length about the Moscow Park of Rest and Culture, which she described as a paradise of freedom compared with such capitalist slave-camps as Kensington Gardens, she declared the meeting open to the public. Were there any questions? I rose to my feet. Yes, I had a question. Here is a shortened version of the ensuing dialogue, which was later quoted with derision by *The Daily Worker*.

B.N.	Do you believe in liberty?
Miss X	What do you mean by liberty?
B.N.	I mean the ability to say, or write, or sing, or otherwise express exactly what I think, when, where and how I like.
Miss X	Yes. That is to say . . .
B.N.	*Do* you?
Comrade	Order! Order!
Miss X	(*Icily*) Let this 'gentleman' ask his question.
B.N.	In that case, will you kindly tell me if I should be allowed to get up in the Red Square at Moscow, blackguard the Soviet Government, and receive the protection of the Soviet police; in the same way that you are allowed to get up in this room, blackguard the British Government and receive the protection of the British Police?
	There was a deathly silence. Nobody moved.
B.N.	I am waiting for an answer.

Suddenly from a corner, a young man with a beard that contrasted oddly with his eunuch voice screamed, 'All that would happen in Moscow is that you would be certified as insane!'

The tension was broken and there was loud applause.

That was published over forty years ago—long before the hideous techniques of Soviet psychiatric torture had been perfected.

I have nearly done with this posthumous review of a book that never really came to life. The only person, who to my knowledge ever took it seriously was Winston Churchill. Shortly after it was published I went down to stay for the weekend with old Mrs

Ronnie Greville at Polesden Lacey, when he was a fellow-guest. He came down to breakfast, where I was sitting alone in the great dining-room. He helped himself liberally, sat down, glared at me, and snorted . . . 'You have been keeping me awake half the night. That book of yours.' Another snort. 'But nobody will take any notice of it.' Another snort. 'I can sympathise. Nobody ever takes any notice of *me*.'

CHAPTER XXII

&&&&&&

ESCAPE

By the time that 1938 was drawing to a close I was physically and mentally exhausted. *News of England* had appeared, and had been received with a deathly silence. To say that I had nothing else on the stocks would be untrue; I had another play, to which I gave the title *Shadow of the Vine*,* but I could not concentrate on it, because it was based on the figure of my father, and he was still unfortunately very much alive, ranting, and raging and vomiting in my brother's vicarage in Cambridge Square, only a couple of miles away from my own house.

I also had a concerto on the stocks, in the form of sheaves of manuscript scattered all over the piano. The sheaves mounted up, usually in the small hours of the morning, when I tried to put on paper all the music that was tormenting me. In retrospect this has its humorous side, because technically my concerto was aimed at the heights; it bristled with cadenzas and double-octave sequences which would have given pause to Rachmaninov. But as a composer I was technically illiterate; it took me hours to write a dozen bars which an educated musician could have polished off in five minutes. If I had been an unmitigated prostitute I would have hired a recording machine and engaged a couple of hacks to put it into shape; after which a bevy of orchestrators and publicity agents

---

* Ten years were to pass before *Shadow of the Vine* was to have its first London production in 1949, and another two years before it was shown on the principal television networks.

would have got to work on it and eventually, no doubt, it would have been produced at the Festival Hall, and received with acclaim.

I had to get away. I was a dried-up stick. A whole bundle of dried-up sticks, waiting for a spark from heaven to set them alight again. For once, in a way, God co-operated. Osbert Sitwell rang up from Renishaw. Could I come up and stay for a few days? For the last time? The phrase puzzled me because I had never been able to visit Renishaw before. Why did he say 'for the last time'?

'Because everything that any of us do in the next few months we shall be doing for the last time. And there are a lot of things I want to do before it is too late. Some of them with you.'

I went up to Renishaw. I took with me a young actor called Cyril Butcher. As I write his name I find myself wondering why I have not written it before. He had already been my constant companion for several years, and still is. Surely forty years of unbroken friendship should have earned him at least a footnote? The only way in which I can explain the omission is by suggesting that in one's life there are some people, men and women, who are so important that they cannot be isolated as characters in their own right. One cannot step aside and watch them from the stalls because one is walking with them on the same stage. Between Cyril and myself there was an almost uncanny rapport. Very soon after we met (it was when we were casting *Evensong* and he stepped out of the wings to audition for a minor part) I realised that here was somebody who was going to mean a great deal in my life. Not because of his physical attraction—(he had just won an all-England prize in some sort of film contest). Nor because of his intellectual equipment, which was considerable, although he had never had a conventional education. Later he was to publish a book of his own —forgotten—a play of his own—forgotten—to serve with gallantry in the navy—forgotten—and afterwards to make a name as a distinguished television director. All forgotten. Today I can dimly understand at least one element that cemented this enduring relationship, and it can be summed up in a single word—*manqué*. From the beginning we both knew that we were destined to miss the boat. In my case, this may sound an exaggeration; I had caught a great many boats, and sailed the seven seas in them, usually occupying a cabin on A Deck. But I had never landed in the right harbour. Cyril had not had such consolations, but he was a happier man, because he took life as it came and did not worry about tomorrow.

We arrived at Renishaw on a dismal evening in late November. When it loomed out of the mist in the distance, gigantic, bleak, and strangely sinister, Cyril stopped the car and said, 'No'.

'No what?'

'We can't possibly stay here. It's twice as large as Buckingham Palace. It'll be icily cold. The plumbing will be ghastly. Anyway, I hardly know Osbert and I want a drink. Let's stay at a pub and ring him up and tell him we've had an accident.'

This outrageous suggestion was ignored.

I shall always remember walking through the front door of Renishaw a few minutes later. It was like stepping into an immense conservatory. Far from being cold, the heat was almost excessive, and it was the exquisite warmth that comes from log fires smouldering in ancient grates. The bitter-sweet tang of the logs mingled with the perfume of white Parma violets. As for Cyril's drink, it was not long in coming, for when Osbert appeared he was carrying a magnum of Louis Roederer 1928. It was opened by an ancient servitor who poured it into Venetian goblets, two of which, I noticed, were cracked.

Are such details worth recording? I think so, because they are echoes of a way of life that is almost extinct. To me, it can be expressed in a single detail, trivial but tremendous. When at last we tottered to our bedrooms, in which the log fires were still smouldering, I closed the door and stared with astonishment at an object in the far corner. It was a large jug of Capo di Monte pottery, standing on a rococo commode. It was covered with a monogrammed towel, and it was filled with very hot water, faintly perfumed with rose-geranium. To the equalitarians of today such an object would be anathema, a symbol of slavery. A bludgeoned housemaid would have been needed to stagger up the labyrinthine staircases in order to pander to my needs. Even if this had been the case, I could not have cared less. I had earned an interlude of luxury, and I slept with a clear conscience.

'For the last time.'

As the days went by, this was the monotonous threnody of Osbert's conversation. It recurred again and again. If one mentioned the ballet he sighed and shook his head and said that when we next saw the curtain fall at Covent Garden it would be for the last time. Soon the opera house would be a heap of rubble.

It was Cyril who briskly switched Osbert out of this melancholy rut. He lifted his glass and observed with the precise diction of a young actor who has been brought up in the hard school of provincial rep . . .

'I may be totally illiterate but I had to learn the Raven at school. You've been saying "Nevermore" ever since we arrived and I refuse to accept it. Let's go for a walk.'

We set out for a tour of the great grey gardens and it was then in the distance that I saw a brilliant flash of blue. It came from a large bed of gentians that Sir George had planted round a statue, and as we stopped and marvelled at this unexpected display we all found ourselves thinking of the same thing. Blue skies, azure seas, purple sunsets . . . magic horizons that we had never seen before.

That night, gathered round the log fire in the great hall, hung with the shadowy portraits of Osbert's ancestors, we decided to go to Mexico.

There was only one snag about this arrangement, as far as I was concerned. Money.

My own bank account, at this time, was deeply in the red, and my assets—apart from the little house in Hampstead—were negligible. I had no life-insurances, and no securities except a small portfolio of shares in companies which were so shady that they almost invariably went into liquidation a few weeks after I had purchased them. At no period in my life, which was already half over, had I managed to accumulate a capital approaching £10,000.

Why? Where had it all gone? I ought to have saved a great deal more after all these years of toil and sweat—at the very least £10,000. This figure began to assume an almost mystical significance. I determined to accumulate it as swiftly as possible. Meanwhile I was about to embark on an adventure that would involve considerable expense. Then, out of the blue a letter arrived from my German publishers with the news that a considerable sum was standing to my credit in Hamburg, but adding that owing to the financial decrees of the Third Reich they were unable to send it in sterling. The utmost they were legally permitted to transfer was ten pounds, for which they enclosed a cheque.

Unfortunately, for them, they added a postscript to the effect that though they could not send any money *out* of the country I could spend it *in* Germany, provided that I spent it on something that was a hundred per cent German. At first this suggestion did not appeal to me at all. Then I had an idea. Anything German, my publishers had said, could be purchased with my hard-earned royalties. Well, I wanted to sail to South America. And if there was anything more Teutonic than the Hamburg-American shipping line, I should be interested to know what it was. So I wrote and instructed them, firmly but politely, to purchase me a suite on the most luxurious of their liners, by name the *Cordillera*, which was sailing for Mexico in December.

Cut to the charming little port of Dover on Christmas Eve, 1938. In the distance are the celebrated white cliffs, veiled in snow. Bringing alongside the S.S. *Cordillera*, which glistens with all the latest German techniques. Introduce Osbert stumbling across the cobblestones shivering in a sable coat, fearing the worst. Go aboard. Walk down the warm corridors. A door is flung open by a Teutonic Apollo who clicks his heels and bows.

I enter the suite. There are two spacious cabins and a central state-room, of such opulence that Onassis would have felt quite at home. Cyril greets us from a sofa. In front of him is a chromium-plated trolley bearing a bottle of champagne and a silver tray, covered by a lid. He lifts the lid and reveals a mountain of iced caviar.

'I've been doing your homework,' he says. 'I've gone into your publisher's contract. And the caviar is on the house.'

We steamed south. All seemed well. For a space I gave myself up to the delight of doing absolutely nothing—not even scribbling little scraps of music on the saloon writing-paper, before throwing them overboard. I had heard the music in my head, and if there were a God in heaven he would also have heard it and filed it for future reference. And obviously there was a God in heaven, for as the weather grew warmer the skies began to be lit by a blue that could only have been mixed on a divine palette—gentian blue, the same blue that had shone from the petals of the flowers at Renishaw.

Most important of all I had escaped from the cage of Page Two. Before setting sail I had sat up half the night scribbling articles for future publications till my wrist ached, and if the art department could not think of any ways of illustrating them, that was their affair. Not that it was so easy to unshackle myself from the chains of the hack. There were several people on board who would have made excellent copy. One of them was a Rothschild—a gaunt middle-aged woman in a scarlet dress who looked rather lonely. I found her wandering about the deck clutching a life of Proust. I thought it would be nice to ask her to our suite for a glass of champagne and a dollop of caviar. I did not know her name and had no idea of her background; I only wanted to give her a little treat. She had probably never tasted caviar before. I was mistaken. She was enormously rich, and she ate our caviar casually as if it were mincemeat. When I discovered who she was I seemed to hear, in the distance, the rattle of journalistic chains. *Beverley Nichols: Caviar with the Rothschilds.* Excellent for the image, and easy for the art department. I did not pursue the friendship and I never saw her again except for a fleeting moment. But I have often wondered from which branch of the glittering hierarchy she was descended. For the Rothschilds, as the reader need scarcely be reminded, were Jews. And I was about to be involved in a Jewish tragedy—a tragedy so poignant that, as I recall it, the memory of the gentian skies seems to be shadowed by the symbol of the crooked cross.

*   *   *

On board the ship there were three hundred German-Jewish refugees. It was only by degrees that one became aware of them, not only because most of them were travelling steerage but because the few cabin-class passengers, when they first showed themselves, had kept to themselves, as though they were only too well aware that they were an inferior race. They huddled together in corners, and when one passed them in the corridors they stepped aside, standing with their backs to the wall, as though they expected to be hit. I found this unendurable. An idiotic fragment of dialogue flashed through my mind. Raging with the injustice of it all I bumped into Osbert on the upper deck. I had been talking to a family of Jewish musicians. The father had sung at Salzburg, and his small son played Mozart with exquisite impertinence. They had been chucked out of Germany like a load of rubbish. All that stood between them and starvation was a sapphire brooch. I said to Osbert: 'This sort of situation makes me ashamed of being an Aryan. If there were a surgeon aboard I should immediately apply to be circumcised.'

'Haven't you been circumcised?'

'No. Have you?'

'I have no idea. One day I must take down my trousers and have a look.'

This was a comedy, it was a tragedy, it was a mix-up, in short it was life. It only became a 'story', in the Maugham sense, when the ship's captain asked me for a drink in his cabin. He was a kindly, intelligent young man, with little of the Nazi about him.

'About all these Jews,' he said. 'You seem to have friends among them.'

'So what?'

'We've just received a cable saying that at least half of them won't be allowed to land. It's nothing to do with our government. It's the Mexicans. They've suddenly changed their immigration laws.'

'But what will happen to them?'

'They'll have to be sent back to Germany. And God knows what will happen to them when they return.'

273

I began to cry out that this was intolerable; it was unspeakable cruelty. Surely they had suffered enough already? He cut me short.

'I'm not completely without a heart. But what can I *do*? My officers are orthodox Nazis. It makes their blood boil to see our waiters serving them at table. They'd be only too delighted to take them back.'

'To the concentration camps?'

He shrugged his shoulders.

I felt sick at heart. 'Why did you come to me about this?'

'I wanted your advice, as an Englishman. I happen to like the English. I'm in a dilemma. Ought I to tell them now, or ought I to wait till the end of the voyage?'

'Does anybody else know about this?'

'Only the radio officer, and he's bound to secrecy.'

'What do you yourself feel?'

'As an officer I ought to be taking immediate action—sorting them out into groups, cancelling their passports, all that sort of thing.'

'And as a man?'

He did not answer. From below we could hear laughter and shouting from the swimming-pool. The Jews always crowded the swimming-pool. They used to plunge into the diamond-clear water as though they were cleansing themselves from sin—not their own sin but the sins of the men who were torturing them.

For a moment we stood there without speaking, while the sound of the laughter drifted through the porthole. Jewish laughter, which in these latter years, had been little heard. I said the first thing that came into my head. 'They sound very happy. A few days' more happiness would mean a lot to them.'

He caught my eye, and then he smiled. A very Aryan smile, with a flash of arrogance but a touch of kindliness. 'You needn't say any more,' he said.

The Jews were not told. The laughter echoed on for a few more days, till suddenly, as we were nearing land, it faded away, and the swimming-pool was deserted. The operation in which they were finally removed was conducted with superb Nazi efficiency. The

274

hour was midnight and as soon as we hove to, little fleets of native boats glided out from the harbour, and the Jews clambered aboard. There were no scenes, no arguments, and total silence except for the occasional whimper of a child in its mother's arms. As I stared through the porthole, I could see little, for the moon was veiled, and the whole world seemed in mourning. Then for a moment the clouds cleared and in the first boat I noticed a gaunt, middle-aged woman in a scarlet dress, sitting proudly erect, staring straight ahead of her. There was a sparkle of diamonds round her throat. The woman whom I had asked to our cabin in order to partake of our precious caviar. Even the Rothschilds, it seemed, were not safe from the octopus tentacles of the Third Reich.

When I was staring out of the porthole my face was wet with sweat, because I was running a high temperature. I will not trouble the reader with the symptoms; I only mention it to excuse the chronological and geographical confusion of the next three months. They are recalled through the mists of a recurrent fever in which Cyril, fortunately, was always by my side.

This was the situation. Osbert departed, en route to Ecuador. Cyril and I were now on our own, and we found ourselves in Venezuela, motoring up the precipitous, corkscrew routes that led to the capital city of Caracas. Why? I have no idea. All I remember is that I was in a rather sombre mood, because the eternal missionary in me was worried about the health of the natives, who were apparently suffering from every known disease. Half the children seemed to be afflicted by trachoma, there was a great deal of tuberculosis, and venereal disease was rampant. The Venezuelan government was making spasmodic efforts to cope with the situation, but their efforts seemed to be confined to plastering the country with alarmist posters. As the coach swept up the mountain road, through scenery of spectacular beauty, we were confronted by one of these posters, so large that it blocked out the view. It posed a simple question, in scarlet letters a foot high.

WHAT HAVE YOU DONE ABOUT YOUR SYPHILIS TODAY?

'What have you done about *your* syphilis today?' demanded Cyril with shameful frivolity.

I said that it was nothing to joke about.

'Perhaps not. But we ought to do *something* about it, and quickly.' He pondered for a moment. Then he gave a broad grin. 'However we obviously can't do it till we get off this bloody bus.'

It was fortunate that I had Cyril with me; throughout this trying period his irrepressible cheerfulness acted as a corrective to my tiresome sensitivity.

We arrived at Panama City. This section of these recollections has the quality of an ancient film documentary, blurred, scratched, and inefficiently cut. In the dockyards I collapsed on the cobble-stones. Crowds gathered round. I have a memory of peering faces, none too friendly, and groping hands, because my jacket had swung open revealing a wad of notes. Cyril lifted me up, commandeered a taxi, and the next thing I remember is waking up in an enormous bed, with a temperature of 104°. There were salacious pictures of naked females on the walls and the ceiling was entirely covered with a mirror.

I blinked at Cyril. 'I feel as if I were in a brothel.'

'You are. The best in Panama City.'

'Why?'

'The taxi-man's idea. Better than any of the hotels, he said, and from what I've seen of them he was right. Very clean, he said. Doctor he come every day to inspect ladies. At last you'll be able to get something done about that syphilis of yours.'

I closed my eyes. The fever burned on. I could not disentangle the dream from the reality. From time to time the door opened softly, to disclose a brightly painted female tiptoeing towards me, pausing in alarm as she caught a glimpse of my ravaged face, beating a hasty retreat. The next thing I remember is a kaleidoscope of trees against the sky, very Cézanne trees, in every shade of green, light and dark, glowing and golden, sullen and sinister.

'Where are we now?'

'In some sort of jungle. On our way to the sea.'

I struggled to sit up in the ambulance. Suddenly there was a sound like a pistol shot and the car braked.

'What was that?'

The driver turned his head. There was a grin on his face. 'Snake, señor. We call him "bushmaster". Very bad snake. I break his back. You wish to see?'

I turned round. Only a few yards away in the middle of the road a magnificent creature, green and mottled black, was writhing *in extremis*. The agony must have been acute because his body was quivering in a gigantic V sign. I had a swift and sharp pain in my own spine, sharing the agony. I shook my head.

As we drove on under the immense tapestry of trees, I could not shake off the memory of the snake's distress. Perhaps it had a family. Perhaps, in the dark shadows, a mate was lurking, and a cluster of small, mottled creatures, waiting for its return. Why should I rejoice in the death of this creature, even if it might have caused my own? God had created the snake. It had not asked to be born a snake. It had made no personal plea for the venom with which God had endowed it.

God, snakes, death, poison . . . under the ever-changing arches of Cézanne's trees, with the scent of sea drifting ever closer towards us. It was all a great puzzlement.

Then I heard Cyril's voice.

'I can read you like a book. And if you've decided to have an emotional crisis about breaking the back of that bushmaster bastard, I shall go on strike.'

As I said before, there was an almost psychic rapport between us.

We arrived at a rambling, haphazard little town called Azuera, which sprawled over a sandy beach lapped by the soporific waves of the Pacific. There was a small hotel by the side of the Ocean, kept by a charming Dane and his rosy-cheeked wife. It was all a great contrast to the brothel—spotlessly clean, with wholesome food, and grace before meals. The jungle seemed far away, but one could still see it in the distance, and always there was the sense of Nature as a cruel powerful presence, spying on us with a thousand hostile eyes. Crouched on the bare branches of a tree outside my window a cluster of vultures kept ceaseless vigil, staring through the window, muttering to one another, like a posse of undertakers impatient for the signal that would tell them that the time had come to pounce and claim the wages of death. Most disturbing were the spectral ranks of land-crabs, grey and ghostly, gathering on the beach. Quite harmless, the landlord assured me, provided that one did not trip up and fall down. They did not look harmless to me. If one stepped forward and shouted at them they retreated, but they held their ranks. There was a flicker of red in their tiny eyes. It was like the opening sequence of a Hitchcock thriller.

So we packed our bags, and went to Havana. Here I give Cyril full marks because he made no protest. He did not particularly want to go to Havana; nor did I; but I was not making much sense, and having got the word 'Havana' in my head I decided that there might be a story in it. He made all the arrangements, booked a suite on a ship called the *Cibonnet*, and rashly handed me the tickets, which I promptly lost. We got onto the *Cibonnet* by very dubious means and when she sailed, in the nick of time, groups of angry little men in shabby uniforms were gathered on the quayside, shaking their fists at us.

As soon as we arrived in Havana it was evident that we had escaped from one jungle only to plunge into another. Though there were no vultures in the trees there were vultures everywhere else, in the hotels, in the restaurants, and of course in the bars. And though, when the sun was setting, there were no sinister lights in the clouds to warn us that God was arranging a thundering spectacular, there were the far more sinister lights of American civilisation. Flickering neon lights in lipstick red and acid green, luring the tourists towards the most squalid entertainments that a primitive and impoverished people can ever have devised for the diversion of the rich. No further comment on Havana, unless we allow ourselves an echo of Voltaire. 'If there had not been a Castro, it would have been necessary to invent one.'

Flash to Vera Cruz. I am beginning to make sense and Cyril is beginning to exert his authority. We really must do something serious about getting to Mexico, so Cyril went off to a travel agency and booked a compartment on a train that was leaving for Mexico City on the following morning. After which he searched for accommodation in a local hotel. When he returned he looked extremely disgruntled.

'What's the matter?'

'It's the hotel.'

'Not *another* brothel?'

'Come and see for yourself.'

I followed him down the winding streets. When we entered the hall we were greeted by a uniformed bandit who showed us up to our bedroom. It was dimly lit; cockroaches scurried over the damp tiles; there was a nauseous odour of decay, and a terrible sense of being shut in a tomb. Apart from all this, there was no bath. Only a rusted spray, dangling from the ceiling, from which there dribbled a reluctant trickle of lukewarm water.

We swept out, ignoring the imprecations of the bandit, turned up a side-street, and sat down in a small café to consider the situation. It seemed as though we were destined to spend the night in the streets. Then there was a tap on my shoulder. I looked up and saw a familiar face . . . Thornton Wilder.

Nobody could have been more welcome. We did not know each other well, but we knew each other well enough to speak the same language. Mutual admiration is not a bad basis on which to build a pleasant evening, and after dinner Thornton—who was also going to Mexico and had suffered the same shock of horror in his hotel—decided that we must all leave Vera Cruz together. At once. By the night train. But *was* there a night train? Thornton blinked through his spectacles. He had no idea. Then we both looked at Cyril.

He drained his glass. 'I must be psychic. I knew something like this would happen. There is a night train, and I took the precaution of booking a suite on it, at enormous expense. But both you gentlemen are so bloody rich that you can afford it.'

Thornton drew in a long sigh of relief.

'Be my guest,' he said.

Cyril grinned. 'I should warn you that it looks like a brothel on wheels. And there are only two beds.'

'In which case,' said Thornton, 'I shall have the great pleasure of sitting up all night and looking at infinity through the windows of a brothel. I can imagine no journey more delectable.'

That long night journey in the train, up and up through the mountains, from the fetid cesspool of Vera Cruz to the glittering miracle of Mexico City, was one of the most unforgettable passages of my life. There we were, all exhausted but all electrically awake, leaning back on our dusty cushions, peering out through the windows and *living*, with an extraordinary intensity. I think we were living in terms of music. As the train panted on, leaving in its wake a long trail of flickering sparks like a golden scarf, we were all hearing music, in our respective ways. Not very clearly perhaps, but clearly enough to identify the passing panorama with the composers who lurked in the back-cloth.

Cyril	These mountains are pure Bach.
Thornton	(*Flinching from a flash of lightning stalking the night sky*) But can't you hear Wagner in the wings?
B.N.	(*Drifting into sleep as the clouds clear away, and there is a glimpse of moonlight*.) Yes. But Chopin has the last word.

On arriving in Mexico City, after bidding an affectionate farewell to Thornton Wilder, Cyril and I sat down in the lounge of what was whimsically described as a 'five-star hotel' and promptly had a blazing row. Sitting there, drinking champagne when I should have been tucked up in bed sipping malted milk, I surveyed the passing scene—the heavy-lidded Mexican ladies, outrageously painted and powdered, swaying their hips and fluttering their eyelashes. I observed, quite politely, that once again he appeared to have deposited me in a brothel. Whereupon Cyril exploded. He too was very tired, he had been sweating his guts out dealing with all the papers and documents, constantly retrieving objects which I had lost, and if I didn't like the fucking brothel I could fucking well go off and choose one for my fucking self. The incident would not be worth mentioning were it not for the fact that over a period of many years this is the only occasion when I can remember either of us using this adjective. It is an adjective that I have always avoided, in the spoken or the written word; it is a sign of weakness rather than strength, demeaning the English language.

After a long pause, in which I stared at Cyril in some astonishment for he was completely out of character, I suggested that his outburst might be due to the altitude.

'Fuck the altitude,' observed Cyril, with total conviction.

And that was the fucking end of the conversation which, in many vicissitudes, has never been repeated.

There now followed a month of physical and spiritual convalescence. As we wandered round Mexico, often far from the beaten track, there were times when I felt very near to heaven. There was a very personal reason for feelings of exaltation; at last, for however brief a space, I was able to forget the gathering clouds of war. In this unique terrain, where savagery and sanctity went hand in hand, there were monuments of beauty which, unlike their counterparts in Europe, were not lying in the shadow of destruction. There were cathedrals where one's eyes could feast on the richly stained windows without seeing, in imagination, the swarm of workmen who—as at Chartres—would soon be stripping the glass from its frames, leaving sockets to stare at the threatening skies. Here the skies were bland and innocent; the glass would remain. Moreover, in Mexico, eight thousand feet up on these soaring plateaux, the aid was so dry and crystalline that it was possible to see early Spanish baroque architecture in almost its original condition. It was as though the churches had been preserved in a casing of cellophane, with the gilding on the frescoes newly minted, the blues still in their midday glory, the crimsons as fresh as blood newly spilt.

So the days sped by and I soaked myself in peace and sunshine and beauty, as a cat soaks itself in sunshine. And then one morning the peace was shattered. A long and somewhat frenzied telegram arrived from London informing me that in two days' time the annual bullfight would be staged in Mexico City and that it was essential for me to attend it and cable back a full report.

This appalling communication hit me like a blow between the eyes. To suggest that a bullfight was not my favourite form of entertainment would be the understatement of all time. Although I had never degraded myself by attending one, I knew by instinct how I should react. I had always refused even to discuss the subject except on one stormy occasion in Paris faced by Ernest Hemingway, in the Ritz Bar. He was holding forth about the glories of the bloody business. I intervened. In a few minutes he had called me a cissy to which I retorted that from him I regarded this as a compliment. It is a pity that this conversation was not recorded, because we both had some talent for invective, and we might have been specially designed to insult one another. Hemingway, in spite of his interludes of genius, was *au fond*, a phoney, like D. H. Lawrence. They were both too proud of the hair on their chests. I have often suspected that in both their cases the hair came from the literary make-up department, and was cunningly attached to their torsos by Elastoplast.

The cable also brought me sharply face to face with my own personality, and my own scatter-brained career, which, as we have seen, was a perpetual conflict between the pro and the prostitute. They went hand in hand. I was being paid a large salary to produce so many thousand words a week, and I was not in the habit of breaking contracts. So I gritted my teeth and went to the bullfight.

The result will be found in the following chapter. It was published on February 26th, 1939, and across the whole of the page Jimmy Drawbell had paid me a personal tribute in his own handwriting. 'This in my opinion is the finest article that Beverley Nichols has ever written . . .'

I did not share his opinion. But at least it was written with my heart's blood, and some of the blood spilt out onto the page.

CHAPTER XXIII

🌸🌸🌸🌸🌸🌸

DEATH
IN THE AFTERNOON

Author's Note. The reader is asked to remember that this chapter is an unedited reproduction of an article written at top speed for a mass-circulation newspaper some forty years ago.

In spite of the passage of time, the article lingers on. Shortly after publication it was translated into Spanish and distributed at the entrance to various bull-rings throughout Spain by gallant little groups of animal lovers, who got into trouble with the police. Like most of my other 'missionary' efforts, it had no permanent effect.

This is what I wrote . . .

I feel physically sick and spiritually dirty. It is five hours since I stumbled out of my seat at the bullfight. Five hours since I left that sun-drenched pit of madness and dust and blood. I have been walking hard most of the time, striding through quiet gardens, trying to cool down, trying to calm my temper, trying above all to forget.

But I can't forget. It's the grey horse I can't get out of my mind.

The matador who staggered away, with the blood running down the purple silk of his breeches . . . him I can forget. Or at least I can consider him fairly calmly. After all, he was a free man. His life was his own. If he chose to toss it away like a counterfeit coin, that was his own affair. Even the bulls I may forget one day, though I doubt it. There are some details which, I fear, will flash back through my memory till I die . . . the lacerated backs that bubbled (yes, literally bubbled) with blood; the tortured whine (there is no other word for it) which they made as they were attacked from every side;

dazzled by the scarlet capes, stung in the front, in the rear, in the flanks by their gallant tormentors. And finally, the quick upward flash of their eyes, dead white, as the dagger was thrust through their brains.

Perhaps there are lies with which I may try to comfort myself when I think of those poor beasts, and though I know they are lies, they may serve their purpose. One can repeat all the glib catchwords of those who are attracted by this 'sport'. One can assure oneself, for example, that the bulls are fierce and evil-spirited. But no; why try to console oneself with such paltry excuses when one knows the truth?—when one knows that these wretched creatures are deliberately maddened for months beforehand, fed on special food, forbidden to breed, shut up in dark boxes, and then without warning let loose in the sunlight amid a whirl of multi-coloured silks and pierced with stinging barbs. Why affront one's intelligence by comparing the 'malevolence' of the animal with the 'bravery' of the man, especially when the man is being paid a hundred guineas for his virtues?

But none of these things gave me quite that feeling of nausea, and even more, of anger that the grey horse did. It was such a lovely animal. And when the horn went into it. . . .

However, that wasn't till the end. Perhaps it would be better if we led up to it a little more gradually.

Why did I go to a bullfight at all? The answer to that is very simple. I am a reporter, and a reporter cannot shut his eyes to life. And in Mexico City, from where I write, 'life' centres round the slaughterhouse. The streets are covered with placards, advertising the Toreo. It is announced that eight *arrogantes y bravos toros*—which translates itself—were to be killed.

There was a wonderful new bullfighter, too.

I thought . . . 'After all, this is a national sport. I may loathe the idea in theory, but it mayn't be so bad in fact. Besides, it's my job to test theory by fact.' So I bought a ticket, in the front row. Even so, I don't think I should have gone if I had not read beforehand that the horses were padded.

That was the first shock. For as we were driving towards the arena, on Sunday afternoon, the chauffeur turned round and gleefully informed me . . . 'This fighter, Señor Z, he doesn't have pads on his horses. No sir.'

'But what happens if . . .'

He shrugged his shoulders. 'Those are very fine horses, he has. Maybe twenty thousand pesos each. He don't want 'em ripped up.'

On that we arrived.

Imagine an immense arena, holding twenty-five thousand people, open to the heavens, crammed to the topmost tier. The colours are so brilliant that they hurt the eyes: the blue of the sky, the vivid orange of the whisky advertisements, the greens and purples and whites of the women's dresses.

As I push forward to my place and study the crowd I think to myself . . . 'It must be all right. If all these elegant females, plastered with cosmetics can enjoy it, presumably it won't be too much for me. Besides, there are children here. Almost babies. The little boy over there, clapping his hands so excitedly, can't be more than four. And though he looks so flushed and hysterical that he ought to be sent to bed with a powder, I suppose his parents know best.'

So I sit down and wait.

I am about ten feet from the edge of the ring. In-between there is a corridor into which the matadors escape when the bull chases them. Over in the far corner is a door, locked and guarded, through which the bull will eventually charge. Four o'clock strikes. There is a fanfare of trumpets. The pageant begins.

Admittedly, at first, it is very charming. Out rides an old man on a grey horse. His black velvet cloak floats in the wind. Then the matadors and picadors, marching in gay procession. Their waistcoats and their breeches are frilled in every imaginable colour, thickly embroidered with gold and silver. Most of their cloaks are not scarlet but magenta. More ceremony and flourishes. Most of them march out again. And now, in rides the celebrated Señor Z. A brave figure indeed, in his golden waistcoat and his purple breeches holding the ribboned 'banderilla' in his hand.

But it is not Señor Z that I am thinking of. It is his horse. A brown horse, sensitive and beautiful, with his body so highly polished that it glistens in the sun. I think of that body, completely unprotected. I think of those horns, like curved knives.

Things are beginning to move swiftly. Through the doors, with lowered head, comes the bull. It is an immense beast, with a black hide and long curved horns. For thirty yards it charges ahead. Then, in the middle, it stops. It looks around. It seems puzzled. As though it was wondering where it was, and who had brought it here, and why there was no grass to eat. Then, quickly, it turns.

Out of the corner of its eye it has seen a matador, waving his cloak. It charges. There is a breathless moment when the matador stands as still as a statue while the bull misses him by inches.

So far, so good. But now Señor Z is bearing down on the bull. A savage flick of the wrist, and he has stuck a ribboned prong in the bull's back. Blood spurts out. The crowd roars its delight. He is back again. He lands another ribboned prong, and yet another. As he makes each thrust he bares his teeth and snarls like a wild animal. And each time those cruel horns just miss his horse's stomach.

Well, the bull is near us now. Look at him! After all, he's only a bull. And we know, we sportsmen, that animals don't feel pain. So we needn't feel revolted when we see a great square of raw flesh into which Señor Z sticks another of his delicate barbs. We needn't worry about that deep, strangled cough that comes out of the beast's mouth, accompanied by a good deal of blood.

Well, they're going to kill it now. Not Señor Z. The others.

The legend is that they do this part of the job swiftly, arrogantly, with a flash of a silver sword. The legend seems to be a little inaccurate. For this is butchery. Butchery dressed up in gold and green and purple. They stab here, there, everywhere. One of the swords goes in the right eye. Never mind. It's only the death of a bull. A slow, bewildered creature sinking to its knees ... a helpless last look at Man, its noble superior. A final, futile effort to avoid the sword. A spasm that shakes the whole body. Then the dagger in the brain, and death, and white up-turned eyes.

Out with him! Away with the silly carcase! It has served its purpose by giving us a moment's thrill. So the doors swing open and four horses are whipped in, who drag him away with chains. A black mass, still warm and twitching.

The girl next to me takes out a mirror and does up her pretty lips. If I am sick, I say to myself (which seems all too probable at the moment), I shall be sick in her direction.

The second fight seems, somehow, more bearable. For suddenly into the arena vaults a newcomer. A slender figure in white and silver, with a scarlet ribbon at his waist and a bright thin sword held negligently in his hand. I do not know why he should seem to catch the attention of the crowd, but he does. I watch him. He is standing only a few yards away. He is young, barely twenty, and you would say he were dreaming of some girl, so arrogant is his poise, so gay the smile on his parted lips. But there is nothing dreamy about his eyes. They are sharp, restless, fixed on every movement of the bull.

His time has come. He turns, clicks his heels, holds out his hat to the girl with the lips. He is dedicating to her the bull which he is about to slaughter.

But something has gone wrong. She shakes her head. The smile fades from the face of the young man. It is replaced by a bitter frown. Contemptuously he tosses his hat to a ragged boy. Then, with a single swift movement, he darts into the centre of the arena.

It is now, and only now, for a few brief moments, that I can see what fascinates people in bullfighting. For now there are no horses, and for some reason most of the other fighters seem to have retired. It is a square fight between a powerful, angry beast and a slim youth armed with a fragile sword. It has a certain beauty. As he twists and turns he has the exquisite elegance of a ballet dancer. And in this case the thing is done swiftly. The barbs are placed true. The bull faces the youth. Each is dead still . . .

Slowly the youth levels his sword. With deliberate, measured steps he stalks towards those fatal horns. Then, with his whole weight, he lunges forward. You can see the sunlight glitter on the sword for a brief instant.

It is all over. I no longer feel sick. That is to say, for the space of about thirty seconds. But with the third fight I feel very sick indeed. Not so much with ordinary nausea as with sheer, choking anger.

For as the third bull is dragged away, the doors swing open, and out ride four picadors. They pass so close that I can see every detail of their horses. I can see that the eyes of those horses are bandaged. That although one side of them is thickly padded, the other side is not, and that this other side is worn and scarred. And I can see that those horses are trembling, sweating, tortured bundles of fear. Better not look. But how can I help looking? It is as though one were hypnotised.

The new bull is already in the ring, and already the scarves are whirling, the 'banderillas' are doing their maddening work.

And now ... Oh, God ... It's got one of the horses. No, the man turned just in time. But the horns are in the pads, and the horse has been tossed, like an old bundle of rags, against the barrier. The horns are shaken violently. Thud, thud, goes that horse against the wood—you can hear the impact of its bones. It is lifted right off its feet. In a sort of sick fury I pray that somehow the pads may hold, that a sudden twist may not shake them loose, that the horse may not stagger.

Another shake. The bull lets go, turns, and charges to the right, I don't look. And yet somehow out of the corner of my eyes, I can see. It is being dragged and scraped all along the barricade. The man is punching its head to keep it facing the right way. These things, looking and yet not looking, I can see. But even if I were blind, I could not help hearing the shrill scream of that horse as the horns got it.

Have you ever heard a horse scream? A rabbit's bad enough, caught in some filthy trap. A dog, run over ... that's not very nice, either. But a horse ...

'Clumsy,' says the girl next to me, and lights another cigarette.

I don't think I can describe the next fight, which made me pull myself to my feet, and get out, stumbling over people's feet.

I'm afraid I shall 'fall down on it' as they say in Fleet Street when you make a mess of a good story. But even if I could describe it, I don't think the editor would care to print it, nor you to read it. For you see, it was now the turn of the grey horse, which I told you about before. And that horse hadn't any pads.

At first it didn't come on. In a sort of haze I saw another bull charge out, the toughest of the lot. I saw more cloaks being waved, more ribboned barbs, drawing more blood. There was one matador, I remember, who gained extra applause by hitting the bull on the nose, and spitting in its face.

Then once again, out rides the great Señor Z. Grander than ever. His gold has changed to lavender, and the lace round his fat neck would delight any woman. How superb he is! Those must be real rubies on his small fingers! But even if he were nothing to look at himself, you could not but admire his horse. As he rides by, I think that it's the sort of horse a great sculptor would be proud to use as a model. Perfect legs, magnificent neck, a coat like pearl-grey satin. The sort of horse that might be your friend too, the sort that would know you, wait for you, miss you if you were gone.

A snarl from the Señor and they are away. A streak of grey against a streak of black. A sickening pause . . . a ribboned barb well placed . . . a swerve, and off again. Right round the arena. Back again. Horse against bull. The crowd roars its approval. The Señor is delighted. Intoxicated. He begins to take risks. Black against grey again. He makes his horse rise on its hind legs for a final sensational attack. The bull charges.

I told you I should 'fall down'. You can guess what happened. All I can remember, as they took the horse away, was wondering, dimly, why its blood had been so dark.

'Brown,' I muttered to myself. 'Deep brown. Not like the bull's. That was quite light. Almost pink.'

I got out . . . just as one of the matadors had been badly slashed in the ribs. It didn't seem to matter much. He asked for it. He'd get his hundred guineas. And his photograph in the papers. And his kiss from one of those girls with scarlet lips.

Well, ladies and gentlemen, that is how I spent my Sunday afternoon. That is why I feel so dirty, mean, and contemptible, even to have ventured near such an exhibition.

And though I have never doubted the existence of God, I should find it difficult, as I throw down my pen, to argue against the existence of the Devil.

CHAPTER XXIV

✿✿✿✿✿✿

NO HIDING PLACE

After Mexico, we went home via New York. Cyril had never been there before and I had the joy of showing to him my own special view of this miraculous city, which reveals itself at dusk, when a million stars, like flights of silver moths, begin to flicker on the skyline. In New York the sense of doing everything 'for the last time' became more urgent than ever. One of the reasons for this conviction was financial. War was only a few weeks ahead and the average intelligent Englishman had little hope that we should win it. A British passport no longer commanded respect, and the pound sterling was already a suspect currency. I had a few pounds left and decided to get rid of them as soon as possible. One of the quickest ways of doing this was to stay at the St Regis' Hotel, where the presiding genius was an international charmer called Prince Felix Yousoupoff. Felix was an old friend who provided us with a millionaire suite where I installed a piano and proceeded to give a succession of parties which usually ended up at Harlem. The very thought of such behaviour today makes me shudder. I could not foot the bill for a single night in such an establishment. As for going to Harlem, one would be taking one's life in one's hands. And yet we used to go as a matter of course, on the spur of the moment, in white tie and tails and diamond cuff-links, leaving the car at the entrance to dance-halls where the vast majority of the revellers were jet black.

Once I went with Cole Porter, who responded to the negro rhythms like a human metronome, flicking his fingers and rising to his feet to try out a dance-step with some amiable monster who looked like President Amin in drag, while little groups of coloured girls formed circles around him, writhing and twisting their scrawny hips. It was all, no doubt, very stimulating, but it was not really my cup of tea. In spite of the superficial friendliness of the 'natives', in spite of the comparative safety of the streets, I was always ill at ease, as though I had strayed into the jungle. I tried to rid myself of this feeling, but I always heard the sounds of the jungle in the dance-halls and even when our parties were going with a swing—with the fashionable photographers flashing away in the background, showing the New York socialites tangling with their coloured buddies, male and female—I was assailed by fears that I could not analyse.

None of this, or anything even vaguely approaching it, could happen in our times. There are so many reasons for feeling apprehensive about the future of civilisation that it is difficult to choose a single over-riding cause for alarm, but it seems obvious that the ultimate battle—the war to end all wars—will be painted in black and white, against a dripping background of scarlet. This primeval conflict will transcend all other conflicts, and make a mockery of all the other political, economic, and religious struggles which are tearing the world apart. The supreme irony of history lies in the fact that such a conflict will be totally unnecessary. But it is on the way, and in one of the literary curiosa of the Nichols *œuvre* I have charted its course in a detailed manuscript which will be published after my death. If it were to appear today it would involve my immediate prosecution under the Race Relations Act.

This last pre-war expedition to New York also marked my final explosion as a controversial journalist. This was the year of the World's Fair, one of the greatest propaganda exercises that even America had ever undertaken. It had already cost £31,000,000 and it had accommodation for 1,000,000 visitors a day. The British press were apparently unaware of its existence. I decided that this situation should be remedied, and made friends with Grover Whalen, who was the moving spirit behind the whole enterprise. He took me on a personally conducted tour of the site, where the giant constructions of the dictators were towering to the skies, overshadowing the pathetic contribution of the British Empire—a ramshackle building which looked as if it had been put up in a hurry on a minimum budget. I cabled back a story which gave a picture of this pathetic exhibit, which was dwarfed by the magnificent Italian contribution. The story made headlines not only in England but in Italy where it caught the attention of Mussolini who splashed it across the Italian press, as an example of British decadence. Not that any further proof was needed, as I was very soon to discover.

Back to Europe. Back to London. To the little house in Hampstead. To Gaskin, immaculate as ever, with a silver tray in his right hand, balancing an icy cocktail shaker. Back to the cats who, true to form, turn their backs, outraged by my long absence, and spring onto the wall, out of reach of stroking, and express their disgust by lifting their legs over their shoulders and delicately attending to their behinds.

Back to the glass bubble of the greenhouse, where the bougainvillaea was stretching to the roof in a shameless profusion of purple blossom. Odd as it may seem, this frail silver folly seemed to me the only place in the city where I could retreat and find refuge. Everybody else was building air-raid shelters at the bottom of their gardens, some of them equipped with shelves lined with tins of expensive delicacies from Fortnum and Mason's. Others were rolling up their shirt sleeves and digging trenches in Hyde Park, under the illusion that they were contributing to the 'war effort'. After an hour's digging they felt they had earned their luncheons at the Ritz. The less fortunate paid furtive visits to the larger tube stations, where they made embarrassed inquiries as to the facilities which would be available to them as soon as the bombs began to fall. The most popular of these potential escape-hatches was Hampstead Tube Station because it was the deepest. This was the tube station nearest to my own house and later, when the bombs had really got going, I was often to have the squalid experience of stepping over rows of prostrate heaps of snoring, malodorous masses of huddled humanity. After which I got out and walked home, down the winding road, under the firework skies, and out into the greenhouse where I closed the door, and touched the flowers, and spoke to them. If I had to die, I would prefer to die with flowers around me.

However, we are anticipating. There were still some weeks to go.

This was not a glorious period in British history, this final run-up to the war. Countless historians have described it, but there is one element that is lacking in all their accounts—the element of humour. A great many things were happening which were, in retrospect, extremely funny. This was evident in the behaviour of my own generation. Most of us assumed that we should be employed in some form of propaganda. But 'propaganda' is an elastic word, and some of the ways in which it was interpreted by the national celebrities were not very helpful. Consider the case of Ivor Novello.

I suppose that there was something he could have done, with his impeccable profile, and his adoring public. But what? One night he arranged a supper party at his flat to discuss possible courses of action. Gladys Cooper was there, and Lady Juliet Duff, and a number of other old cronies including myself. Did we think that he ought to join up? The Navy perhaps? Oh no, protested Juliet, he was far too precious, though of course he would look divine in the uniform of a naval officer. Then what about the Air Force? The protests grew even louder, because some of us remembered that during the First World War Ivor had in fact had a short spell of flying, for which he was so eminently unfitted that as soon as he stepped into a 'plane there was alarm and consternation among all within crashing distance.

Then Gladys clapped her hands. 'I have it,' she cried. 'You must write a song. You must write another "Keep the Home Fires Burning"!'

There was a chorus of approval. 'Keep the Home Fires Burning' —does anybody remember it now?—had been a national theme song in the first war.

Ivor beamed. Strange as it might seem, this was exactly what he had in mind. Indeed, the song was already written. Would we care to hear it? We could not wait to do so. Whereupon he stepped onto the little platform, sat down at the piano, and proceeded to play a song of such unbelievable banality that none of us knew where to look. I can remember nothing of the tune, which was a lifeless hotchpotch. And I can remember only three lines of the lyric, but these were more than enough. They were . . .

> So we'll grin, grin, grin,
> Till we win, win, win,
> And the boys come home again.

There was the usual confused babel of adulation when he stepped down from the platform. I only once heard the thing sung in public, on a wet matinée, in a transitory production a few days after the beginning of the phoney war. When I stepped out into the street at the end of the performance, I did not go round to see Ivor. I knew him too well to put on an act. I was not grinning. There was nothing to grin about.

My own experience of the propaganda machine was startling. It was inevitable that sooner or later I should be approached by the authorities to serve in some sort of capacity, and I was more than willing to do so; but when the call came, shortly after my return from America, the suggestion they made was of a nature that made me feel that history was repeating itself. My duties in the First World War had been ridiculous enough, but the role that was now suggested verged on insanity.

I cannot remember the name of the office to which I was directed, and I never discovered the name of the genius in whose brain the plan originated. Presumably it was some bigwig in a branch of the Ministry of Information. But I remember, very clearly, the hypnotic stare of a man behind the desk as he outlined his fantastic proposition.

He spoke in a near whisper and constantly glanced over his shoulder, as though spies might be working behind the curtains.

Did I know why I had been summoned? Was I prepared to take risks? Here, on my part, was a slight but I hope not too perceptible pause; I had a fleeting fear that he might be about to send me somewhere in some sort of submarine. But I kept my chin up. Yes. Of course I was prepared to take risks.

Then came another question, out of the blue. Was I still connected with the Oxford Group? No? But I had once written very enthusiastic articles about them? Yes ... but ... Never mind the 'buts'. I *had* written the articles? Yes. And I had not retracted them? No.

Then the story came out. The Oxford Group, apparently, was giving the British considerable cause for concern, particularly in the United States. Dr Buchman's relationships with the Nazis were too intimate to be healthy. He appeared to be on excellent terms with Himmler. And though he was far too clever to indulge in activities which could lead to an open confrontation with the British or the French, there was no doubt where his sympathies lay. He had to be stopped.

But how?

This was where I came in. Would I go to America and initiate a rival religious movement, which would act as a counter-force to the Group's influence? I had a 'name'. I had numerous important 'contacts'. I knew how to conduct myself on the lecture platform. If I were given the funds and the necessary diplomatic support, would I go to America and take charge of the whole operation?

How was I to answer these questions? How was I to explain that the whole conception was midsummer madness? To set off to New York, at a moment's notice, to create an 'image', to establish an organisation, to engage a band of disciples, to fire them with enthusiasm, and to fly here there and everywhere delivering a 'message' which would convince a vast population that God was on our side—whatever that might mean, even if it were true ... No.

I forget how I managed to conclude the interview without losing my temper. All I remember is that when I got home I wrote a curt note rejecting his proposition. My explanation was short and to the point. Dear Sir, I told him, I am too much of a coward to return to America at this moment, even on such an exalted mission. If I did so, everybody would say that I was running away.

* * *

But I *was* running away. I was seeking a hiding-place. But where was the hiding-place? I could not continue to sit in the greenhouse, studying the bougainvillaea, which in any case was beginning to be attacked by black-fly.

So I went to Lourdes.

When I arrived at the office to tell Jimmy Drawbell of my intentions he heaved a deep sigh. 'So we're back to God again?'

'We haven't mentioned God on Page Two for a couple of years.'

'I'm thinking of the art department. How do we illustrate God?'

I suggested that this was his job. And anyway, for at least the last hundred articles I had provided the art department with a constant stream of pictorial copy. Dukes, duchesses, film stars, cabinet ministers, débutantes. I had presented them against an ever-changing background that had taken me half way round the world.

A long pause. 'You really care about God, don't you?'

'In some form or another.'

'What is that supposed to mean?'

'That is what I hope to find out.'

'O.K. So you go to Lourdes. I'll send somebody down to be ready for you when you pay your respects at the shrine of Sainte Bernadette. . . .'

The key to this conversation lay in the words 'in some form or another'. Those words are really the key to my whole life-story, the only words that can give it any sort of moral justification or artistic unity. Ever since my schoolboy sonnet to the buttercups ('God's money') there has been this spiritual motif in my life, like a musical theme, which would not leave me nor let me rest. Even when I was being most ridiculous, even when I was swept in by forces which I now realise were false and cheating, such as the Oxford Group, I still, as Jimmy Drawbell had reminded me, 'cared about God'. Even when I was in white tie and tails.

The expedition to Lourdes was a perfect example of my persistent conflict between the sacred and the profane. On the night before I set out there was a party which went on till dawn. After the party I flew to Paris and picked up a car outside the Ritz in the Place

Vendôme. I spent the night studying the Abbé Périgord's classic volume of the Miracles of Sainte Bernadette. It was not easy reading, for it was copiously illustrated with medical diagrams and X-ray photographs which I could not pretend to understand. But I persisted with it because—as always—I was in search of a faith that would stand up to scientific scrutiny. Such a search is perhaps doomed to failure. Or is it? I did not know then, and I do not know today. All I know is that it is the most important search on which any man can embark on his journey through this world.

The next two days of this pilgrimage are a blank, in which I motored through France alone, wondering what life was all about and why I was making such a mess of it. This mood of near despair was short-lived because by a happy chance I arrived at Lourdes at dawn, fired with enthusiasm and unaffected by fatigue. In those days I must have had the constitution of an ox and the obstinacy of a mule. As the car crested the hill the sun came out, gilding the roofs of the old grey houses and painting the river with streaks of silver.

After a breakfast of freshly baked croissants and scarlet cherries I began to prowl around, and at every moment my spirits mounted. For here was a city built, quite literally on faith. It shone from every shop window; it was inextricably entangled in the most humdrum affairs of the community. Some people who go to Lourdes are shocked by the commercialism of it all; I do not share their disapproval. There was something warm and comforting in these winding streets, through which there drifted a haunting odour of sanctity, and I did not care that the sanctity was to some extent synthetic. I stood enchanted by the windows of the confectioners whose boxes of bonbons were painted with scenes from the Nativity. I joined the groups of children who were pressing their noses against the glass of the toyshops, enraptured by the clockwork dolls who were strutting around against a background of silver paper—dolls that were not equipped with the uniforms of soldiers but dressed in the raiment of the saints.

At the end of a long day I climbed the stairs to the attic bedroom which was all I had been able to find in the way of accommodation in a city where there was very little room to be found in any of the inns. I make no apology for quoting the last words of the article in which I tried to capture the emotions of that crowded day which, in after years, I have lived again, and yet again . . .

Of all the nights of beauty that I have ever known, few will ever equal the beauty of the night when I joined the throng of pilgrims who paraded the city, in the gathering darkness, singing songs and carrying tapers. Those tapers formed a chain of gold, a mile long; the sky was wearing all her stars; but the brightest light of all came from the Grotto of Sainte Bernadette, blazing with a thousand candles, to which we were wending our way. One walked in a dream, yet it was a dream in which all the senses were curiously alert; I can still see individual faces in the crowd, the ecstasy in the eyes of a young German, the smile of ineffable happiness on the thick lips of a Negro. At last, when all the multitudes were gathered together, when all the nations were blended in a great mass that stretched to the far distance, there was silence. Never have I heard anything so beautiful as that silence. Nor is that a contradiction in terms, for true silence, the silence of the spirit, is not negative. It is no more a mere absence of words than darkness is a mere absence of light. Rather is it a harmony of all gentle sounds, a gathering of whispers, a sweet symphony of rest.

From Lourdes I sped to Cannes, from the sublime to the second-rate, from the pure radiance of Christianity to the neon glitter of café society. This confession might be cited as a damning proof of my lamentable superficiality. If the inspiration of Lourdes had been genuine, surely one would have sought a few days' solitude in the hills. But I had not only myself to think about; in Cannes there were several old friends who were incapable of looking after themselves, and I felt a moral obligation to help them. There was an old lady with a tiny villa which I had rashly promised to shut in case things came to the worst; there was an old man who was sick; and another with a broken-down car which had to be transported to England.

Cannes was a lunatic asylum, of which the focal point was the great terrace of the Carlton Hotel. For twenty years this had served as a parade ground for the world's playboys and playgirls; this was where the millionaires had strutted with their mistresses, where the bronzed and beautiful young people had flaunted their latest *affaires*, and where there was a nightly firework display of jewels from Cartier and Boucheron. I had been part of this scene, from time to time, and it would be hypocrisy to suggest that I had not enjoyed it. But tonight, as I wearily steered the car towards the hotel, I realised that the whole place had gone mad. The streets were blocked with cars being loaded up with petrol, any sort of petrol at any sort of price, and it was being poured into the cars by hysterical women, some of them still in beach-pyjamas. As soon as they had got their petrol they threw their jewel-cases into the boot, and fled to the north. Panic had set in because the French radio was in a state of hopeless confusion, and there had been several premature announcements that war had actually begun—rumours that were enhanced by the tramp, tramp of soldiers' boots marching up the promenade—the French army on its way to man the Italian frontier. And what an army it was! Weary, slouching, ill-equipped, ill-disciplined, and across the face of every man was written the message of *je m'en fiche*.

I parked the car, and made my way to the cocktail bar. I had expected it to be crowded but it was almost empty. I drank a glass of champagne; it tasted bitter and Charles the barman, who was an old friend, pushed aside the note that I offered him. 'We used to drink together, Monsieur Beverley,' he said. 'But now there is nothing left to drink to, except to the fall of France.'

I walked out onto the terrace. This too was almost empty. One had an uncanny feeling of being the last passenger left on a sinking ship. Then over in a corner, smoking a cigarette and staring out to sea, I saw a figure who might have been specially placed there by some film director with a superb sense of casting. It was Elsa Maxwell, who for years had been acknowledged by the gossip writers of America and Europe as the Queen of Pleasure—Elsa, who was always giving, or about to give, the most stupendous party of all time—Elsa, who had done more than any other living woman to brighten the lives of the very rich. I walked across to her. She rose and folded me in a strong embrace. As we kissed I found myself wondering what it would be like to have an affair with a lesbian. Would one be crushed to death? How could our respective roles be interpreted? I knew, of course, the physical answer to these questions, but what about the emotional side? I have always had a feeling that inside every lesbian there is a frightened little woman trying to get out.

'Come up to the villa and dine,' said Elsa. 'It may be the last time that I can ever ask you.'

There were eight of us. The villa was high up in the hills, and after dinner we sat looking out over the bay, whose beauty was enhanced by the diamond necklaces of light that line the shore. Suddenly the lights went out. The bay receded into darkness. The glittering fringe of civilisation had been wrenched away.

'I wonder,' said Elsa, 'how long it will be before the lights will go on again.'

So did I. I also wonder if I was the only person at that party who realised that they would never really go on again at all. Oh yes . . . after five years of slaughter the switches would come back into action. The fabulous coast would again be illuminated in all its glory. But the glory would be tarnished and the scene that the lights revealed would be vulgar and degraded. A civilisation was collapsing, the death-throes of the Mediterranean had begun. Elsa went over to the piano and lit a candle. She lifted her fingers and let them sink back on the keyboard. 'Beverley—come and help. I wouldn't know how to play the sort of music for this occasion.' I sat down at the piano, which was an ancient Bluthner, slightly out of tune. So much the better, for the whole universe was out of tune. I wondered what to play. Chopin, as always, came to the rescue. This was the moment for the Marche Funèbre. An excellent choice, for it is a very easy piece, and I was not very sober. I got through the first section, which was accompanied by a somewhat inappropriate chorus of cicadas from the gardens in the background. Then came the middle movement. The ghost of Chopin drifted across the terrace, lifted a spectral finger, and told me to stop. I have always listened to Chopin, always loved him, always bowed to his authority. We have a very special relationship. So I did not finish the piece, and there was silence.

*   *   *

301

After the silence, we began to talk. If there had been a tape-recorder in the background it would have provided valuable copy for some of the novelists and scenario writers who in the years to come were to attempt to capture the atmosphere of that period. There was no recorder. But there was the old pro, myself. When dawn was breaking I was driven back to the Carlton by a raddled Franco-American 'princess' who, after a few ineffective dabs and pecks and gropes, lost patience and pushed me out into the Croisette, to finish the journey on foot. I believe, and sincerely hope, that shortly afterwards she crashed into a lamp-post opposite the Hotel Martinez.

I walked upstairs to my suite (the lifts were already out of action), sat down at the window, and began to write. Here is the gist of what I wrote. It is only a fragment, but it catches the authentic essence of the moment. It was a composite of all our heartaches and all our fears, and through it there ran a theme of three words . . . 'Do you remember?' There cannot be many people still alive who were personally acquainted with those whom we were recalling. But it was a star-studded cast.

Do you remember Max Reinhardt's parties at Salzburg? What will happen to that lovely city? Shall we have to bomb it? Do you think they've moved all the pictures from the Louvre? And is it true that Eddie Molyneux is somewhere in Biarritz, hiding his paintings by Cézanne, Degas and Sisley? What is Noël Coward up to? Do you remember the first-night of *The Vortex* at the tiny Everyman Theatre, and how we all stood up on our rickety seats and cheered? Where is Cecil Beaton? Will he photograph the war? Will he draw it? Behind Cecil's deceptively rococo façade there lurked, we all suspected, a dynamic genius but it had not yet found true expression.

Do you remember the Lido? And the parties at Constance Toulmin's palazzo on the Grand Canal? Do you remember the Marchesa Casati . . . a monster who might have been created by Beardsley . . . and how she stalked into that fabulous ball accompanied by a page whom she had caused to be encased in gold leaf, and was it really true that as a result of this treatment the page has expired from asphyxiation? If so, what had happened to the body? Would we ever learn the answer to such questions, which once had so enthralled us?

Do you remember Mussolini, and the audiences he used to give in Rome, which had always left us bewildered—those of us who had been privileged to attend them? Do you remember when old Lady Charnwood went to see him and hobbled across the floor and sank into a gilded chair and stared at him boldly in the face? And how, when he asked her if she spoke Italian, she replied, 'Yes, your Excellency, but only in the imperative.'? Was it true that Mussolini had syphilis, and was on the verge of insanity, and if so would he bring Italy into the war? Would that mean that we had to bomb Venice? Why did not the Pope do something? Why didn't he at least *say* something? Could any of us recall a single whisper of comment that had echoed from the Vatican during this ultimate crisis of Christendom? No, we could not. None of our party, as far as I can remember, was of Catholic persuasion, but when next we met Evelyn Waugh we must ask him for an authoritative decision. But would we ever meet him again? Where was he? What was he up to? Something mischievous, no doubt. Possibly something heroic. Even better, something funny. But humour was not the key note of this macabre occasion.

What would the Labour people do now? They had passionately resisted any attempt to enforce conscription. Would they continue to do so? And Oswald Mosley, would they shut him up? And was it not a supreme tragedy that one of the most brilliant men of our age, who might have talked to Hitler in a language that he would have understood, should have been shuffled off the stage as though he were a criminal?

Do you remember Budapest? And the little bars where one went to drink Tokay at six o'clock—and dancing through the night with the loveliest women in Europe? And then, still dancing, waltzing with them to the Danube, and plunging into its magical waters which though they were not blue seemed to have an elixir of their own? Do you remember Ludwig's fairy castles? Would they be bombed? Would we use gas? What about old ladies in gas-masks, particularly those whose faces had been lifted? Would they be able to fit them over their wigs? And would babies have to wear them? And animals? Somehow the animals worried me most.

The grim and the trivial were mingled in hopeless confusion. If Italy came in did that mean that the Ivy Restaurant would have to close down and would our dear Mario be interned. . . . Mario, the proprietor, to whom Noël had dedicated *Bitter Sweet*? Why hadn't we been nicer to that beastly Edda Ciano when her husband was Italian Ambassador in London? Why had nobody gone to her parties? She'd probably given Mussolini the foulest reports about us.

Do you remember Le Touquet and Syrie Maugham's villa with the great white and silver drawing-room and the bowls of white lilies on ivory chairs reflected in the long slatted mirrors? And how we used to troop off to that little restaurant with the striped parasols to join old Selfridge drinking champagne with his *chères amies* the Dolly Sisters? And speaking of Le Touquet, supposing the Germans got the Channel ports. Could the French be trusted? What about Laval? Supposing . . .

And then the pen dropped from my hand. The old pro had done his duty, recording the passing scene. I fell asleep at the desk, lulled by the ceaseless echo of the tramp of soldiers' feet on the promenade below.

On the following morning I set out for home.

INDEX

Mozart, Wolfgang Amadeus 210, 233
music 92, 137, 142, 210, 220, 233, 251
Mussolini, Benito 174, 293, 303

Nancy 199
Nash Brothers 55
Nazimova 239
Nazis 296
New England 80
Newport, Rhode Island 79, 80
News of England 261, 262, 267
New Statesman, The 164, 172, 182
New York 87, 196, 291, 292
New Yorker, The 136
New York Times, The 129
Nichols, Alan (brother of Beverley) 6
Nichols, Beverley, his parents 2, 6, 8,
  24, 34, 57, 74, 89, 91, 97, 108, 112,
  122, 164, 208, 267; influence of Miss
  Herridge 5; at Marlborough College
  1–3, 19–28; fascinated by Mesmer
  15; joins army 32; joins Labour
  Corps 35; is commissioned 39;
  joins Secret Service 45; buys overcoat in Hanover Square 49; visits
  U.S.A. 76–88; father withdraws
  financial support 91; goes to Oxford
  University 91; is President of Union
  91; edits *Isis* 91; gains degree 92;
  debut as concert pianist 92;
  founds and edits *Oxford Outlook* 92;
  publishes first novel 92; recreates
  Oxford University Liberal Club 92;
  leaves Oxford 108; in Venice 155–
  158; addresses League of Nations
  Meeting in Albert Hall 165; accepts
  offer from *Sunday Chronicle* 186; is
  pyscho-analysed 202; suffers nervous breakdown 220, 221; addresses Oxford Group meeting 222;
  visits mining community 259–261;
  goes to South America 271–282;
  attends bullfight 283–290; his love
  of flowers and gardens 5, 6, 18, 131,
  207–210, 217–219, 254; his love of
  music 18, 90, 137, 210; his love of

poetry 18; his religious ideas 5–13,
  29, 98; his ideals 177; his masochism
  262; his dislike of flying 262
Nichols, John (father of Beverley) 2,
  8, 24, 34, 57, 74, 89, 91, 97, 108, 122,
  164, 208, 267
Nichols, Paul (brother of Beverley) 6,
  8, 23, 57, 114, 116
Nightingale, Florence 95
Northcliffe, Lord 218
Norway 203
Novello, Ivor 176, 242, 294, 295

Observer, The 178
O'Casey, Sean 7
Olivier, Sir Laurence 103
Olympic Games, 1936 227, 231
opera 102
oratory 93, 96, 97, 102
Oreste, Dr 118
Orthodoxy 11
Orwell, George 178, 187
O.T.C., Marlborough College 32, 33
Outlook, The 43, 50
Oxford 1, 16, 91–93, 103–108, 111,
  112, 221–223
Oxford and Asquith, Countess of 118
Oxford Group 222, 223, 296, 297
Oxford, Margot 118
Oxford Outlook, The 92, 104
Oxford Union 91, 93, 96, 97, 106

pacifism 59, 163, 164, 172–174, 230,
  231, 241
Paganini, Nicolo 38
Panama City 276
Paris 246, 247
Patchwork 111, 112, 123, 159
Patinir, Joachim 147
Patriot, The 52
Peg o' my Heart 84
Penrose, Evelyn 17, 18
Pepys, Samuel 36, 141
Philip of Hesse, Prince 130
Picasso, Pablo 51, 55
Picture of Dorian Grey, The 51